D0882050

# DARWIN'S HOUSE OF CARDS

# DARWIN'S
# HOUSE OF CARDS

## A JOURNALIST'S ODYSSEY
## THROUGH THE DARWIN DEBATES

## TOM BETHELL

SEATTLE          DISCOVERY INSTITUTE PRESS          2017

## Description

In this provocative history of contemporary debates over evolution, veteran journalist Tom Bethell depicts Darwin's theory as a nineteenth-century idea past its prime, propped up by logical fallacies, bogus claims, and empirical evidence that is all but disintegrating under an onslaught of new scientific discoveries. Bethell presents a concise yet wide-ranging tour of the flash points of modern evolutionary theory, investigating controversies over common descent, natural selection, the fossil record, biogeography, information theory, evolutionary psychology, artificial intelligence, and the growing intelligent design movement. Bethell's account is enriched by his own personal encounters with of some of our era's leading scientists and thinkers, including Harvard biologists Stephen Jay Gould and Richard Lewontin; British paleontologist Colin Patterson; and renowned philosopher of science Karl Popper.

## Copyright Notice

Copyright © 2017 by Discovery Institute. All Rights Reserved.

## Library Cataloging Data

*Darwin's House of Cards: A Journalist's Odyssey Through the Darwin Debates* by Tom Bethell

294 pages, 6 x 9 x 0.6 in. & 0.9 lb, 229 x 152 x 16 mm & x 400 g

Library of Congress Control Number: 2016961820

SCI034000 SCIENCE/History

SCI027000 SCIENCE/Life Sciences/Evolution

BIO015000 BIOGRAPHY & AUTOBIOGRAPHY/Science & Technology

BIO025000 BIOGRAPHY & AUTOBIOGRAPHY/ Editors, Journalists, Publishers

ISBN-13: 978-1-936599-41-7 (paperback), 978-1-936599-42-4 (Kindle), 978-1-936599-43-1 (EPUB)

## Publisher Information

Discovery Institute Press, 208 Columbia Street, Seattle, WA 98104

Internet: http://www. discoveryinstitutepress.org/

Published in the United States of America on acid-free paper.

First Edition: January 2017.

*To Donna*

# CONTENTS

# INTRODUCTION

Doubts about evolution first arose in my mind when I looked at the title page of *The Origin of Species*. I read, and then re-read that page:

On the Origin of Species
by Means of Natural Selection,
or the
preservation of favoured races
in the struggle for life
by Charles Darwin, M.A.
1859

The words "preservation" and "favoured" stood out. Was there any way of knowing what "races" (meaning species, or individual variants) were favored other than by looking to see which ones were in fact preserved? Can *favored* be distinguished from *preserved*?

It was in 1960 that my doubts arose. There was a lot of publicity about Darwin's theory at the time, and especially at Oxford University. Exactly one hundred years earlier, Thomas Henry Huxley and Bishop Samuel Wilberforce had engaged in a famous debate at the university's Museum of Natural History. Twice a week, en route to tutorials at the Psychology Department, I would walk past that museum on Parks Road. "Psychology, Philosophy and Physiology" was my "major," although we didn't use that word.

Psychology aims to study the mind, but the intractable problem was (and remains) that you can't see the mind from the outside. You can only experience it from within, and that means you can't touch it or measure it. As they said at the time, the mind is a "black box." By the mid-twen-tieth century, psychology was worshipping at the feet of science, and ob-serving and measuring are fundamental aspects of science. So an obvi-ous question arose: Could science penetrate the black box of the mind?

In an attempt to circumvent it, a discipline called behaviorism had been established by John B. Watson. He in turn was influenced by Ivan Pavlov. The goal was to reduce psychology to behavior, thereby sidestep-ping the black box problem. Responses ("outputs") would be compared to stimuli ("inputs"). As long as a predictable relationship could be es-tablished between the two, the mind and consciousness could be quietly ignored and even (as far as science was concerned) assumed not to exist. Thought was assumed to be covert speech.

Both behaviorism and neo-Darwinism "derived their inspiration from the same *zeitgeist* of reductionist philosophy which prevailed dur-ing the first half of our [twentieth] century," Arthur Koestler wrote. He characterized the conventional wisdom of that time as the belief that biological evolution was nothing but random mutations, preserved by natural selection.[1] It remains the conventional wisdom to this day.

Experimental psychology could also study the brain directly—as-suming it to be the mind's "location." So researchers began dipping into the brain with electrodes. Today, that field is called "neuroscience." Meanwhile, the mind remains as intangible as ever. A part of the brain lighting up is one thing, and the individual sensation of "blue" is another. In fact they are incommensurable things.

## Survival of the Fittest

As TO natural selection's preservation of the "favored races," Herbert Spencer—a prominent figure in his day—said that Darwin's mecha-nism could be summarized as "the survival of the fittest."[2] Darwin was not impressed by Spencer, but he gratefully accepted his survival-of-the-fittest formula, and incorporated it into the fifth edition of *The Origin of Species*.

So the question remains: Is there any way of deciding what is "fit" other than by seeing what survives? If not, maybe Darwin was arguing in a self-confirming circle: the survival of the survivors.

One day I mentioned the problem to my philosophy tutor, E. J. Lemmon, who had studied under Alfred Tarski. Esteemed for his clarity, Dr. Lemmon gave weekly lectures in the "schools" building on Oxford's High Street. The vast hall would be packed with undergraduates hoping to get through their logic "prelims."

Lemmon saw that the meaning of "fitness" was something that the leading field of Oxford philosophy—the "ordinary language" school, dominated by John L. Austin—might find interesting. Can we describe the fitness of an organism (or of one of its traits) without waiting to see what survives and what doesn't? It was not a question that Dr. Lemmon had been thinking about, but he allowed that it was worth considering. A few years later he was hired away by Claremont Graduate School in California. Despite a weak heart, he climbed a hillside and was felled by a heart attack right there. He can't have been more than forty years old. An austere volume, *Beginning Logic*, has survived him. When I look at its bleak truth tables, I feel that it doesn't do justice to the man.

I had arrived at Oxford naïvely imagining that philosophy taught us the meaning of life. I went to public lectures by Gilbert Ryle, whose book *The Concept of Mind* was then in fashion. It was plainly written but, like the psychologists of the day, Ryle aimed to reduce mind to behavior. I even attended a seminar by A. J. Ayer, until I realized that I didn't understand half of what was said, not least by his voluble graduate students. In 1936, at the age of twenty-six, "Freddie" Ayer had written *Language, Truth and Logic*, declaring most philosophical problems to be meaningless—especially the ones that undergraduates were likely to find interesting.

Late in life—he died in 1989—Ayer had a "near-death" experience. A resolute non-believer, he nonetheless wrote an article titled "What I Saw When I Was Dead." He told his attending physician: "I saw a Divine Being. I'm afraid I'm going to have to revise all my books and opinions."[3]

Later he said the experience had weakened "not my belief that there is no life after death, but my inflexible attitude towards that belief."[4]

"Oxford philosophy" was in some ways (intentionally) disillusioning, but later I came to see its usefulness. Many problems in philosophy had flourished over the years because the words formulating them often had no clear meaning. Philosophers had sometimes even indulged that imprecision. "Fitness," at any rate, seemed worth analyzing, especially if its vagueness had misled biologists into believing that a mechanism of evolution had been discovered. Maybe they had only discovered that saying the same thing in two different ways could be so construed.

The 1860 encounter between Huxley and Bishop Wilberforce was seen as a debate between religion and science. It was the first time, but far from the last, that Darwinism would generate such a conflict. Over the next 150 years science and religion were routinely portrayed as antagonists, as they still are today. But it is a modern conceit. A counterclaim was persuasively made by Cambridge University's James Hannam in *The Genesis of Science* (2010). Medieval Christianity actually laid the groundwork for the blossoming of science, Hannam argued. Newton, Faraday, and Clerk Maxwell, to name just three, embraced religion even as they advanced science.

Nonetheless, the "religion versus science" stereotype did arise after Darwin's *The Origin of Species*, and in consequence of it. In 1925 it was reinforced in America, when John Scopes was indicted for teaching evolution in defiance of a Tennessee statute. The trial was a "media circus"—perhaps one of the first. Clarence Darrow derided William Jennings Bryan's fundamentalism and scientific questions about Darwinism hardly arose. Ridicule carried the day. To this day, those who question Darwinism are sometimes still suspected of hostility to reason.

At any rate, the validity of evolution as science is the key question to be addressed in this book. I hope to do so with minimal regard to religion. Stephen Jay Gould once wrote that the "magisteria" of science and religion don't overlap; nonetheless, keeping them separate has never been easy. The main reason is that Darwin's supporters are eager to blur the distinction. Often they resemble inquisitors, hunting for a heretical motive whenever criticism of evolution is raised.

Darwin himself frequently argued his case in *The Origin of Species* by favorably contrasting his theory of "descent with modification," with the old story of "independent creation." The former, obviously, was more plausible to him. Nonetheless, we plainly see evidence of design in complex, self-reproducing organisms. But Darwin and his modern disciples have insisted that that is a delusion. I question whether it really is, and discuss the intelligent design movement in a later chapter.

In his correspondence—often less inhibited than his books—Darwin was disposed to give theological reasons for rejecting the evidence of design. "There seems to me too much misery in the world," he wrote to Asa Gray in 1860. "I cannot persuade myself that a beneficent and omnipotent God would have designedly created the *Ichneumonidae* [digger wasps] with the express intention of their feeding within the living bodies of caterpillars, or that a cat should play with mice."[5]

After I graduated from Oxford the evolution question faded from my mind; it wasn't revived until ten years later. Then, in America, I came across a surprising book, *Darwin Retried* (1973). Its author, Norman Macbeth, was a Harvard-trained lawyer. We may think of him as the forerunner to Phillip Johnson, the law professor at U. C. Berkeley who did so much to launch the intelligent design movement.

Macbeth's book carried impressive endorsements by Jacques Barzun, Arthur Koestler, and Karl Popper. "I regard the book as most meritorious and as a really important contribution to the debate," Popper wrote.[6] A philosopher who was taken seriously at Oxford, Popper argued that to be certified as scientific, theories must in principle be falsifiable. It must be possible to devise experiments that can put such theories to the test, maybe corroborating them, or more critically, showing them to be false.

Was that possible with Darwin's theory? Popper's criterion has since been challenged, but his principle of falsification is sound. True, a theory that is sufficiently hedged and qualified can be protected against all opposition. But hedged theories make for poor science and when the Popperian test is weakened, so are the claims of hedged theories.

Macbeth's book cited such pillars of Darwinian orthodoxy as Ernst Mayr, George Gaylord Simpson, and Sir Julian Huxley (grandson of T. H.). I was delighted to see that one of the authorities cited by Macbeth—Conrad Waddington of Edinburgh University—confirmed my earlier doubts. A developmental biologist and a member of the small group of evolutionists who had shaped what became known as the neo-Darwinian synthesis, Waddington said in 1959:

> Darwin's major contribution was the suggestion that evolution can be explained by the natural selection of random variations. Natural selection, which was at first considered as though it were a hypothesis that was in need of experimental or observational confirmation, turned out on closer inspection to be a tautology, a statement of an inevitable although previously unrecognized relation. It states that the fittest individuals in a population (defined as those that leave most offspring) will leave most offspring. Once the statement is made, its truth is apparent.[7]

Norman Macbeth and I soon became friends and we discussed this and many other things. He lived near Manhattan, and he introduced me to biologists and curators at the American Museum of Natural History in New York. I would learn that they had much more to say on related topics. I also had lengthy discussions with Colin Patterson, Gary Nelson (an expert on fossil fishes), and Norman Platnick (an expert on spiders).

In his autobiography, Karl Popper said he had come to the conclusion that "Darwinism is not a testable scientific theory, but a metaphysical research program."[8] To say that a species now living is adapted to its environment "is almost tautological," he wrote. "Adaptation or fitness is defined by modern evolutionists as survival value, and can be measured by actual success in survival. There is hardly any possibility of testing a theory as feeble as this."[9]

Further controversy ensued, for Popper—apparently under pressure in England—partially recanted in 1978. Later, in 1988, I had a chance to interview Popper myself, when he spent a week at the Hoover Institution at Stanford University. I immediately brought up the issue of natural selection. He told me that his opinion had not changed. He also said he thought that natural selection had in fact been falsified "by Darwin's own theory." Distortions introduced by sexual selection sometimes meant that offspring were not better adapted than their parents, he said.

When I mentioned that Darwinism had evidently benefited from the idea of Progress, widely accepted in the mid-nineteenth century but widely rejected in the late twentieth, Popper said that "I have been one of the people who have destroyed it." He said he had "preached" along those lines in his book *The Poverty of Historicism*.

Popper's comment that Darwin's theory is "feeble" is certainly true, and Darwinism can also be viewed as a "research program." But it's not clear that natural selection can ever be falsified in any particular context. (See my Chapter 5.) Suffice it to say that evolutionists cling to natural selection, and have done so tenaciously ever since Darwin. It is the main mechanism of biological improvement, or progression from molecules to man, that has been attributed to the undirected or random operations of the natural world.

Both Popper and Koestler suggested that Darwinism was a child of its time, inspired more by the *zeitgeist* than by science strictly construed. What about today? In his posthumously published book, *The Discarded Image* (1964), C. S. Lewis argued that the scientific facts that seem important in one age may be seen quite differently in another, or may be ignored altogether.

The question whether our time is significantly different from Darwin's is an important one, and I discuss it in my first chapter.

# 1. DARWINISM IN OUR TIME

IN 1949, C. S. LEWIS WROTE TO A FRIEND THAT "EVOLUTION, ETC." was the "assumed background" of modern thought.[1] Then, in *The Discarded Image*, he argued that "a developing world," by which he meant an evolving one, was "obviously in harmony with the revolutionary and the romantic temper."[2] He was specifically thinking of Darwin's theory.

As history unfolds, he continued, later generations are likely to look for a new "Model," or worldview. That search may well precede any evidence pointing to or requiring such a transformation. But when the desire for a new outlook matures, scientists "go to work and discover the evidence."[3]

Nature, Lewis went on, "has all sorts of phenomena in stock and can suit many different tastes." In short, the "model" of a particular time "reflects the prevalent psychology of an age almost as much as it reflects the state of that age's knowledge."[4]

The worldview of Lewis's day was likely to change sooner or later, and we seem to be in such a transition period today and perhaps have been for a decade or longer.

Three or four such changes are worth noting. The first and perhaps most important is the loss of the idea of Progress (throughout, "Progress" is capitalized to denote the philosophy as it existed in Darwin's day). (See Chapter 21.) In Darwin's day, Progress was thought of as an all-embracing fact. In his *Autobiography* Darwin said that "man in the distant future will be a far more perfect creature than he now is."[5] He also said at the end of *The Origin of Species* that "all corporeal and mental endowments will tend to progress toward perfection."[6] Few believe anything like that today.

The word "evolution" does not occur once in *The Origin*. ("Evolved" appears once—it is the last word in the book.) Instead Darwin referred to *improvement*, which does convey the idea of progress. Either *improved* or *improvement* appears dozens of times.

Victorian philosophers, Darwin among them, were immersed in the idea of Progress. They were, Lewis wrote, "favoured members of the happiest class in the happiest country in the world at the world's happiest period."[7] They took progress for granted.

One only has to read statements by our environmentalists to see how much things have changed. Mankind today is seen as the ruination of the planet. The alleged extinction of recent or contemporary species is blamed on human carelessness, while "climate change" (assumed to be anthropogenic) has become a major cause. Supposed remedies take precedence over such mundane matters as economic growth and the well-being of the poor. They are embraced by the ruling class all over Europe and the Western world.

The second change is demographic: Fertility rates have fallen below replacement level right across the Western world. Food production widely outpaces population growth, and obesity exceeds hunger as a health risk. Thomas Robert Malthus would not have expected that. According to his calculations, population increased geometrically and was destined to outrun food-supply. Furthermore, Darwin's theory of evolution was directly inspired by the Malthusian doctrine.

The worldview underlying Darwinism conformed to the spirit of its age—that of the late Enlightenment. As long as the two were broadly aligned, Darwin's philosophy was accepted by most scientists, and therefore by most educated laymen. Articles in academic journals were waved through the familiar checkpoints. "Peer review," for example, is sometimes used as a barrier to entry for non-approved science. Within the academic world, dissenters from Darwinism could be "expelled." As for biology departments, no dissent is permitted for untenured faculty.

*Creationist* has become the accusation of choice against dissenters, while authoritarianism or "scientism" is frequently substituted for science.

Nonetheless, we are seeing a tide that is slowly turning. Faith in evolutionism—and it is a faith—has declined along with the new hostility to Progress. That is to be expected because a progressive philosophy was built into Darwinism from the beginning. At the same time, large holes have begun to appear in the science.

The intelligent design movement, which rose to prominence in the 1990s and was promptly dismissed by the academy, has flourished. The philosopher and mathematician William A. Dembski, one of the founders of the movement, said recently that it has grown internationally and has:

> pressed Western intellectuals to take seriously the claim that life and the cosmos are the product of intelligence. To be sure, many of them reject this claim. But their need to confront and refute it suggests that our mental environment is no longer stagnating in the atheistic materialism that for so long has dominated Western intellectual life... With atheistic materialism now itself in question, Christianity is again on the table for discussion.[8]

As an additional change, one might also mention the digital revolution, and with it the Internet. It is comparable in magnitude to the change wrought by the printing press in the fifteenth century. What the long-term effect of the digital revolution will be no one can foresee. But it is decentralizing the flow of information and, to the previously marginalized, the cost of information has been greatly reduced. One might say that the flow of information is being democratized. In particular, criticism of Darwin's theory of evolution now reaches many more people than it did when journals like *Science* and *Nature* were able to dominate science news.

For a decade or two, Darwinism's promoters and beneficiaries, most of them lodged within universities, will pretend that nothing much is happening. But the auguries are not good. Those who claim to live by science will eventually die by science.

Historians thrive because it is difficult to know in detail what happened a hundred years ago, let alone a thousand. Darwinists benefit from the great difficulty of knowing what happened a million years ago, not to mention a billion. They are pleased to think that because some skeptics reject their extrapolations and conclusions, they are opposed to "science."

But, as I hope to show in the following chapters, the science of neo-Darwinism was poor all along, and supported by very few facts. I have become ever more convinced that, although Darwinism has been promoted as science, its unstated role has been to prop up a philosophy—the philosophy of materialism—and atheism along with it.

## Darwin's House of Cards

DARWINISM WAS once a well-fortified castle, with elaborate towers, moats, and battlements. It remained in that condition for well over 100 years—from the publication of *The Origin of Species* in 1859 to the Darwin Centennial and then for perhaps three decades after that. Today, however, it more closely resembles a house of cards, built out of flimsy icons rather than hard evidence, and liable to blow away in the slightest breeze.

David Gelernter, who survived one of the Unabomber's mailed explosive devices, said in 2014 that "attacking Darwin is the sin against the Holy Ghost that pious scientists are taught never to forgive."[9] That is mostly still true today, but the times are changing. In November 2016, the Royal Society in London, one of the world's most eminent scientific societies, convened a group of scientists to discuss "calls for revision of the standard theory of evolution," acknowledging that "the issues involved remain hotly contested."[10] The meeting itself appears to have been a dud, with nothing genuinely capable of rescuing the standard theory having been proposed. But the fact that the meeting was convened at all is telling. It offers hope that the issues to be discussed in the following chapters may yet receive a serious airing.

# 2. DARWIN'S MISTAKE

## Warm Little Pond

DARWIN'S CLAIM to fame was the discovery of natural selection, widely regarded as the mechanism of evolution. But before taking a closer look at that, we should consider the origin of life itself. How did that happen? In the second (1860) edition of *The Origin of Species*, Darwin speculated, "[P]robably all the organic beings which have ever lived on this earth have descended from some one primordial form, into which life was first breathed by the Creator."[1]

"First breathed *by the Creator*." The last three words, not present in the first edition of 1859, were perhaps a tactful concession toward the advocates of "special creation" who were still dominant in 1860. In the same 1860 edition, Darwin made a similar addition to the end of the book: "There is grandeur in this view of life, with its several powers, having been originally breathed by the Creator into a few forms or into one."[2]

Here he allowed that life might have been "breathed into" matter more than once, by special actions of "the Creator." But no such intellectual evasion was needed twelve years later, when he wrote to his close friend and supporter, the botanist Joseph Hooker:

> But if (& oh! what a big if!) we could conceive in some warm little pond with all sorts of ammonia & phosphoric salts, light, heat, electricity &c present,— that a protein compound was chemically formed, ready to undergo still more complex changes...[3]

Now he was hoping to find that life might have originated in a "warm little pond." But in the ensuing 145 years, numerous attempts to generate life in test tubes have been made, and all have failed. The Miller-Urey experiment of 1953 produced mainly a simple amino acid (along with traces of some others) under conditions that did not match the early earth environment it intended to replicate.

No further progress has been made. "The origin-of-life field is a failure—we still do not have even a plausible coherent model, let alone a validated scenario, for the emergence of life on Earth,"[4] Eugene Koonin said in 2011. A Russian immigrant at the NIH and a senior investigator at the National Center for Biotechnology Information, Koonin also said that "A succession of exceedingly unlikely steps is essential for the origin of life," making "the final outcome seem almost like a miracle."[5] Koonin also writes:

> Scientists have also been unable to find life on Mars or anywhere else. The question how life began, and why it seems to be unique here, remains a conspicuous difficulty for the materialistic view of life.[6]

Life has this remarkable feature: Organisms can reproduce themselves. Darwin and just about everyone else took their self-reproducing capacity for granted. It does happen, obviously. Bacteria do it asexually. Cells in the body do it. But a big leap of faith was required to accept that the accidental collision of molecules—even given billions of years—could generate self-reproducing entities called cells. Bear in mind that natural selection can play no role at this stage, because it assumes the prior existence of self-reproducing entities.

We also need to remind ourselves just how improbable such things are. No non-living thing has ever been able to reproduce itself without assistance from an intelligent (human) agent. If it could be done, factory assembly lines might well become a thing of the past.

As to natural selection, it also seems remarkable that the machinery of evolution should be built automatically into self-reproducing organisms. But that is what many of those with scientific aspirations came to believe after *The Origin of Species* was published.

What do we really know about natural selection? To summarize the current view: As a source of innovation, mutations in the DNA molecule generate random variations, and natural selection then acts as a filtering device. "Unfit" variants rarely survive even the early stages of development. As a matter of observation, then, what we find when organisms reproduce is that descendants incorporate small changes. Offspring differ a little from their parents, and their offspring differ even more from their grandparents. And so on. So the reproduction that we see is imperfect. All die in the end, but some variant forms contrive to leave more offspring than others.

Darwin was a materialist, and his theory was as materialistic as his philosophy. So he could not rely on anything beyond or outside the natural world—a designer for example. In fact, *The Origin* deliberately set out to explain life in all its complexity without any appeal to a designer or creator.

Darwin and his later supporters have assumed that in order to qualify as science the study of nature must appeal exclusively to natural causes. Science and religion must be kept separate; miracles are ruled out. Darwin wanted to establish that the study of nature had been updated, with no role allowed for design or the supernatural. Indeed, if his theory was true, no such designer was needed.

## A Letter from Wallace

DARWIN WAS conducting his own leisurely researches, first in London and then at his country house in Kent, when he heard from Alfred Russel Wallace, a naturalist who had spent time in the Malay Archipelago. In 1858 he sent a letter to Darwin, proposing a theory so similar to Darwin's as to be virtually identical. Wallace's "Ternate Essay," titled "On the Tendency of Varieties to Depart Indefinitely from the Original Type," spurred the dawdling Darwin into action. His patient note-taking became *The Origin of Species* within a year.

Coincidentally, both Darwin and Wallace had read Malthus's "Essay on the Principle of Population," first published in 1798, and expanded in later editions. A free-market economist, Malthus made the argument that population increases geometrically, while food supply grows only arithmetically. The former will rapidly outpace the latter, putting pressure on many organisms and causing many to die of starvation.

Darwin found that Malthus ("that great philosopher") had given him a theory "with which to work." The doctrine of Malthus equally applied "to the animal and vegetable kingdoms," where there could be "no artificial increase of food, and no prudential restraint from marriage," Darwin wrote.[7] Without such restraint, "the earth would soon be covered by the progeny of a single pair." Darwin sounded like a modern-day environmentalist in positing that there would one day "literally not be standing room."[8]

In his *Autobiography*, Darwin said that he first read Malthus in 1838:

It at once struck me that under these circumstances favorable variations would tend to be preserved, and unfavorable ones to be destroyed. The result of this would be the formation of new species.[9]

Wallace said something very similar. Perhaps the most important book he had read, he said, was Malthus's *Principle of Population*. It eventually gave him "the long-sought clue to the effective agent in the evolution of organic species."[10]

In short, both Darwin and Wallace read the same book and responded in the same way: Organisms would find themselves pressured by the Malthusian math, somehow causing them to increase in complexity and to speciate, thereby generating the fitter and then the fittest, allowing the fittest of all to survive.

"How extremely stupid not to have thought of that!"[11] said Thomas Huxley, when he first read Darwin's argument. The philosopher Bertrand Russell was a little more careful: "Darwin's theory was essentially an extension to the animal and vegetable world of laissez-faire economics."[12]

Darwin relentlessly pursued his insight. Organisms live by the Malthusian "struggle." Lighten the pressure, "mitigate the destruction ever so little, and the number of the species will almost instantaneously increase to any amount."[13]

It was as though he thought of new species as waiting in the wings. All organisms had to do was to increase their rate of reproduction and ever more species would appear on stage. At its heart, Darwin's theory was a theory of competition, with free market insights applied to "struggling" animals.

As to Wallace's "indefinite departure from the original type," it is the focal point of what I have called "Darwin's Mistake." Here is the problem in summary:

We all know that small differences are observed between the generations. Offspring may be slightly smaller than the parents, or slightly larger, or different in many other ways. Darwin's mistake was to assume that these differences somehow accumulate over the millennia, so that one species eventually transforms itself into another.

Without evidence, Darwin's supporters today still accept that intergenerational differences accumulate, eventually transforming their phenotype, or bodily form. But such a transformation has never been observed. No species has ever been seen to evolve into another. What scientists do observe is something quite different: reversion to a mean. Such reversion can be analogized to commuting, or going back and forth. But Darwin's theory perceives intergenerational changes as something more resembling an incessant journey. In short, Darwin's mistake was one of extrapolation. Although extrapolation can be a legitimate procedure in scientific analysis, it is always a risky one, and if done without due care can lead to erroneous conclusions.

Wallace's biographer, the science historian Michael Flannery, has pointed out that later in life Wallace changed his mind and embraced what is now called intelligent design. "To me," Flannery said in an interview, "the best source on this is the very title to his book, *The World of Life: A Manifestation of Creative Power, Directive Mind and Ultimate Purpose* (1910)."

In the book, Wallace cited examples of the evidence for design in the natural world. For example, he wrote:

Looking at it as a whole, the bird's wing seems to me to be, of all the mere mechanical organs of any living thing, that which most clearly implies the working out of a preconceived design in a new and apparently most complex and difficult manner, yet so as to produce a marvelously successful result.[14]

Today, Wallace's defection from Darwin's camp is usually either played down or widely ignored.

## Two Questions

EARLY ON, Darwin said that he would offer only "general conclusions" about the origin of species—"that mystery of mysteries."[15] But he would add "a few facts in illustration." Publishing "all the facts, with references," was something that he hoped to do "in a future work."[16] But that work was never written; *The Origin* was merely his "abstract."[17] He rushed to complete it when he saw that Wallace had the same idea and might publish first.[18]

The Malthusian forces are usually balanced, Darwin thought, but a trifling event will give "the victory to one organic being over another." What checks the tendency of a given species to increase? We don't know, even in a "single instance," he allowed.[19] This, too, he would discuss in his future work, and "at considerable length," although he never did.

In *The Origin*, Darwin instead addressed two great questions: Given that offspring are imperfect "copies" of the parental generation, can natural selection on its own really bring about the transmutation from simple to complex forms, generating new species en route? To that question, Darwin's followers have consistently answered yes.

Second, did such organisms form an unbroken parent-offspring chain throughout the history of life? This is the question of universal common descent. It boils down to this: Did life emerge from non-life only once? Or could it have happened several (or many) times?

Because time-travel is impossible, it is difficult to answer the question—other than by looking at fossils or (more recently) at DNA evidence. Even then, the evidence may not be able to resolve the question decisively. Both questions therefore pose a continuing challenge to Darwin's theory.

His own study of domesticated animals provided Darwin with ideas and clues. He joined pigeon-fancier clubs in London and marveled at their diversity: the carrier pigeon, the tumbler, the pouter, the trumpeter, the fantail. An ornithologist, if shown these specimens, might well see them as distinct and "well-defined species." Meanwhile, we should recall that pigeons—whether specially bred or living in the wild—have never been observed to evolve into anything else. Pigeons they have always remained.

Darwin's claim was that, in the natural world, selection "accumulated" differences, just as human breeders accumulate them under domestication. Animal breeders had indeed shown that some hereditary modification is possible. Breeders knew how to cultivate certain traits (color, length of feather or wool, for example), and often found that that the offspring of selected mates had the desired character more abundantly, or more noticeably than its predecessors. So it could be said a small amount of "evolution" has occurred between one generation and the next.

By analogy, then, Darwin argued that the same process arises in nature—only this time much more effectively. With a rhetorical flourish, he wrote in *The Origin*:

> How fleeting are the wishes and efforts of man! How short his time! And consequently how poor will his products be, compared with those accumulated by nature during whole geological periods. Can we wonder, then, that nature's productions should be far 'truer' in character than man's productions; that they should be infinitely better adapted to the most complex conditions of life?[20]

He was saying that whatever man could do, "nature" could do better. Just as human breeders selected those individuals best suited to their needs to be the progenitors of the next generation, so, Darwin argued, nature "selected" those organisms that are best fitted to survive the ongoing struggle for existence. In that way, progressive change would persist.

Darwin then claimed that nature's selection was as "superior to man's feeble efforts as the works of Nature are to those of Art."[21] But here he was speaking metaphorically, not appealing to evidence.

So there it was: improving machinery was built into nature, "daily and hourly scrutinising," Darwin wrote, "silently and insensibly working... at the improvement of each organic being."[22] In this way, Darwin thought, one type of organism would inevitably be transformed into another. He went so far as to write (in the first edition of *The Origin*) that he could see no difficulty in bears becoming "more and more aquatic in their structure and habits, with larger and larger mouths, till a creature was produced as monstrous as a whale."[23] (He abandoned his bears-to-whales speculation in later editions.)

"If feeble man can do much by his powers of artificial selection," he said, he could see no limit "to the beauty and infinite complexity of the co-adaptations between all organic beings."[24] But he failed to point out that "feeble man" is able to "select" because he has a rational mind, whereas it has yet to be shown that nature has any such thing.

## Nature as Agent

IN DARWIN's hands, natural selection resembled a magic wand. It was capable of doing whatever a creator could do. But his theory also introduced something else: the underlying mechanism was no longer supernatural. It had been turned into a naturalistic and "scientific" claim. It was pleasing to the nineteenth century for that reason, as it still is to the modern age more generally.

Paul Nelson, a philosopher of science with Discovery Institute, points out that when Darwin made his arguments, he saw no need for proof. He said, in effect: "Tell me why these minor changes should not add up, over time, to major differences." Of course, asking why a particular thing should not happen evades the duty of a hypothesis to explain how it does happen. It was one of Darwin's favorite rhetorical devices, and he used it repeatedly in *The Origin*.

For quite some time, Darwin's mechanism was not seriously examined. Then the renowned geneticist Thomas H. Morgan, winner of the Nobel Prize for his work in mapping the chromosomes of fruit flies, suggested that the whole thing looks suspiciously like a tautology. "For it may appear little more than a truism," he wrote, "to state that the individuals that are the best adapted to survive have a better chance of surviving than those not so well adapted to survive."[25]

Darwin often wrote as if nature were imbued with purpose. Just as breeders could magnify the differences between their varieties by careful selection of breeding stock, so "nature" itself "selected" varieties in the wild, eventually generating the species that we see. But can "nature" make choices in the same way that a farmer can when he is deciding which variants to select? That it could was one of the main arguments in *The Origin.*

In response to Darwin, the philosopher Jerry Fodor, the author of *What Darwin Got Wrong* (with Massimo Piattelli-Palmarini, 2010) said that natural selection can't make decisions. Fodor also wrote that natural selection "can't run experiments," and it "can't consult the intentions of the builder."

> Doing any of those requires having a mind, and, by general consensus, natural selection doesn't have one. All natural selection can do is respond to correlations between phenotypic traits and fitness. And that doesn't help because, by assumption, if either of the confounded traits is correlated with fitness, so too is the other.[26]

Fodor's point was that whole organisms leave offspring, and they include numerous traits that are inevitably conflated. So when they leave offspring, it is impossible to say which of the conflated traits has been selected for. Fodor's criticism has never been rebutted.

## Running Wild

AT ONE point, Darwin brought up an objection to his own theory: Naturalists claimed that domestic varieties, when set free and run wild, "gradually but certainly revert in character to their aboriginal stocks."

If so, "no deductions can be drawn from domestic races to species in a state of nature."[27] Here, in effect, Darwin himself was bringing up the "extrapolation" objection.

But Darwin partly raised the issue himself. "Many of the most strongly-marked domestic varieties could not possibly live in a wild state,"[28] he allowed. Being conspicuous, they would be selected against.

"Reversion," as he called it, also implied that varieties don't stray far from a mean, or what Wallace called the "original type." Unanswered, that criticism might revive the theory of "archetypes," as proposed by Darwin's contemporary and opponent, Richard Owen, who founded London's Natural History Museum. Darwin firmly rejected archetypes—the original pattern on which all things of the same kind are based—because they would set sharp limits to variation, and that would be fatal to his theory.

That such limits to variation do exist was "assumed by most authors,"[29] Darwin allowed, although he claimed not to know of "a single fact" on which their claim was based. But neither could he point to a single case of the unlimited variation that his theory required. All was based on his willingness to extrapolate from the small variations that we do routinely see *between successive generations*.

In *The Origin*, Darwin gave one imaginary illustration of natural selection. He supposed a place where wolves are hard-pressed for food and prey is scarce. In that setting, he could "see no reason to doubt that the swiftest and slimmest wolves would have the best chance of surviving and to be preserved or selected."[30]

But there is indeed a "reason to doubt" victory to the swiftest, as I shall argue in Chapter 5. In much the same way, he went on, man can "improve the fleetness of his greyhounds"—by "methodical selection."[31] But the two cases are not remotely comparable. The selection of greyhounds by human breeders for speed is a purposive, goal-directed act; while the wolf case is not. In Chapter 6, I discuss the cases of natural selection that have actually been observed.

Darwin also asked why, if species have descended from others by fine gradations, we don't see "innumerable transitional forms." Furthermore, why are species so "well defined"? Why is "all nature" not "in confusion?" These were good questions. He tried to answer them by saying that the same process that "improved" and transformed some varieties extinguished their predecessors: "Both the parent and all the transitional varieties will generally have been exterminated by the very process of formation and perfection of the new form."[32]

So once again, his understanding of natural selection as an all-powerful force came to his rescue. It could account both for the appearance and the disappearance of intermediate forms, whichever was needed. Meanwhile the intermediate forms that his theory required have remained (mostly) elusive to this day.

Darwin said at one point that if "any complex organ" could be shown to exist, which could not have been formed by "numerous, successive, slight modifications," then his theory "would absolutely break down." But he could find "no such case." True, an organ "so perfect as the eye" was enough to "stagger anyone." But for any organ,

> [I]f we know of a long series of gradations in complexity, each good for its possessor, then, under changing conditions of life, there is no logical impossibility in the acquirement of any conceivable degree of perfection through natural selection.[33]

Notice the weakness of his response. To say that "perfection" was not logically impossible for natural selection leaves unanswered the question: was it physically possible? In his book *Darwin's Black Box*, Lehigh University biochemist Michael Behe refuted Darwin's claim that complex organs could be formed by a long series of steps. (See my Chapter 14 for more on Behe's objection.)

What about instinctive behavior? Such acts are performed by young animals "without any experience" and without knowing their purpose. Darwin mentioned the precise honeycomb structures of bees, and the even more complex edifices built by ants. Instincts, he argued, were similar to habits. They can be modified by "the will or reason." Mozart performed at the age of three, but even he had to practice. Similarly, it would be an "error" to suppose that instincts were acquired in a single generation.

As Darwin saw, a "degree of variation in instincts" was indispensable for natural selection to apply. Everything had to appear in the step-by-step fashion that his theory decreed. In fact, he wrote, "the canon... 'Natura non facit saltum' [nature doesn't make jumps] is applicable to instincts as well as to corporeal structure."[34] The problem for Darwin was that he knew of no cases of gradually acquired instincts. Instinctive behavior, therefore, really does seem to involve "jumps," without trial and error. Mozart indeed had to practice, but hive-making bees don't.

## Fossil Record

DARWIN CANDIDLY accepted that his theory predicted a "finely graduated organic chain,"[35] which geology failed to show. It was the "gravest objection which can be urged against my theory."[36] Then he added a further complication: We should be looking for common ancestors, not intermediates between two forms. We don't expect to find intermediates between the horse and the tapir, for example. What we do expect are links "between each and an unknown common parent."[37] But that only magnified his problem: "The number of intermediate and transitional links... must have been inconceivably great. But assuredly, if this theory be true, such have lived upon this earth."[38]

Why then don't we see the intermediates that "must" have existed? Because "new and improved varieties will inevitably supplant and exterminate the older, less improved and intermediate varieties."[39] So "species are rendered to a large extent defined and distinct objects."[40] Here, perhaps surprisingly, he brought in the phenomenon of extinction to rescue his theory. He argued that species need environmental "slots" if they are to flourish. "The number of places in the polity of nature is not indefinitely great,"[41] he said. The extinction of old species therefore opened up new spaces for new ones.

To strengthen his case, Darwin said that only a small portion of the Earth had been explored. So a poor fossil record was to be expected. Still, Darwin allowed, if we study a single formation, it is "difficult to understand, why we do not therein find closely graduated varieties between the allied species which lived at its commencement and at its close."[42] (More recent analyses of the fossil record have shown that it is more complete than most people realize. I discuss the issue in Chapter 10.)

When it came to classification, Darwin was a "lumper," not a "splitter."[43] He concluded that there is "no fundamental distinction between species and varieties."[44] This worked greatly to his advantage, because mutation and natural selection can be shown to increase the number of varieties but not to generate new species. To this day such species-transformations have not been demonstrated. They would be headline news if they had.

He restated his faith in unlimited variation. The claim that it is limited was "incapable of proof," he wrote. Since we see both variation and "a powerful agent always ready to act and select," why should we doubt that more variation "in any way useful... would be preserved?" He saw "no limit to this power."[45]

Again, we find Darwin arguing not that his theory had been shown to be right but that his opponents had failed to show that it was wrong.

Darwin wrote that when The Origin was published "eminent naturalists" had rejected his theory. Why so? Because they were convinced that species are immutable. Also, as Darwin saw it, we are slow to admit any great change when "we do not see the intermediate steps."[46] Yet to this day species still do seem to be immutable and the intermediate steps are still largely missing.

In the following chapters I shall look more closely at Darwin's various claims, in the light both of new evidence against them and of the failure of Darwinians to unearth much in support of them. But first, in the next chapter, I shall briefly review the copiously documented Darwin Centennial, held in Chicago in 1959, with Darwin's grandson Sir Charles in attendance. Darwinism probably reached its greatest level of support at about that time.

# 3. Darwin's Curia at the Centenary

Darwin's centenary proceedings, celebrated at the University of Chicago in 1959, give us a good picture of the conventional wisdom about Darwinism prevailing at that time. All the eminent evolutionists of the day were assembled in Chicago—Sir Julian Huxley, Ernst Mayr, Sewall Wright, George Gaylord Simpson, Louis Leakey, Theodosius Dobzhansky, Ledyard Stebbins, Hermann J. Muller, E. B. Ford, and C. H. Waddington. In an inspired moment years later, the well-known Harvard naturalist Edward O. Wilson referred to them as Darwin's "Curia."

In 1959, the opinions of biblical fundamentalists on evolution were ignored. National polls, showing that only a minority outside the academic world actually believed in undirected evolution, had not yet been undertaken. The school of thought known as intelligent design did not exist. In short, Darwin's theory encountered few centennial challenges.

Furthermore, earlier problems had been resolved. In the 1860s, an apparently fatal criticism of Darwinism had been raised by a Scottish engineer named Fleeming Jenkin. Helpful variations, he thought, would inevitably be blended and diluted away by bad mutations in later generations. But Mendel's laws of inheritance, which Darwin had not known about, showed the criticism to be in error. "Genes" don't blend, and are preserved from one generation to the next. Meanwhile, in an attempt to solve the non-problem that he faced, Darwin took refuge in Lamarckism—the inheritance of acquired characteristics. But that in turn was shown to have been an unnecessary move. (Recently, the field called epi-genetics may have shown that acquired characters can be transmitted to future generations, but such claims are controversial. I review them briefly in Chapter 14.)

In other ways, the post-Mendelian dispensation was highly accom-modating toward Darwinism. Throughout the twentieth century (but not in the twenty-first), genes could be invoked without being observed, and one or many genes could be thought of as contributing solely or jointly to any trait. Ronald A. Fisher, Sewall Wright, and other mathe-matically inclined population geneticists went to work, and by the 1940s had cobbled together what seemed to be a satisfactory solution to all problems. The melding of natural selection and Mendelian genetics be-came known as the neo-Darwinian synthesis.

At the centenary, other difficulties were minimized or ignored. The double helical structure of DNA, coiled within the nucleus of every cell, recently described by James Watson and Francis Crick, was seen as a solution to old problems rather than a source of new ones. In 1956 the chromosomes were reliably counted for the first time—forty-six in the case of humans. But beyond that, the cell remained largely *terra incog-nita*.

With the aid of powerful microscopes, it was felt, the hidden things of this world would soon be brought to light, and any remaining doubts would be swept away. Such was the temper of the time.

In the Chicago discussions, harmony usually displaced argument. At one point Dobzhansky said, "I agree with both Mayr and Stebbins."

Julian Huxley: "That's bad. We're all agreeing."

Huxley to Wright: "I take it you entirely agree with Stebbins."

Wright: "I agree with everybody."[1]

In short, they presented a united front.

But in a late interview with *Skeptic*, published in 2000, Ernst Mayr showed that that harmony was short-lived. At the age of ninety-five, he was out of sorts and displeased with a number of his colleagues. For ex-ample, he said of George Gaylord Simpson, the author of *The Major*

*Features of Evolution*, that he never really understood the species concept, "because he didn't have a personal acquaintance with nature."[2] Mayr also said that "there are two kinds of scientists: media scientists and scientist's scientists." Stephen J. Gould, Richard Dawkins and E. O. Wilson were "media scientists in the sense of publishing for the public." (Wilson himself later called Dawkins a "journalist.")

Sir Charles Darwin (1887–1962), grandson of the great man, crossed the Atlantic and joined them in their deliberations. He took the occasion to express "enormous admiration for Julian's grandfather," T. H. Huxley, the hero of the Oxford debate in 1860. Sir Charles described T. H. as having defended evolutionary theory, then a novelty, against a dissenter "who insisted that a species was a species." Huxley had wittily admonished the doubter: "Do you really believe that at one moment all the molecules jump together suddenly somewhere in space to create a perfect full-grown rhinoceros?"[3]

Darwin himself made a similar remark at the end of *The Origin*. "Do they really believe that at innumerable periods in the earth's history certain elemental atoms have been commanded suddenly to flash into living tissues?" he asked.[4] But it was the image of an abruptly materializing rhinoceros that had aroused Sir Charles's admiration.

Speaking at the Chicago event, Sir Julian—he was knighted after serving one term as Director General of UNESCO—could say of evolution: "It simply is not just a theory any longer. It is a fact, like the fact that the earth goes around the sun."[5] Leading Darwinists today, among them Richard Dawkins and the University of Chicago's Jerry Coyne, still repeat that mantra word for word. No one is permitted to step out of line, and in 1959 few were inclined to do so.

In the centenary proceedings, the Harvard astronomer Harlow Shapley outdid all the others in adulation. He told a television audience that the most difficult test of all had been met. An experiment had been conducted at the University of Chicago, assuring us:

> of what we had rather suspected for a long time: that one can bridge the gap between the inanimate and the animate and that the appear-

ance of life is essentially an automatic biochemical development that comes along naturally when physical conditions are right.[6]

"We can evolve [life]," Shapley added. He even told skeptics that "during the coming week we shall hear about evolving it in test tubes."[7]

He was referring to an experiment by Stanley Miller, conducted with his PhD advisor, Harold Urey. Later known as the Miller-Urey experiment, it showed that if electricity is passed through chemicals simulating the earth's early atmosphere, some of the simpler amino acids are precipitated.

But amino acids are about as far from life as nuts and bolts are from a finished automobile and no one today thinks that Miller-Urey bridged the gap between life and non-life. Miller himself, who became a professor of chemistry at UC-San Diego, said almost forty years later: "The problem of the origin of life has turned out to be much more difficult than I and most other people imagined."[8]

The astronomer and cosmologist Carl Sagan said that the Miller-Urey experiment was "the single most significant step in convincing many scientists that life is likely to be abundant in the cosmos."[9] But, despite a great deal of searching and NASA funding since then, no extraterrestrial life has yet been discovered.

Adlai Stevenson, the Governor of Illinois and Democratic presidential candidate, participated in one of the panels. He rejoiced that "we are much more enlightened now."[10] For example, he said, we have learned how to tolerate different philosophies and we know that we have to teach this tolerance to our students.

In contrast to this newfound harmony, said Julian Huxley, the conflict of worldviews in earlier centuries had been extreme. It had involved totally different religions—for example Islam and Christianity.

"One can't say that there is complete reconciliation between Islam and Christianity even now," Huxley added. "But at any rate the religious difference is not a source of political or even of violent ideological conflict."[11]

The revival of Islam, so conspicuous in our own day, was not even a rumor in 1959. Nor were participants inclined to challenge Huxley's optimism.

"You achieve coexistence," said the Chicago anthropologist Sol Tax, who organized the conference and later edited the proceedings for publication. You reach "a new pattern of thought," agreed Huxley, who continued, "the really evolutionary outlook is able to comprehend many apparently disparate facts" and reconcile them.[12]

All seemed to accept that God was no longer needed. Nor did any participants appeal to design. In fact, Darwinism had "come of age." The "most striking phenomenon in biological evolution is the emergence of mind out of an apparently mindless universe,"[13] Huxley crowed.

"Does mind evolve?" Adlai Stevenson wondered.[14]

It only became noticeable "fairly late, with the appearance of well-developed vertebrates and higher mollusks,"[15] instructed Sir Julian, who was never at a loss, no matter how difficult the question.

"This is where you and the religionists diverge," said the emcee, Irv Kupcinet of the *Chicago Sun-Times*. "Most of them go part of the way with Darwin and agree that perhaps God created man out of a number of animals, but they attribute mind and soul to God alone."

Huxley, undeterred, declared that "Darwinism removed the whole idea of God as the creator of organisms from the sphere of rational discussion."[16]

William Paley in his *Natural Theology* (1802) could treat the human eye as so well-adapted that it was obviously designed, Huxley allowed, summarizing pre-Darwinian opinion. And design entailed a designer. But evolutionary theory had long since come to the rescue. Darwin had "pointed out that no supernatural designer was needed," so no further argument was called for.[17]

In fact, Huxley, reassuring the few skeptics who might have remained, reaffirmed evolution's credo that "[natural selection] could account for any known form of life, [so] there was no need for a supernatural agency in its evolution."[18] There was no dissent from other panelists on that score. Darwin himself had limited his antagonism to theism by confining it to his personal correspondence. But by 1959 such caution was no longer needed.

Trying to spice up the proceedings, Irv Kupcinet said that churches still say "it was God alone who instilled spirit and soul and mind into man."

Huxley quickly slapped him down. "That too is completely contrary to the facts," he said. "There was no sudden moment during evolutionary history when spirit was instilled into life." Nor was there any reason to accept such an "arbitrary theological postulate." He was confident that "we can dismiss entirely all thought of a supernatural overriding mind being responsible for the evolutionary process."

"I do, entirely," Darwin's grandson agreed.

"And biologists do, with very few exceptions," said Huxley.

The astronomer Harlow Shapley mentioned his numerous contacts with "the liberal clergy of America" who "accept evolution without objecting to it or worrying about it." So maybe there was little to worry about from the clerical quarter. Still, it was true that the Pope "doesn't deny God," Shapley added—"and you don't either."

"I certainly do," said Huxley.

"Oh, no. If you defined God you wouldn't."

Huxley: "Now don't go into semantics."

Shapley: "You're not an atheist, Julian. You're an agnostic."

Huxley: "I am an atheist, in the only correct sense, that I don't believe in the existence of a supernatural being who influences natural events."[19]

Theodosius Dobzhansky, a Christian, said a few months later (in 1960) that Huxley was "militantly and virulently anti-religious,"[20] and referred to "the wholly justified irritation with Julian Huxley's use of evolution as a weapon to combat religion."[21]

Dobzhansky's comments at the Chicago centenary were often a moderating influence. More than once he reminded his colleagues of how little was known about the topic under discussion. But he was the exception.

Did the Curia bring any new evidence to back up evolutionist claims? There was indeed a bit of novelty, divulged by Edmund B. Ford (1901–1988), a long-time professor at Oxford University. He mentioned an article recently published by Bernard Kettlewell in *Scientific American*, describing the spread of dark-colored moths in polluted English woods. Ford had supervised Kettlewell's research, which had enumerated the *Biston betularia* moth varieties in the woods around the industrial city of Birmingham and also the rural woods of Dorset. Kettlewell's influential article was headlined "Darwin's Missing Evidence."

"Black moths have spread in the industrial areas of Britain within living memory," said Professor Ford.

Not to be outdone, Huxley tossed in, "I might add that the blackness is definitely adaptive and that the black form has got blacker."[22]

Later, the experiment became controversial, as we shall see. Nonetheless, its frequent invocation over the following fifty years showed not only how precious this little gem of evidence was to evolutionists but also how modest it was.

When the panelists were asked what public issues most concerned them, the hydrogen bomb and the population explosion were high on their lists. Contraceptives were urgently needed to cope with the latter. Sir Charles thought that "world government is the obvious answer." But he also admitted it might not work:

> Supposing a world government limits population but one part of the world says 'we don't like your limitations. We are going to have more children because we are more important than anyone else, and you can't have too many pigmies in Central Africa'—or whatever race it may be. What is the world government going to do? Kill them?[23]

"That is a highly hypothetical situation," said Sir Julian. But Sir Charles had a point, surely.

Huxley then aired his own eugenic ambitions. Lots of bad mutations are out there, he warned, and in earlier centuries "natural selection wiped out bad mutations."[24] Now, we keep many carriers of these mutations alive. "For instance people with hemophilia, who would undoubt-edly have died otherwise."

He emphasized that "the whole point of Darwin and his revolution in thought" was that "time is of the essence," and that if our interference with the course of nature continued indefinitely, "the whole genetic ca-pacity of man will be much weakened."[25]

Sir Charles also said that he was greatly impressed by the new "cal-culating machines that are already pretty good at doing the sums we set them." Was something afoot there? A bright young man once told him that to teach machines anything we must train them with rewards and punishments. Then, over time, they will become habituated. Eventual-ly—"and not so many years hence"—they won't need this drill. Then they will "proceed to take charge and tell us many things we don't know."[26]

He was anticipating artificial intelligence, strong claims for which have since been made by Raymond Kurzweil and others. (Kurzweil once predicted that computers will rival human intelligence by 2029.) But even in 1959 it was expected that artificial intelligence would soon over-take the human variety. But half a century later, AI (as it is now called) has been a continuing disappointment. All the evidence today is that computers do what they are told—if they don't crash first.

The discovery of extraterrestrial life also seemed probable—even im-minent, in 1959. Harlow Shapley was looking for "high sentient beings," who suffer from this "neurotic complex we call intelligence." It's "a pretty common quality," he thought. "It is not confined to man but goes down through the animal world."[27]

Shapley mentioned that $10^{20}$ stars are visible with the help of tele-scopes, many of which have been involved in useful (because planet-forming) collisions and accidents. He didn't see why humans—living on the periphery of our galaxy—should consider "our own planet the only blessed place." He added this:

> You see, there was a time when we might say we swore by a one-planet god, or deity, or something of that kind. That's over! We have to realize that this is an enormous universe, and it should be a plea-

sure to be in such a big operation. Fancy the myopic predictions and concepts of the ancient Church Fathers compared with what we can get now from the laboratories or from the philosophers who are following them.[28]

But extraterrestrial life has turned out to be another let-down. Over half a century later, the laboratories and telescopes have shown us little that we didn't already know was out there in 1959.

An interesting aspect of the centenary was the survival of the faith in Progress. In the nineteenth century it had played a key role in persuading people that evolution was a reality. That faith was already waning by 1959—not surprising considering the two world wars that had intervened—but it was confidently reiterated by the geneticist Hermann J. Muller:

> Even as our own culture could not mean very much to the most superior ape, the culture of a mere million years from now will be so rich and advanced in its potentialities of experience and accomplishment that in it we, with our genetic constitution, would be like imbeciles in a palace. And so I believe that not only our cultural but also our biological evolution will go on to now undreamed-of heights.[29]

Muller sounded like Leon Trotsky, who had predicted that "the average human type will rise to the heights of an Aristotle, a Goethe or a Marx." Like Trotsky, Muller had lived in the Soviet Union in the 1930s; but unlike Trotsky (assassinated in 1940) he lived to tell the tale.

Muller had been awarded the Nobel Prize in 1946. His claim to fame was his study of the effects of X-rays on fruit flies. In an article titled "New Discovery Speeds Up Evolution," *Scientific American* reported in 1928 that "evolutionary changes, or mutations, can be produced 150 times as fast by the use of X-rays as they can by the ordinary processes of nature."[30]

Today, all attempts to "speed up evolution" with X-rays, which are always destructive to the experimental animal, have been abandoned.

Technological progress still proceeds apace, but faith in the benign transformation of human nature is dead today. That may be one of the most important cultural changes since Darwin's day. Signs of its fading were already appearing in 1959.

Harlow Shapley, for example, ventured to say that "it begins to look as if the human race is one of the worst things that has happened to the Earth."[31] That would have shocked Darwin. But it is widely shared by environmentalists today. Shapley even referred to human intelligence as a "mental disease."

But Julian Huxley never lost the progressive faith that had animated both his grandfather and Darwin himself. He praised Muller for stressing "the long term importance of genetic improvement." We should take care to build in "some kind of conscious eugenic selection" in our own experiments, to guard against backsliding. We should also recall the "equally essential improvement of purely psychosocial organs"—by which Huxley meant the human mind.[32]

At the end of the conference Huxley delivered a speech—some called it a sermon—from the pulpit of the Rockefeller Chapel. He echoed the sentiments of Herbert Spencer, the leading apostle of progress in Darwin's day.

"Our evolutionary vision now includes the discovery that biological advance exists," Huxley said, each step or grade being "characterized by a new and improved pattern of organization."[33] At about the same time, he said that man was on the verge of becoming "business manager for the cosmic process of evolution."[34]

Huxley and Muller were not just Spencerian but also Darwinian in adhering to this faith. Darwin himself had written at the end of The Origin of Species that "all corporeal and mental endowments will tend to progress toward perfection." In his Autobiography, Darwin expressed his belief "that man in the distant future will be a far more perfect creature than he now is."[35]

Today, putting it mildly, we no longer believe that.

Perhaps the main change between the centenary in 1959 and the 150th anniversary of The Origin in 2009 is that Huxley, Shapley, Darwin, Muller, and others were more confident and relaxed in their views than we might expect from a comparable gathering today. They were united, they expected no challenge or dissent, and they received none.

It's also time to point out that Darwinian evolution never did have much in the way of evidence to support it. Today, following Julian Huxley's lead, it is often embraced more for the support that it gives to atheistic philosophy than for its science. The scientific evidence for evolution is not only weaker than is generally supposed, but as new discoveries have been made since 1959, the reasons for accepting the theory have diminished rather than increased.

An important issue that arose in the twenty-first century is the reliability of claims made by Darwin and his followers on behalf of universal common descent. That is the subject of my next chapter.

# 4. COMMON DESCENT:
# FACT OR THEORY?

THE PHRASE "TREE OF LIFE," CLAIMING THAT ALL ORGANISMS ARE related, occurs only once in *The Origin of Species*. Darwin illustrated a part of that tree in the book's single diagram. The best-known depiction of the tree of life was published by the German physiologist Ernst Haeckel, in 1879. It was titled "The Pedigree of Man."

"Universal common descent" is another way of making the same claim: the claim that all organisms are cousins, however distant their cousinship may be. "Common ancestry" is a deduction from universal common descent. If common descent is true, then any two species must have a common ancestor, no matter how dissimilar they may appear to be. Branches must meet somewhere if the "tree" is real. Twigs can't just hang in mid-air.

Cats and dogs, for example, both belong to the order *Carnivora*. They may have had a common ancestor about 60 million years ago. Chimpanzees and humans are assumed to have shared a more recent common ancestor, perhaps six million years ago. But we don't know what any of these ancestral creatures looked like. Richard Dawkins, as we shall see, discussed some of the difficulties in visualizing them.

Notice that the claim of chimp-human common ancestry is not the same as saying that chimpanzees themselves are *ancestral* to humans. Biologists rarely claim that one species evolved into another. But if it's true that all organisms are cousins, what eventually became humans and chimps must at some earlier point have been united at a branching point.

That theoretical creature is usually called an "ape"—or more technically, a non-human hominoid.

The last common ancestor of chimps and humans was certainly not fossilized, and amazingly, the only known fossil of *any* chimpanzee was found only twelve years ago (in 2004). That fossil (which came in the form of teeth), was said to be alive half a million years ago.

As an aside, chimpanzees played a role in Darwin's formulation of *The Origin of Species*. They were brought to London's Zoological Garden for the first time in the 1830s. Queen Victoria visited the zoo, but was not amused. She found the chimpanzees "painfully and disagreeably human."[1] But Darwin was impressed. Coming from a wealthy family, he was admitted into the cage of a chimp named Jenny who was kept inside the heated giraffe house during the winter. When a keeper sternly addressed the chimp ("Jenny, if you will stop bawling and be a good girl, I will give you the apple"), Darwin felt sure that she understood every word.

Today, common descent is mostly accepted as a fact within the academic world. Louis Pasteur is said to have called the claim that all life comes from other life the "law of biogenesis." The immunologist Peter Medawar defined that law as the claim that "all living organisms are the progeny of living organisms that went before them." Alternatively, if a creature were shown not to have parents, the theory of evolution would collapse.

Medawar (1915–1987), who won the Nobel Prize in Physiology or Medicine in 1960, added this comment:

> The Law of Biogenesis is arguably the most fundamental in biology, for evolution may be construed as a form of biogenesis that provides for the occasional begetting of a variant form.[2]

Biogenesis is not fully law-like, however, because by definition the first living organism was not the progeny of anything living. We may therefore ask: If a "law" has one exception, might it not have more than one?

Biologists are not in total accord on the issue today. Some accept a single branching tree, Darwin-style—the monophyletic position. Others think that different branches of life originated independently—the polyphyletic position. For them, the history of life resembles an orchard, not a single exfoliating tree. These "orchard" theorists, as they are called by some, may differ among themselves as to how many separate "trees" there are.

For example, the late microbiologist Carl Woese (1928–2012) argued that "Extant life on Earth is descended not from one, but from three distinctly different cell types." Those three types are found today in the archaea, the bacteria, and the eukaryotes.[3] However, Woese added, "the designs of the three have developed and matured, in a communal fashion, along with those of many other designs that along the way became extinct." Other biologists, differing from Woese, think there may have been more than three original forms.

For Darwinists, the monophyletic position is usually treated as a given. In fact, it is treated as a postulate. According to Casey Luskin, then with the Discovery Institute:

> The truth is that common ancestry is merely an assumption that governs interpretation of the data, not an undeniable conclusion. Whenever data contradicts expectations of common descent, evolutionists resort to a variety of ad hoc rationalizations to save common descent from being falsified.[4]

University of Tufts philosopher Daniel Dennett took the conventional position when he said that Darwin started out with "facts that everyone knows"—that "all of today's living things are the offspring of parents, who are the offspring of grandparents, and so forth." Extrapolating from that, Darwin himself (eventually) decided that "there is a single tree of life."[5]

Theistic evolutionists, whose position is epitomized by BioLogos (founded in 2006 by Francis S. Collins, who later became the Director of the National Institutes of Health), believe that "the diversity and interrelation of all life on earth are best explained by the God-ordained process of evolution with common descent."[6]

BioLogos, too, accepts a single tree of life.

## Turnips Our Cousins

RICHARD DAWKINS once said that we are distant cousins of turnips.[7] In 2004 he wrote an article for the *London Sunday Times* with Richard Harries, then the Bishop of Oxford, who accepted that "evolution is a fact."[8] Others, including the Archbishop of Canterbury, were only too happy to agree. We may recall that Samuel Wilberforce, the earlier and rather more skeptical bishop of Oxford—he debated T. H. Huxley in 1860—drily referred to our "unsuspected cousinship with the mushrooms."[9]

In any event our alleged cousinship, whether with turnips or mushrooms, has certainly not been observed. Since we are unable to go back in time, it's hard to know what could confirm such a claim. But we should retain the skepticism that is appropriate to science and inquire further: Can we really know how many times life appeared from non-life? If once, maybe it did so often.

Early on, Darwin himself raised that as a possibility. He ended *The Origin of Species* with the comment that there was "a grandeur" in his view of life, which he believed was originally "breathed into a few forms or into one."[10] A few forms? Here Darwin was candid enough to admit that he didn't know how often life had arisen from non-life. We still don't know today. In a letter to Joseph Hooker in 1871, Darwin speculated that a "warm little pond" might have been the source of life.[11] His comment serves to remind us that observation often plays little or no role in these ruminations.

Here it is important to add a caution: The theory of common descent is not the same as Darwin's theory of evolution. Darwinism is the more severe doctrine, admitting only material causes. Its goal is to explain the whole of nature within a purely naturalistic framework, with natural selection doing all the work.

Common descent, on the other hand, can embrace design and/or supernatural intervention, and still remain true. All organisms (save the first) could and perhaps did have parents. At the same time, speciation events in the history of life could have been guided by interventions from a source that is external to nature.

Some advocates of intelligent design today accept common descent. The best known is Michael Behe. In his book *Darwin's Black Box* he was the first to set forth the idea of "irreducible complexity." On the other hand, William Dembski, a leader of the intelligent design movement, mildly disagreed with Behe. "Common descent seems to me not all that well established," he said in a brief interview.

> Certain fossil and molecular evidence suggests that a fair amount of evolution may have taken place (perhaps to the level of families, orders, or even classes), but the grand picture of evolution ("monad to Man," as Michael Ruse calls it) seems to me unsupported. Indeed, the evidence seems to be against it.[12]

Others who are critical of Darwinism, but not committed to ID, do accept common descent. For example James A. Barham, an independent researcher, told me that he prefers to assume a God who created

> a natural order that is capable of producing whatever exists under its own steam, without His further intervention. At least, that seems to me the best working assumption, because it forces us to continue to try to think beyond the boundaries of our current understanding.[13]

He argued, not that God "worked a series of miracles," but that "the natural order must somehow contain within it the possibility for our existence. Our job is to investigate the natural order further, so that we may understand how this has been possible."

What is the best evidence for common descent? In his 2009 book *The Greatest Show on Earth*, Dawkins addressed the question and made a genetic argument:

> Today we are pretty certain that all living creatures on this planet are descended from a single ancestor. The evidence… is that the genetic code is universal, all but identical across animals, plants, fungi,

bacteria, archaea and viruses. The 64-word dictionary, by which the three-letter DNA words are translated into twenty amino acids and one punctuation mark, which means 'start reading here' or 'stop reading here,' is the same 64-word dictionary wherever you look in the living kingdoms (with one or two exceptions too minor to undermine the generalization).[14]

Dawkins went on to say that if "some weird, anomalous microbes called the harumscaryotes were discovered, which [used]... a triplet code but not the same sixty-four-word dictionary—if any of these conditions were met, we might suggest that life had originated twice: once for the harumscaryotes and once the rest of life."[15]

He then added a related reason for believing that the genetic code must be universal:

> The reason is interesting. Any mutation in the genetic code itself (as opposed to mutations in the genes that it encodes) would have an instantly catastrophic effect, not just in one place but throughout the whole organism. If any word in the 64-word dictionary changed its meaning, so that it came to specify a different amino acid, just about every protein in the body would instantaneously change, probably in many places along its length. Unlike an ordinary mutation... this would spell disaster.[16]

We might compare Dawkins's "disaster" to an error on a computer keyboard which shifts all letters one position to the left, unbeknownst to the user. This could well render all typed words unintelligible. A simple typo, on the other hand, would introduce an error only into a single word.

Dawkins's argument about the universality of the genetic code seemed impressive at first. But there was a problem. He had accepted one or two exceptions to its universality, but he thought they were "minor." Since that time, however, the National Center for Biotechnology Information, a government agency, has compiled a list of seventeen known variant genetic codes. When it came to the genetic code, then, the exceptions were not minor. Dawkins had not kept up with the latest evidence.

Harvard's Ernst Mayr made the same mistake. He wrote in 1986:

Was Darwin right about common descent? Certainly. The last link in the chain of evidence was the demonstration by molecular biology that all organisms have the same genetic code. There is a historical unity in the entire living world which cannot help but have a deep meaning for any thinking person.[17]

In *One Long Argument* (1993), Mayr doubled down, writing that common descent "has been gloriously confirmed by all researches since 1859." Everything we have learned about the physiology and chemistry of organisms since then "supports Darwin's daring speculation," he wrote.[18]

But J. Craig Venter, a biochemist who was one of the first to sequence the human genome, is among those who have challenged this claim. He forthrightly denied that the genetic code is universal. The bacterium Mycoplasma has a non-universal code, he pointed out. He also said he found it implausible that all organisms on Earth share a common ancestor.

This was publicized in a science forum held at Arizona State University in February 2011, a little over a year after Dawkins's *Greatest Show* was published. The physicist Paul Davies and others, including two Nobel Prize winners, participated in the event, which was videotaped. Richard Dawkins himself was on the panel. The forum addressed the question, "What is life?"

Most of the panelists accepted that all organisms on Earth represent a single kind of life because they believed that the genetic code is universal. The NASA scientist and panelist Chris McKay made the case that this single form of life—a "sample of one"—should encourage us to further explore Mars and other planets for signs of life.

Craig Venter then disputed the premise. He challenged the claim "that there's only one life form on this planet." We have "a lot of different types of metabolism, different organisms," he said. He turned to Paul Davies and added: "I wouldn't call you the same life form as the one we have that lives in pH 12 base. That would dissolve your skin if we dropped you in it."

"Well, I've got the same genetic code," said Davies. "We'll have a common ancestor."

"You don't have the same genetic code," replied Venter. "In fact, the Mycoplasmas use a different genetic code that would not work in your cells. So there are a lot of variations on the theme…"

At that point Paul Davies interrupted Venter: "But you're not saying [Mycoplasma] belongs to a different tree of life from me, are you?"

"The tree of life is an artifact of some early scientific studies that aren't really holding up," Venter replied. "So there is not a tree of life."

The moderator then turned the microphone over to Richard Dawkins, to see what he had to say.

"I'm intrigued at Craig saying that the tree of life is a fiction," Dawkins responded. "The DNA code of all creatures that have ever been looked at is all but identical."

But Venter had just denied that, telling the forum that his experimental bacteria read their DNA using a different coding convention.

Dawkins began to show his own uncertainty:

"Surely that means that they're all related?" he asked Venter. "Doesn't it?"[19]

Casey Luskin, who has studied the videotape (available online), commented that "as nearly as we can tell from the video" Venter "only smiles."[20]

Earlier, the evolutionary bioinformatics specialist W. Ford Doolittle had said in *Science* that "the history of life cannot properly be represented as a tree."[21]

## What Do Common Ancestors Look Like?

If the ancestors of separate organisms are conjoined at branching points, what do those common ancestors look like? Are we able to identify them in particular cases? And how do they compare with their descendants? In *The Greatest Show*, Dawkins candidly set forth some of the difficulties. He considered, for example, the (postulated) common ancestor of a herring (a vertebrate) and a squid (a mollusk):

It is possible that one of them resembles the common ancestor more than the other, but it doesn't follow that this has to be the case. There has been an exactly equal amount of time for both to have diverged from the ancestor, so the prior expectation of an evolutionist might be, if anything, that no modern animal should be more primitive than another. ["Primitive" has various meanings in biology, but Dawkins clarified that it means "resembling ancestors."] We might expect both of them to have changed to some extent, but in different directions, since the time of the shared ancestor... Moreover, the different parts of animals don't all have to evolve at the same rate.[22]

Dawkins also discussed the common ancestor of monkeys and earthworms. Probably it would look more like an earthworm than a monkey, he allowed, but again we don't really know, because both branches have had so much time to diverge. In the case of chimpanzees and humans, he thought it "a fair bet" that the common ancestor we share with them "was more like a chimp than like us"; it "probably didn't walk upright as we do"; it "probably was a lot hairier than we are," and so on.[23]

But this should remind us that neither Dawkins nor anyone else knows what common ancestors looked like. In fact, their very existence is a deduction from the "tree of life." In the second edition of *The Origin* (1860) Darwin laid down the law (forgetting about his earlier "a few forms or one"): "All the organic beings which have ever lived on this earth have descended from some one primordial form."[24]

Nonetheless Darwin's tree, and with it common descent, is still hypothetical. Craig Venter said it is an "artifact." And as we have seen, the genetic code is not universal. So the question persists: have common ancestors ever been identified?

## Transformed Cladists

I ONCE toured the exhibits at the Natural History Museum in London with Colin Patterson, then the senior paleontologist at the museum. That was in 1984. He told me that he was looking for cases where the actual common ancestor of two given species was identified in the diagrams on display. These would be at the "nodes" in the tree of life. But all the nodes shown in the museum were vacant, comparable to the branching points on roads, all of which are unidentified.

Patterson told me that as far as he could see, nodes are always empty in diagrams of the tree of life. He also doubted we would ever have access to a tree of life that we could regard as "factual." His text for an earlier exhibit of the Natural History Museum began: "If the theory of evolution is true…" It attracted a huge amount of attention from *Nature* and other publications, most of it hostile.

Patterson was a key figure in a group of taxonomists, or systematists, known as cladists (rhymes with "sadists"). In fact he became the unofficial leader of a more radical group called "transformed cladists." They insisted that the morphology and structure of living organisms and their fossils are all that we know. Lacking birth records or death certificates, our ideas about ancestry can best be determined by the most parsimonious arrangement of the known traits of organisms.

As to fossils: We sometimes do see exceptionally well-preserved examples, and they are well-publicized. But usually, Patterson told me, a fossil is little more than a "mess on a rock," telling us very little. Patterson was joined in his dissent by a few paleontologists at the American Museum of Natural History in New York, notably Gareth Nelson, who for a time was chairman of the Ichthyology Department, and Norman Platnick, one of the world's experts on spiders.

We shall return to cladistics, to Patterson, and to his supporters and critics in a later chapter. These dissenters are important because they laid down an important challenge to Darwinism, and did so from within the academic establishment.

Meanwhile, it seems fair to say that the verdict on common descent must be: "unproven." The evidence for it is weak. The genetic code is not universal. And even when the supporters of intelligent design accept common descent—as Michael Behe does—they add design requirements that put the claim of universal cousinship beyond the naturalistic domain.

That is a forbidden move within present-day biology, which is dominated by a materialistic philosophy, or "methodological naturalism," as it is sometimes called. I devote Chapter 13 to a more detailed look at materialism.

# 5. NATURAL SELECTION: A CLOSER LOOK

CRITICISM OF NATURAL SELECTION BEGAN TO APPEAR WHILE LATER editions of *The Origin of Species* were still being written. In *The Genesis of Species*, for example, the English biologist St. George Jackson Mivart (1827–1900) expressed doubt whether selection could explain the early stages of useful structures—the eye in particular. Darwin replied (in his sixth edition) that in several cases, the animal kingdom showed sensitivity to light in different stages. But the cases he cited were not related by descent. It was as though an architect were to show cave dwellings and then Chartres Cathedral, with thatched cottages as intermediates, to demonstrate that cavemen could have built the cathedral.

"We ought to look exclusively to its lineal progenitors," Darwin allowed, "but this is scarcely ever possible."[1] In that case, how can we know that eyes evolved step by step? We can't. In fact, such a claim is a deduction from Darwin's theory.

Mivart's criticism of natural selection has been repeated ever since. Harvard Professor R. C. Lewontin made the same point in a 1999 interview. In his book *The Deniable Darwin* (2009), David Berlinski criticized claims by Dan Nilsson and Susanne Pelger, based on computer calculations, that the eye could have evolved one bit at a time. Conveniently, they start by assuming an organism endowed with a light-sensitive patch.[2]

Mivart's comments also resembled A. R. Wallace's, in that neither believed the human mind could be solely a product of material causes. Mivart, who became a Roman Catholic, quarreled with the anti-Catholic T. H. Huxley, although Huxley had at first impressed him. ("As to natural selection," Mivart said, "I accepted it completely and in fact my doubts & difficulties were first excited by attending Prof. Huxley's lectures at the School of Mines."[3])

Mivart also attacked Darwin's later book, *The Descent of Man* (1871), for which Darwin seems not to have forgiven him.

A number of modern academics have also doubted whether natural selection is sufficient to cause speciation and everything else. James Shapiro, a molecular biologist at the University of Chicago, believes that "spontaneous genome organization" must somehow be involved. Comparably, Mivart over a hundred years earlier saw "an internal force or tendency."[4] But neo-Darwinian rules exclude reliance on such forces, whether internal or spontaneous. As a source of variation, randomness must prevail.

In the twentieth century, criticism of natural selection rarely appeared before the Darwin centennial. Then, in a symposium at the Wistar Institute in 1966, it was attacked by C. H. Waddington, who had also criticized it a few years earlier at the Chicago centenary. The Wistar symposium was entitled "Mathematical Challenges to the Neo-Darwinian Interpretation of Evolution."

This time, Waddington said that some of the statements of neo-Darwinism are "vacuous." Darwin's understanding of fitness was later turned into "a lot of mathematics," Waddington said, and then redefined "simply in terms of leaving offspring." It was "smuggled in" that the animals leaving the most offspring are going to be the fastest horses, "or something of that sort," but nothing like that was explicit in the theory. All it said was that some organisms will leave more offspring than others. Then Waddington added: "The whole real guts of evolution—which is how do you come to have horses and tigers and things—is outside the mathematical theory."[5]

The probability of generating new genetic information by random DNA mutations was also discussed by Wistar participants, among them MIT engineering professor Murray Eden and R. C. Lewontin (who was then at the University of Chicago). The problem that Prof. Eden addressed was logically prior to natural selection, which can only "select" something if random mutation has already generated it.

The skeptics at Wistar argued that assembling a new gene or protein is mathematically highly improbable "because of the sheer number of base or amino-acid sequences," as Discovery Institute's Stephen Meyer wrote in *Signature in the Cell* (2011).[6] For every combination that produces a functional protein, there exist literally billions of other combinations that do not. (This argument will be further explored in my chapter on intelligent design.)

## A Conflict with Gould

IN 1976 I published an article in *Harper's Magazine* about some of these issues—but without delving into the "mathematical challenges." I did bring up Waddington's discussion of natural selection, saying it seemed unlikely that a criterion of fitness independent of survival could ever be identified.

The article received a good deal of attention, both hostile and friendly. One who responded was Stephen Jay Gould, who had only recently inaugurated his monthly column in *Natural History* magazine. One of his earliest articles, "Darwin's Untimely Burial," was reprinted in his book *Ever Since Darwin* (1977). Surprisingly, Gould did propose an independent criterion of fitness. But first he said this:

> Bethell's argument has a curious ring for most practicing scientists. We are always ready to watch a theory fall under the impact of new data, but we do not expect a great and influential theory to collapse from a logical error in its formulation.[7]

He conceded that Darwin's attempt to establish an independent criterion of fitness by analogy with artificial selection had failed. "The pigeon fancier knows what he wants," Gould said. "The fittest [pigeons] are not defined by their survival. They are, rather, allowed to survive because they possess desired traits." Then he came to his key point:

Certain morphological, physiological and behavioral traits should be superior *a priori* as designs for living in new environments. These traits confer fitness by an engineer's criterion of good design, not by the empirical fact of their survival and spread.[8]

Well, what about an "engineer's criterion of good design"? Animals certainly look well designed, but Darwinians are obliged to regard that as an illusion. Richard Dawkins famously said that "biology is the study of complicated things that give the appearance of having been designed for a purpose."[9] The illusion arose, Dawkins thought, because those "complicated things" went through millennia of "improvement" by natural selection.

But to return to Gould, in his next book, *The Panda's Thumb* (1980) he corrected himself. He said that the panda's thumb is a "contraption, not a lovely contrivance"; it is a "somewhat clumsy but quite workable solution." Pandas are all thumbs when they strip bamboo stalks, but they do it effectively enough. Gould then added that an "engineer's best solution is debarred by history," meaning that the thumb had to be added on to other irreplaceable panda structures. So the panda's thumb "wins no prize in an engineer's derby."[10] Gould made a similar criticism of orchid design. (Darwin wrote a short book about orchids in 1862.)

So Gould's "engineer's solution" didn't work in particular cases. In fact, Gould is among those biologists who regard bad design as good evidence for evolution. After all, he said, if we can bring a designer into the picture, we are surely entitled to assume that he is a good designer.

In 1983, Gould wrote that "evolution lies exposed in the imperfections that record a history of descent." Discussing the limbs of rats, bats, and porpoises, for example, he said that "an engineer, starting from scratch, could design better limbs in each case."[11]

But "bad" design in nature can hardly be regarded as evidence that a Designer doesn't exist. Brown University biologist Kenneth Miller, whose book *Only a Theory* (2008) was a lengthy attack on the intelligent design movement, saw that the "bad design" argument was a poor one:

Consider the Edsel or the Yugo, or any other poorly designed piece of automotive machinery. However bad the results, there is no doubt that these cars were in fact designed—maybe not very well, but designed nonetheless. Imperfection, therefore, does not argue for evolution.[12]

A few years later, Gould threw caution to the winds and used a misleading analogy to show how natural selection might work. In *An Urchin in the Storm* (1987) he responded to criticism by the astronomer Robert Jastrow. Jastrow had questioned whether man could possibly have arisen "as the product of a succession of chance events occurring during the last 4 billion years."[13]

It was a teaching moment for Gould. Jastrow's claim "rests on a basic misunderstanding of Darwin," Gould wrote.

> If, in the hoary metaphor, monkeys type at random, we will never get the *Aeneid* if we must start each trial from scratch. But if we may keep the letters that, by chance, turn up in the right places and start each new trial with these correct letters in place, we will eventually get "Arma virumque cano" and all the rest.[14]

Richard Dawkins used the same argument, applying it to the line in Hamlet, "methinks it is like a weasel." Monkeys will arrive at that, too, if they are allowed to "keep" the letters positioned correctly by accident, Dawkins wrote. But that argument assumed what Gould, Dawkins and all other Darwinians disallow: that evolution has a goal. Inconsistently, Dawkins was positing that an intelligent agent was conveniently on hand, looking over the monkeys' shoulders, scrutinizing the gibberish they typed and preserving the correctly placed letters.

Where did that intelligent agent come from? Darwin's theory had supposedly removed the need for any such intelligence, but further study of the problem has shown intelligence to be essential.

## Encounter with Lewontin

I wrote to Gould and asked if I could go and see him. He replied that he would be happy to talk but that a better choice would be his colleague Richard C. Lewontin, a geneticist and by then the Alexander Agassiz

Professor of Zoology at Harvard. Appointed in 1973, he was earlier a student of Dobzhansky's at the University of Chicago. Gould told me that Lewontin was interested in these same questions, so I went to see him. He welcomed me into his office.

It is impossible to talk to Lewontin for five minutes without being impressed by his intelligence. He is a man of the Left, and like Gould was also known to proclaim his Marxism. (Gould said he learned it "at his daddy's knee.")[15]

The field called Sociobiology had been brewing at that moment; in fact brewing in Edward O. Wilson's office, right above Lewontin's in the same Harvard building. Wilson's *Sociobiology: the New Synthesis* was published in 1975. Most of Wilson's book dealt with social insects, but the final chapter dealt with human behavior, which he said was partly shaped by genes. This was judged to be "determinism," and demonstrations against it were promptly mounted by a group called "Science for the People." But that gets us into the sociobiology story which I explore in Chapter 16.

Lewontin indeed was critical of natural selection, which (like Bertrand Russell) he saw as an invasion of biology by economics. Karl Marx felt the same way. Some thought that in raising Marxian objections to Darwinism, Lewontin was importing his own philosophy into biology. But he had a point, surely. It was the laissez-faire economist Thomas Robert Malthus whose ideas had suggested natural selection to Darwin in the first place. (On reading Malthus, Darwin wrote in his *Autobiography*: "Here then I had at last got a theory by which to work.") And decades before Lewontin, Julian Huxley had referred to "the planetary system of laissez-faire that we call natural selection."[16]

Lewontin elaborated on his criticism of natural selection in his book *Biology as Ideology* (1991):

> Darwin's whole theory of evolution by natural selection bears an uncanny resemblance to the political economy of early capitalism as developed by the Scottish economists. Darwin had some knowledge of the economic survival of the fittest because he earned his living from

investment in shares he followed daily in the newspapers. What Darwin did was take early nineteenth century *political* economy and expand it to include all of *natural* economy.[17]

Lewontin also made a key substantive criticism of natural selection. He repeated it several times, but the best version came in an article he wrote for *Nature*, "Testing the Theory of Natural Selection." According to Karl Popper's "Logic of Scientific Discovery," Lewontin wrote, the first rule for any scientific hypothesis is that it ought to be possible to think of an observation that would contradict it:

> For what good is a theory that is guaranteed by its internal logical structure to agree with all conceivable observations, irrespective of the real structure of the world? If scientists are going to use logically unbeatable theories about the world, they might as well give up natural science and take up religion. Yet is that not exactly the situation with regard to Darwinism?[18]

Lewontin gave the example of a species of bird with a small beak that evolved a larger one, and did so because some aspect of the environment had changed, causing larger-beaked birds to leave more offspring. "Such a theory can never be falsified, for it merely asserts that some environmental difference created the conditions for natural selection of a new character," Lewontin wrote. The claim "is existentially quantified, so that the failure to find the environmental factor proves nothing, except that one has not looked hard enough."[19]

"Existential quantification" can be put more simply: If a new character appears, it is not explained by saying that something in the environment changed. We need to know what changed. Such a claim can then be tested, and perhaps shown to be false.

Oddly enough, two decades after Lewontin wrote that, a real case of increased beak size was reported—in finches on the Galápagos Islands, no less. Darwin had spent a few weeks there onboard *H.M.S. Beagle* in 1835. Peter and Rosemary Grant's research on the Galápagos finches was publicly reported in the 1980s.

Further, the size in beak change they reported was associated with a particular environmental change—drought. The problem was that after the drought ended, the average beak size of the birds reverted to normal. "There was no net evolution, much less speciation," wrote Discovery Institute's Jonathan Wells.[20] All the finch changes oscillated about a mean, and did not produce what Darwin had called an incipient species.

The Galápagos Islands are sometimes said to have been the source of Darwin's ideas about evolution. The variety of finches on the different Galápagos Islands may have played a role, but the laissez-faire economic outlook prevalent in England at the time is a much better candidate.

Darwin gave a rare (and imaginary) illustration of natural selection in *The Origin of Species*, illustrating Lewontin's point. Darwin supposed an environment in which wolves were hard-pressed for food and prey was scarce. He could "see no reason to doubt that the swiftest and slimmest wolves would have the best chance of surviving and to be preserved or selected."[21]

Let's accept Darwin's scenario. Imagine that by an accidental mutation a wolf is indeed swifter and outruns all the others. Then the wolf must really catch a deer, eat it, find a mate, leave more offspring, transmitting the new "swift" gene to them. And so on.

The problem is that once a different environment is postulated—and a change in the animal's constitution counts as such—there is no limit to the number of possibilities that can account for a different outcome, an outcome in which the swift wolf in practice fails to survive. Darwin recognized the problem, because he added this proviso: "provided always that [speedy wolves] retained strength to master their prey at this or at some other period of the year."[22]

But we can't just assume that only the wolf's speed is affected. Let's assume that a researcher in the field decides that a swift wolf will be "selected for." After investigating the outcome he finds that his theory is false. How does he react? Does he phone *Nature* and say, "Hold the space! I have just falsified Darwin's natural selection"?

Of course not. He concludes that *some other* factor was acting in that environment. "I don't know what it is right now," he might say, "but I'll keep looking." As Lewontin said, "the failure to find the environmental factor proves nothing, except that one has not looked hard enough."[23]

In short, we can't simply say "swiftness confers fitness," because maybe it does and maybe it doesn't. It depends on reactions within that ever-changing thing called the environment. The problem is that the "environment" in which variations appear has literally thousands of components and they can never be exhaustively specified or "controlled for." In assuming that nothing else does change, Darwinians do their own "controlled" (i.e. thought) experiments and see them through to a conclusion that is satisfying to them.

The next day Lewontin invited me to join him with some students on the lawn outside the Museum of Comparative Zoology. Here he made the basic point that a new adaptation won't be "selected for" unless it displays some relative advantage at the outset—which was Mivart's initial point about the eye. Later, Lewontin repeated the argument, and on the record, in an interview with *Lingua Franca*. The journalist who wrote the article quoted Lewontin as saying, "we'd be better off flying":

> "It would increase our fitness, we'd be better able to flee from predators. But if we flap our arms, we don't get any lift." He stands up and starts flapping his arms to illustrate. "Even if I picked up a pair of Ping-Pong paddles, it wouldn't help." He's walking around the room now, madly flapping his arms and still not getting any lift. "Until you're doing something, you're not doing it," Lewontin says by way of summary, "and natural selection can't help. What natural selection does is to make more efficient what the organism is already doing."

His argument was that "natural selection alone can't explain the origin of flight or of any complicated new function." Unless a small change gives an animal an advantage, "the change won't be selected for, and obviously a little bit of a wing doesn't do any good."[24]

Lewontin's commitment to materialism is another aspect of his worldview that should be stressed. Consider the following comments in the *New York Review of Books*. They made a big impression at the time because they were so forthrightly expressed:

> We take the side of science *in spite of* the patent absurdity of some of its constructs, *in spite of* its failure to fulfill many of its extravagant promises of health and life, *in spite of* the tolerance of the scientific community for unsubstantiated just-so stories, because we have a prior commitment, a commitment to materialism.

> It is not that the methods and institutions of science somehow compel us to accept a material explanation of the phenomenal world, but, on the contrary, that we are forced by our *a priori* adherence to material causes to create an apparatus of investigation and a set of concepts that produce material explanations, no matter how counterintuitive, no matter how mystifying to the uninitiated.

> Moreover, that materialism is absolute, for we cannot allow a Divine Foot in the door. The eminent Kant scholar Lewis Beck used to say that anyone who could believe in God could believe in anything. To appeal to an omnipotent deity is to allow that at any moment the regularities of nature may be ruptured, that miracles may happen.[25]

His point was that materialists don't believe in their philosophy because they are convinced by evolutionist claims. It is the other way around. They believe that the history of life can be explained by evolutionary processes "because of their prior commitment to materialism."

His argument can be restated this way: Complex, self-replicating organisms certainly exist, but in a purely material world they can only arise by the slow accumulation of fortuitous changes—one after the other. So Darwinism, or something very similar to it, is close to being a deduction from a materialist premise.

One who saw what was going on was Karl Marx. Writing to Engels in 1862, he said that for Darwin, "the animal kingdom figures as civil society":

> It is remarkable how Darwin recognizes among the beasts and plants his English society with its division of labor, competition, opening up of new markets, 'invention,' and the Malthusian 'struggle for existence'.[26]

Marx admired Darwin, not of course for his economics, but for his materialism. Recommending *The Origin* to Ferdinand Lasalle, he wrote that "despite all deficiencies," Darwin had for the first time dealt a death-blow to "teleology in the natural sciences."[27]

Darwinism forbids any reference to purpose, or teleology, as it does to causes "beyond" the physical world. In fact, it seemed to make such causes redundant. In that sense, Darwin and Marx were comrades indeed.

In the museum's elevator (no sign of E. O. Wilson coming down, and therefore no hushed silences), Lewontin asked me out of the blue why I thought sexual reproduction had appeared among living things. It had not occurred to me that that presented a problem for Darwinism. But years later the biochemist Michael Behe told me that it does.

"In the Darwinian view," Behe said, "the whole point of reproduction is to get your genes into the next generation. But with sexual reproduction you only transmit half; the other half being contributed by your partner. So why does that happen? Nobody knows." Lewontin implied that he didn't know either.

Lewontin's worldview encouraged him to take a critical look at natural selection, which Darwinians have almost always been reluctant to do. Today, in fact, some of those who might well agree with Lewontin about natural selection are likely to remain silent lest their unorthodoxy should attract reprisals within the academy. Lewontin had no such fears, and he made an impression on me and many others for that reason.

But we need to look at a related issue: What is the modern, scientific evidence that natural selection has really been observed? That is the subject of the next chapter.

# 6. What is the Evidence for Natural Selection?

IN RECENT YEARS, DARWIN'S THEORY OF NATURAL SELECTION HAS been ever more extravagantly praised, even as counter-arguments have increased. Daniel Dennett, the author of *Darwin's Dangerous Idea*, went further than most when he wrote:

> If I were to give an award for the single best idea anyone has ever had, I'd give it to Darwin, ahead of Newton and Einstein and everyone else. In a single stroke, the idea of evolution by natural selection unifies the realm of life, meaning and purpose with the realm of realm of space and time, cause and effect, mechanism and physical law.[1]

An atheist, Dennett once said: "You'll never see a horse shoe making a blacksmith. You'll never see a pot making a potter."[2] According to Richard Dawkins, however, natural selection provides "a workable process that does that very counter-intuitive thing."[3]

Dawkins and Dennett, both at Oxford at the same time, once worked as an unofficial team. The idea that a pot can make the potter is what made Darwin's "contribution to human thought so revolutionary and so loaded with the power to raise consciousness," Dawkins wrote.[4] The pot-to-potter claim is in fact quite helpful because it shows just how extreme—Dawkins says revolutionary—Darwin's idea was. It raised Dawkins's own consciousness. We can be excused if it fails to raise ours, at least until we hear some evidence for the claim.

Elsewhere, Dawkins said that natural selection "is the explanation for the existence and apparently purposeful form of all life." Furthermore, it is something that we "know" to be true. It is an "automatic process."[5] Julian Huxley, for one, was already on board. He said in 1959 that Darwin "pointed out that no supernatural designer was needed, since natural selection could account for any known form of life."[6]

In *The Origin of Species*, Darwin provided one (imaginary) example of natural selection (described in the previous chapter). Since then a handful of examples have been endlessly recycled and Darwin himself could well have mentioned them—had he known what to look for. But they are not quite what he had in mind. He regarded natural selection as the mechanism that transforms one species into others. The modern examples show something far less impressive than that. So let's review them in turn and see what they show.

## The Peppered Moth

THE MOST frequently cited example of natural selection is a change in the ratio of speckled and melanic (dark) moths in Britain. Ever since the Chicago centennial, it has been promoted as providing the best support for Darwin's theory. (In Chapter 3 I briefly covered the moths.) Dark moths had spread in the industrial areas of Britain "within living memory," said Prof. E. B. Ford of Oxford. Julian Huxley added that the naturalist Bernard Kettlewell had shown that birds "picked off a majority of those moths that did not match their surroundings." It was "an actual quantitative experiment."[7]

Kettlewell began by collecting the two moth varieties and marking them for later recognition. Then he released them in two wooded areas; one polluted, near Birmingham, the other in rural Dorset. In the polluted areas where trees were blackened, the dark moths were abundant. But in the rural woods, where lichens thrived on tree trunks, the light moths did best. The predators were sharp-eyed birds, so Kettlewell concluded that camouflage was the key to their differential survival.

Kettlewell's experiment was later criticized because he released the moths during daylight hours and they fluttered to the nearest resting place, tree trunks. Later it was discovered that the moths do not rest there. Their normal resting place turned out to be high among the leaves in the crown of the trees. So there were complaints—even accusations of fraud.

An amended version of the experiment was then done by a British biologist, Michael Majerus, but he died before he could publish his results. Other biologists then came to his aid, posthumously. His results, published in *Biology Letters*, weakly supported the bird-predation and camouflage theory.

Jonathan Wells included a chapter on these much-studied moths in his book *Icons of Evolution*. He reviewed Kettlewell's data, but in a sense it was all irrelevant. As Wells later wrote, Darwinian evolution requires much more than the selection of beneficial traits,

> and much more than a shift in the proportions of light- and dark-colored moths. It requires the descent with modification of all living things from one or a few common ancestors. Darwin did not write a book titled *How the Proportions of Two Pre-existing Moth Varieties Can Change through Natural Selection*; he wrote a book titled *On the Origin of Species by Means of Natural Selection*.[8]

The real question, Wells added, is whether natural selection can produce "new species, organs and body plans." That is not answered, or even addressed "by shifts in the proportions of pre-existing varieties of the same species."

Majerus said in a 2007 lecture that the moth story is important because it is "is one of the most visually impacting and easily understood examples of Darwinian evolution in action." Therefore "it should be taught. It provides after all the Proof of Evolution."[9]

Wells commented: What matters, evidently, is that the moth story "is a useful tool for indoctrinating students in Darwinian evolution."

Jerry Coyne, the author of *Why Evolution Is True* and an early critic of the Kettlewell deception, embraced the Majerus revision. "I am delighted to agree with this conclusion, which answers my previous criticisms about the *Biston* story," he wrote. (*Biston betularia* is the Latin name of the moth species.) Coyne then continued:

But we have to remember that the evidence for natural selection never rested entirely—or even substantially—on the bird predation experiments, but rather on the data-sets documenting allele frequency changes that were consistent, parallel on two continents, and then reversed when the environment changed.[10]

Coyne's last seven words are significant. After Britain enacted its Clear Air Act, the polluted woods recovered and the dark moths lost their relative advantage. The ratio of dark and speckled moths ("allele frequency changes") then reverted to normal. In the unpolluted environment, the light-colored moths regained the "adaptive" title.

It is sometimes said that natural selection caused the moths "to adapt to their environment." But notice that no individual moth changed color or acquired a novel adaptation. The dark and light varieties existed before the experiment began and were still with us after pollution controls were in place. The dark (melanic) variety simply became relatively more numerous. It might be said that the moth "population" adapted, but that only serves to disguise the point that individual moths did not.

The persistent invocation of the moth experiment despite its obvious weakness shows that evolutionists do not have more persuasive examples to offer.

## Resistance to Antibiotics

As a popular example of natural selection, bacterial resistance to antibiotics is a close runner-up to the moths. So let's hear the drum roll from Richard Dawkins: Bacterial resistance illustrates "the wondrous power of natural selection".[11]

What is that wondrous power?

Bacteria are single-celled organisms, found all over the world, in our gut (*E. coli*) and deep underwater. Some can replicate asexually in a matter of minutes and their short generation-span accounts for their popularity among lab researchers. If Silicon Valley were ever to achieve self-replication, it would indeed demonstrate a "wondrous power." But it is something that engineers have not yet been able to manage with any artifact designed by humans.

Bacteria subsist on a wide variety of nutrients drawn from their environment. Now add a poison to the mix: for example, an anti-bacterial substance such as penicillin (discovered by Alexander Fleming in 1928). What happens? Some or many of the bacteria will die, but others will survive the onslaught.

The number of bacteria species is not known but it is thought to be in the millions. Some may well be immune to the poison, and so they will survive. The ones that do survive ("the fittest," of course) will have greater access to nutrients. They will flourish. So that is what bacterial resistance to antibiotics amounts to: differential survival (once again). Some bacteria flourish; others don't. But this does not explain how any bacterium was generated in the first place.

As with the moths, then, bacterial resistance to antibiotics explains how we get more of something that already exists.

Now let's complicate the picture a little, with help from Michael Behe, the biochemist at Lehigh University. In *Darwin's Black Box* (1996) he famously drew attention to the "irreducible complexity" of the bacterial flagellum—an outboard "propeller" that transports bacteria through fluids. Behe's message was that if you try to build the flagellum one part at a time, it won't function. All the parts need to be in place from the beginning. In that respect it is like a mousetrap, Behe said. Part of a mousetrap placed on the floor won't catch a few mice; it won't catch any.

In a recent interview, I asked Behe if any new features of an organism have been shown to arise by natural selection.

"As far as I know the strongest such evidence comes from antibiotic resistance in bacteria," he told me.

But what about the argument that it gives you more of what you already have?

That is usually true, Behe replied, but an experiment can begin with just one bacterium, "and that sometimes does show something new."

He reassured me that you can indeed start an experiment with a single bacterium, "[a]nd one that has no resistance to antibiotics." You can grow that up, and as they grow into large numbers, mistakes in the DNA are made, comparable to errors in a manuscript that is repeatedly copied. "But what you find," Behe added, "is that most of these mutations involve the loss of an activity or function that the bacterium once had."

In such cases, some of those mutations might "luckily help it survive in the presence of an antibiotic, or something else in the environment," Behe said. In that way, a mutated bacterium develops antibiotic resistance even though its progenitor was unprotected. But it also shows something else.

"It is good evidence that mutations can do little more than break things," Behe went on. "And occasionally those breaks have a beneficial side effect." But it "certainly isn't building anything."

We shall hear a similar story from Behe in Chapter 16, dealing with Richard Lenski's multi-generational experiment at Michigan State University. Lenski has bred bacteria non-stop in his lab since 1988 and is continuing to do so. Again, he showed that when a mutation breaks a bacterial bond, it can be as "liberating" to bacteria as it is to a prisoner who breaks his chains. Nonetheless, Lenski's bacteria remain the same species of bacteria to this day.

According to Lee Spetner, all cases of antibiotic resistance in bacteria involve such "breaking," which is a loss of information in the genome. When the antibiotic is removed from the bacterial environment the bacteria revert to their natural form, which is more robust. Losing information is not the kind of evolution that leads to greater complexity and new structures.[12]

The main point is that experimental evidence on antibiotic resistance has not shown us how we get bacteria, or any other microbe. All it has shown is how we get relatively more (or fewer) of one variety or another. Meanwhile, something else has come up. If you search online for antibiotic resistance you will find it presented not as a triumph of Darwinism but as a problem for public health. This is from the Center for Disease Control:

> Almost every type of bacteria has become stronger and less responsive to antibiotic treatment when it is really needed. These antibiotic-resistant bacteria can quickly spread to family members, schoolmates, and co-workers—threatening the community with a new strain of infectious disease that is more difficult to cure and more expensive to treat.[13]

## Galápagos Finches

IN THE 1980s, we began to hear that finches in the Galápagos Islands provide one more example of natural selection. This is our third illustration. Darwin spent a few weeks there in 1835 when on board *H.M.S. Beagle*. He brought finch specimens home to England, but he was not much interested in them at the time. Over a hundred years later the ornithologist David Lack published *Darwin's Finches* (1947), proposing that different beak sizes on the different islands were adaptations caused by natural selection.

According to Lack, the finches "started a train of thought which culminated in the *Origin of Species*."[14]

But Darwin's involvement in this story is less important than what happened later.

The key Galápagos research, done by Peter and Rosemary Grant, starting in 1973, was described in detail by Jonathan Weiner in *The Beak of the Finch* (1994). He called the Grants' work "the best and most detailed demonstration to date of the power of Darwin's process."[15]

The Galápagos finches are distinguished mainly by the size of their beaks. A key event was a drought in 1977, when rainfall was a fraction of normal. The finches eat seeds, and with the drought small seeds became scarce. To crack open the more abundant large seeds a larger beak helped. Natural selection therefore "favored" the finches with larger beaks. It was a "selection event," said the Grants. They concluded that only about twenty such events would be needed to transform an average Galápagos finch into an entirely different species.

Here the Grants were extrapolating, and as Jonathan Wells said, their extrapolation depended on the assumption "that increases in beak size are cumulative from one drought to the next."[16]

A few years later the El Niño current brought heavy rainfall, and small seeds were once again abundant. The average beak size then returned to its previous level. In 1987 Peter Grant and his graduate student duly reported in *Nature* a "reversal in the direction of selection." Smaller beak size was "favored in years following very wet conditions, possibly because the food supply is dominated by small soft seeds."[17]

"Selection had flipped," wrote Jonathan Weiner. "The birds took a giant step backward after their giant step forward." The finch population was oscillating back and forth. Wells concluded in *Icons of Evolution*:

> Thanks to years of careful research by the Grants and their colleagues, we know quite a lot about natural selection and breeding patterns in Darwin's finches. And the available evidence is clear. First, selection oscillates with climatic fluctuations, and does not exhibit long term evolutionary change.... [Yet] evidence for oscillating natural selection in finch beaks is claimed as evidence for the origin of finches in the first place.[18]

In *Why Evolution Is True*, Jerry Coyne picked up the story—or a part of it. He attributed the finches' "adaptation" to an anomalous change in the climate. The large-beaked survivors left more offspring, and then, by the next generation:

> natural selection had increased the average beak size by 10 percent (body size increased as well). That is a staggering rate of evolutionary change—far larger than anything we see in the fossil record... Everything we require of evolution by natural selection was amply documented by the Grants in other studies.[19]

But there was one thing Coyne didn't tell his readers: That when the rains returned with El Niño, the average beak size returned to normal.

Darwin might well have been dismayed if the meager evidence for natural selection, assembled over many years, had been presented to him 150 years after *The Origin* was published. "A change in the ratio of pre-existing varieties? That is all you have been able to come up with?" he might reasonably have asked. It is worth bearing in mind how feeble this evidence is, any time someone tells you that Darwinism is a fact.

## Armchair Philosophy

IN AN article he wrote for the journal *Evolution*, Richard Dawkins commented on the astronomer Fred Hoyle's claim that natural selection is as likely to build organic life as a tornado blowing through a junkyard is to create a Boeing 747. Dawkins said Hoyle didn't seem to realize that in Darwin's theory, selection is cumulative: "small gains are saved." The hurricane doesn't "spontaneously assemble the airliner in one go." Small improvements are added bit by bit.[20] Adaptive evolution "must be gradual and cumulative," Dawkins continued, because "nothing except gradual accumulation could, in principle, do the job of solving the 747 riddle."

Thus, the evolution of the vertebrate eye "must have been progressive." "Ancient ancestors had a very simple eye," and "we don't need evidence for this (although it is nice that it is there)":

> It has to be true because the alternative—an initially complex eye, well endowed with features good for seeing, pitches us right back to Hoyle country and the sheer cliff of improbability. There must be a ramp of step by step progress toward the modern, multi-featured descendant of that optical prototype.[21]

Dawkins added that "modern analogues of every step up the ramp can be found, working serviceably in dozens of eyes dotted independently around the animal kingdom." But even without them, we could be confident that "there must have been a gradual, progressive increase… Without stirring from our armchair, we can see that it must be so."[22]

Dawkins's underlying method is revealed by his repeated assertions that something must be, must have been, had to be true. What this shows is that his science is subordinate to his philosophy. Since (in his view) evolution is true, and since complex organs like eyes certainly exist, it follows that they must have been accumulated bit by bit. Darwinism itself obliges us to believe that.

We don't even have to study the evidence. Dawkins's armchair philosophy tells him what must be true before he is under the obligation to observe anything.

Dawkins does claim that evidence shows us dozens of eyes "working serviceably" and "dotted independently around the animal kingdom." But as we saw in the previous chapter (and as Darwin recognized), they do not even remotely form a parent-offspring chain. That is why Dawkins inserted the word "independently."

In the same way, the six words "methinks it is like a weasel" can be found dotted independently around any library, but that does not mean that someone else was "independently" on his way to writing *Hamlet.*

Let us give the last word to the Columbia University geneticist Thomas Hunt Morgan (1866–1945), who almost a hundred years ago was skeptical of the claims being made about natural selection. He won the Nobel Prize in 1933. In his *Drosophila* experiments, he kept on attempting to increase the number of bristles in fruit flies. But the number would always reach a plateau which could not be exceeded. He then commented—and perhaps this should be engraved in stone:

> Selection, then, has not produced anything new, but only more of certain kinds of individuals. Evolution, however, means producing new things, not more of what already exists.[23]

That is all that modern researchers have been able to show in our day, too. And it raises a further question. The finch observations on the Galápagos showed oscillations about a mean. They did not confirm what Alfred R. Wallace in 1858 called "indefinite departure from the original type." In fact they tended to disconfirm it.

Which leads to the important question: Has any researcher ever been able to show such "indefinite departure from the original type"? If not, what reason do we have for accepting that Darwin's theory is true?

Meanwhile, natural selection is perpetually affirmed by proponents as the mechanism built into nature that can account for whatever is observed to exist. Its details do not have to be observed. Whatever exists, natural selection explains it. Darwin continues to be the hero of materialism because he "discovered" an unguided mechanism that can be brought on stage to explain everything that exists in biology, without having to resort to the supernatural.

So far, however, there is no evidence to show that this process is actually responsible for the fantastically diverse array of species that populate our world. Natural selection functions in the realm of philosophy, not science.

# 7. On Extinction

THE CLAIM THAT EVOLUTION IS A FACT OFTEN RESTS ON THE ASsumption that evolution means "change over time." As no one doubts that change over time is a reality, it's an easy case to make. But by evolution we understand something much more precise than that. Extinction, on the other hand, is a fact any way you look at it. Dinosaurs make the case quite effectively. So what does extinction tell us about evolution, and about our own times?

By one estimate, 99.9 percent of all species that ever lived are now extinct. If so, we might reasonably assume that, just as we all are destined to die, so all species are destined to go extinct. The most famous modern example is that of the passenger pigeon. "Martha," the last living specimen, died at the Cincinnati Zoo in 1914. The last known Tasmanian wolf died in the Hobart Zoo in 1936.

There are said to have been five mass extinctions, very roughly at 100-million-year intervals. The fifth is thought to have been caused by a meteorite, about 65 million years ago, killing off the dinosaurs. But no one is sure where it landed or whether it really caused their extinction. A large under-water crater in the Yucatan is the current favorite. Others now suggest that climate change may have been the villain. There have also been numerous "background" extinctions, which seem to be continuous. Some say that background and mass-extinctions blend into one another.

Many paleontologists and commentators think that we are now experiencing the sixth and worst mass extinction—the one caused by human beings. Anyone searching the subject online today will find that extinction of the old-fashioned kind has almost been submerged by the supposedly high current rate of extinction, a rate attributed to human carelessness and indifference. Leading the list of indictments has been the destruction of habitat, the loss of biodiversity, and global warming. I shall have something to say about these issues—best thought of as political—later in this chapter.

Meanwhile, what caused all those earlier extinctions, whether "mass" or "background"? Darwin discussed the issue at some length in *The Origin of Species*. Extinction, he argued, is "intimately connected with natural selection," his all-explanatory mechanism. Selection preserved "favored forms" (a truism), which duly survived. But he further claimed that most geographical areas are "already fully stocked with inhabitants," from which it followed that, as the favored forms "increase in number, so, generally, will the less favored decrease and become rare. Rarity, as geology tells us, is the precursor to extinction."[1]

Darwin conceded (correctly) that we don't have any way of knowing that any given region really is "fully stocked" with species. But that also meant there was no way of testing his theory. Later, he repeated his "extinction" argument in a slightly different form:

Each new form will tend in a fully-stocked country to take the place of, and finally to exterminate, its own less improved parent or other less-favored forms, with which it comes into competition. Thus extinction and natural selection will, as we have seen, go hand in hand.[2]

The alternative was to believe "that the number of specific forms goes on perpetually and almost indefinitely increasing." But he believed that no such increase had been observed, as "geology shows us plainly." Indeed, he added, we can see why the number of species should not have increased, "for the number of places in the polity of nature is not indefinitely great."

Darwin's argument can be analogized to a building with a flat roof and no side barriers. As new people—better adapted ones—keep coming up an escalator into the limited space on top, others—already on the roof and less well adapted—get pushed off and fall to their deaths.

Such is the philosophy of progress that animated Darwin and his contemporaries. Well-adapted organisms kept on replacing less well-adapted ones. The fit are replaced by the fitter, and the fittest inevitably survive. And so life keeps right on improving.

It hardly needs saying that such a philosophy has been overthrown in our own day. In the Western world, humans are widely seen as the villains of creation—an ongoing threat to many other life forms. It follows for the idea's proponents that our numbers should (ideally) be reduced, or at least minimized. Alan Weisman's book *The World Without Us*, in which humans have disappeared without explanation, became a surprise best-seller in 2007. Weisman called his book a "fantasy," but it was widely seen as an optimistic one.

Darwin resumed his discussion of extinction later on in *The Origin*. This time he compared the philosophies of uniformitarianism and catastrophism. The biblical Flood was the primeval catastrophe. But by Darwin's day it was already seen as a myth. Enlightenment ideas were fast replacing biblical ones. "The old notion" was that the earth's inhabitants had been "swept away by catastrophes," Darwin wrote. But that view was being abandoned, "even by those geologists [and here he named three] whose general views would naturally lead them to this conclusion."[3]

Darwin thought the study of "tertiary formations" gave us good reason to accept a more uniformitarian philosophy, in which species gradually disappeared, "one after another, first from one spot, then from another, and finally from the world." ("Tertiary" refers to the geologic period from 66 million to about 2.5 million years ago.)

Throughout the nineteenth century, the philosophy of gradualism replaced catastrophism, with Darwin's *The Origin* greatly contributing to the new worldview.

Oddly enough, physical evidence for past global catastrophes has accumulated in recent years, leading to a revival of interest in catastrophism. In the uniformitarian (or gradualist) view, supported by the geologist Charles Lyell and then by Darwin, physical causes acting now are assumed to be the same as those that acted in the past. Therefore the present is a reliable guide to the past. Modern science itself was partly an offspring of the uniformitarian worldview. Predictions, for example, can only really be tested in an environment that is roughly unchanging and so "predictable."

Catastrophism, in contrast, introduces unforeseen events. Abrupt novelties, such as meteorites plunging into the earth and (maybe) wiping out the dinosaurs, could happen at any time.

In the modern "polity of nations," to use Darwin's phrase, revolutions are often admired—at least by those on the political Left. To them, parliaments are old-fashioned affairs, and the rule of law, with its slow, incremental changes, is a little on the dull side—perhaps too predictable.

Stephen Jay Gould, who was partly responsible for the renewed popularity of catastrophism, wrote in his introduction to David M. Raup's book, *Extinction: Bad Genes or Bad Luck* (1991):

> The extra-terrestrial theory of mass extinction—easy to conceptualize but proposed with good supporting data for the first time only in 1980—may revolutionize not only our view of life's history but our entire concept of historical change by making a legitimate catastrophism respectable again.[4]

So, again, what caused all those earlier extinctions? In *Darwin Retried*, my old friend Norman Macbeth quoted Gavin de Beer as saying that it "remains unclear why any given species has disappeared."[5] De Beer was director of London's Natural History Museum and president of the Linnean Society in the 1950s.

Macbeth also saw that extinction's difficulty parallels the one besetting natural selection: "It is all too easy to say that a species becomes extinct because it failed to adapt, while establishing its failure to adapt only by its becoming extinct."[6]

The Harvard evolutionist Ernst Mayr did say something close to that. In 1963, he claimed that extinction was due to the inability of animals "to respond to new selection pressures." Then he added: "The actual cause of the extinction of any fossil species will presumably always remain uncertain."[7]

George Gaylord Simpson said much the same thing: "Particular cases of extinction, other than those evidently due to competition, are usually hard or impossible to explain in detail." The basic problem was that there are too many possibilities to choose from, just as there often are with establishing the cause of an individual death in the absence of a pathologist.[8]

In 2013, Charles Marshall of U.C. Berkeley's Museum of Paleontology offered "the failure to evolve" in relation to the environment as a cause of extinction. A decrease in the origin of new species seemed to be driving some mammals to extinction, he thought. Notice that Darwin saw an increase in speciation as a driver of extinction; for Charles Marshall a decline has the same effect.

## Raup's Caveats

PERHAPS THE most open-minded book on the subject today is the late David M. Raup's 1991 work, *Extinction: Bad Genes or Bad Luck?* A paleontologist at the University of Chicago and a member of the National Academy of Sciences, he also wrote *The Nemesis Affair: The Story of the Death of Dinosaurs and the Ways of Science* (1986). His extinction book includes the following passage, echoing de Beer, Mayr, and Simpson:

> The disturbing reality is that for none of the thousands of well-documented extinctions in the geologic past do we have a solid explanation of why the extinction occurred. We have many proposals in specific cases, of course: trilobites died out because of competition from newly evolved fish; dinosaurs were too big or stupid; the antlers of Irish elk became too cumbersome. They are all plausible scenarios, but no matter how plausible, they cannot be shown to be true beyond reasonable doubt. Equally plausible alternative scenarios can be invented with ease, and none has predictive power in the sense that it can be shown a priori that a given species or anatomical type was destined to go extinct.
>
> Sadly, the only evidence for the inferiority of victims of extinction is the fact of their extinction—a circular argument. The weakness of the argument does not of course invalidate the notion that ex-

tinction is based on fitness: it may only reflect our ignorance. For example, mammals of the late Cretaceous may have actually been better adapted than the dinosaurs, but our knowledge of these animals may not be good enough for us to recognize that superiority.[9]

Raup's comment about extinctions is a mirror image of Darwin's about speciation. Just as in no case do we have a "solid explanation of why the extinction occurred," so in no case does Darwin give us a solid explanation of why speciation occurred.

David Raup (1933–2015) was refreshingly non-dogmatic, frequently offering alternative ways of looking at the evidence. Extinction is a "difficult research topic," he allowed. He thought that there might be 40 million species alive today and that a thousand times that number were extinct. Species are "temporary" phenomena. An average duration of 10 million years for a particular species is "unusually long." Yet even that is only a small fraction (0.25 percent) of the duration of life on earth.[10]

His outlook is sometimes Darwinian, as when he accepts that some disappearances are what he calls "pseudo-extinctions": one species may "disappear" by transforming itself into another. Yet he also accepts that "true extinction" is real, and prevalent.[11]

But he also challenged Darwin, as when he questioned the importance of competition. For Darwin, whose master was Malthus, competition was the beating heart of natural selection. Raup allowed that evolutionary biologists have long emphasized competition, but more recently, ecologists "have downplayed its role." Competition, Raup thought, "may not be as crucial as once thought, especially in extinction."[12] In Darwin's view, it was the force of competition that kept driving new "productions" onward and upward in a progressive direction.

We have heard of "living fossils," such as sharks, horseshoe crabs, the gingko tree, and the coelacanth, which seem to have endured forever; but in none of those cases "is the living species the same as the fossil species." In detail, the Jurassic types of shark and horseshoe crabs are not to be confused "with those living today."[13]

Raup also discussed the amazing flying reptiles, known as pterosaurs, which lived from about 200 million years ago to the Cretaceous-Tertiary extinction (the one thought to have been caused by a meteorite). One of the pterosaurs was "larger than many airplanes." Its wings had no feathers, but were formed of large folds "or extensions of skin suspended from greatly lengthened bones of fingers," somewhat like the wings of modern bats. Furthermore, pterosaurs were capable of taking off from level ground and of powered flight. Yet they left no descendants. Faced with such marvels, an agnostic Raup seemed to be saying, "Who knows how all these things happened?"

> [Pterosaurs] were merely another successful group that appeared, flourished for a time then disappeared. Lest I give the impression of the pterosaur interval as being short-lived, note that their time on earth was thirty times longer than ours, so far.[14]

Like Darwin, Raup believed that extinction encouraged evolution. The fossil record shows that many "adaptive breakthroughs—bursts of speciation accompanied by the origin of new families and orders—occur after the big mass extinctions."[15]

Perhaps another way of looking at the matter is to suggest that the history of life on earth is analogous to a six-act play, with the five great extinctions ringing down the curtain at the close of each act. Humans appear only toward the end, in the last act.

Meanwhile, bacteria seem to be an exception to the theory that extinction drives evolution. Visible in the pre-Cambrian period, bacteria "do not appear to have changed much during their long tenure on earth," Raup said. They are difficult to kill and "many of the earliest bacteria are indistinguishable in shape and structure from their living counterparts."[16]

As a side-note, Karl Popper called bacteria immortal. When a bacterium divides, where is the individual that preceded the division? If one of those new bacteria dies, is that any different from the death of a skin cell? In other words, the entire population of a bacterial species may be compared to a single individual.

Raup was a strong supporter of the Search for Extraterrestrial Intelligence. Only by discovering life elsewhere in space will we "really have the means to know whether our own biological system has predictable patterns not yet recognized."[17] No extraterrestrial life has yet been found, of course.

He noted that sea level, whether high or low, may have been associated with extinction, and that the level at present is "somewhat lower than it was during most times in the past." Raup was not among today's climate-change alarmists. While temperature fluctuations are "large," he wrote, the overall trend "as the present day is approached is one of cooling."[18] That was written in 1990, so maybe the Earth has warmed up a little since then.

## The Sixth Great Extinction

THE LEADING proponents of the claim that humans are causing the Sixth Great Extinction have been former Vice President Al Gore and Harvard emeritus professor E. O. Wilson. In 2014, Wilson visited England for a symbolic ground-breaking of the Mass Extinction Memorial Observatory, to be built in Dorset, the county where we found an abundance of those speckled moths. (On this occasion, in a BBC interview, Wilson dismissed Richard Dawkins as a mere "journalist.")

The Memorial Observatory is on the "World Heritage Jurassic Coast" (why had one not heard of that?), and it will highlight "17,000 species under threat worldwide." It will also function as "an information and exhibition centre dedicated to the 860 species of animals, birds, insects and sea life that have been identified as extinct since the demise of the dodo in the seventeenth century."[19]

Notice the big disparity between the number of "threatened" and "identified" extinctions—the former twenty times greater than the latter. If there have been 860 known extinctions since the time of dodo (approximately 1650 A.D.), that would be close to two species a year possibly attributable to human action. Is that figure shockingly large?

Estimates of the number of species alive today range from 8.7 million[20] to one trillion.[21] It is generally thought that perhaps as much as ninety-nine percent of the species that ever lived are now extinct. Even at the low end of the current inventory, that would mean that nature has done away with far more species than the human race has.

Denyse O'Leary, the editor of a website called *Uncommon Descent*, considers that a real possibility. But it all depends on your point of view. She gave the example of the black bear, which has been doing well in the Canadian province of Ontario:

> Bears can live off stuff humans throw out. So can raccoons, skunks, etc. Deer like horticultural gardens just fine. Many people feed wild birds, squirrels, chipmunks, rabbits. In Toronto, where I lived for nearly 50 years, thousands of Canada geese no longer migrate, as people feed them, and they can gobble lawns in milder winter weather.
>
> Agriculture has not hurt the woodchuck or the grasshopper one bit. Human prosperity has not hurt wildlife here, if you go by the hugely increased premium food supply humans create. But that's just me. Maybe if I lived in the rainforest, I would see something different.[22]

In an interview at Harvard, Wilson recently gave a more global account, showing the high degree of uncertainty:

> We are on a little-known planet. We have knowledge of two million species, but for the vast majority we know only the name and a little bit of the anatomy. We don't know anything at all about their biology. There are conservatively at least eight million species in all, and it's probably much more than that because of the bacteria and archaea and micro-organisms we're just beginning to explore. The number of species remaining to be discovered could easily go into the tens of millions.[23]

Well, is it eight million, or tens of millions? No matter; the great drive to indict the human race seems unstoppable—reflecting the huge loss of self-confidence that overcame Western elites in the latter part of the twentieth century. It is a development that would have amazed Darwin himself. A *Washington Post* review of Wilson's latest book, *The*

*Meaning of Human Existence*, was headlined "Is Earth's Dominant Species Doomed to Self-Destruct?"[24]

In recent years, exaggerated concern about human activity has become the norm. In 1980, the *Global 2000 Report* predicted that fifteen to twenty percent of all species would become extinct by the year 2000.[25] In 1993, Aaron Wildavsky and Julian Simon concluded that those numbers were based on "pure guesswork."[26] More recently, Wilson updated that, saying it is "entirely possible" that we will lose half the world's species by the end of the twenty-first century.[27]

A British newspaper reported that for the first time since the dinosaurs disappeared, "humans are driving animals and plants to extinction faster than new species can evolve." One might add that no subject is more susceptible to influence by fashionable opinion than claims about extinction. The crisis is driven by "hunting, the spread of alien predators and disease, and climate change," according to the newspaper report.[28]

The Center for Biological Diversity said in 2010 that although extinction is a natural phenomenon, occurring at a "background" rate of about one to five species per year, "scientists estimate we're now losing species at 1,000 to 10,000 times the background rate, with literally dozens going extinct every day." The center added that as many as thirty to fifty percent of all species could be heading for extinction by mid-century.[29]

Maybe, in the end, we shouldn't take either these extinction numbers or their explanation too seriously. Natural selection is enlisted to explain either the origin of a species or its extinction. Did the organism flourish? That's natural selection for you. Did it die out? That's the failure of natural selection. First it got the job done and but then it put the organism in a fix with no solution. We should be every bit as skeptical about extinction rates as of claims about natural selection.

# 8. Is Variation Indefinite or Limited?

Wallace's *Ternate Essay* was sent to Darwin in 1858 and titled "On the Tendency of Varieties to Depart Indefinitely from the Original Type." It was published by the Linnean Society along with Darwin's own contributions. At the end of his essay Wallace wrote:

> We believe we have now shown that there is a tendency in nature to the continued progression of certain classes of varieties further and further from the original type—a progression to which there appears no reason to assign any definite limits.[1]

Wallace's title clarifies what evolutionists must show today: small, heritable changes that keep on accumulating. Making a similar case, Darwin accepted "indefinite departure" as true. In his "1844 Essay" he argued: "That a limit to variation does exist in nature is assumed by most authors," but he was "unable to discover a single fact on which this belief is grounded."[2]

But Darwin himself failed to provide a single fact to overturn what most authors had accepted. He would certainly have done so, had he known of any. The birds his pigeon-fancier friends bred always remained pigeons, and he was well aware of that. Neither Wallace nor Darwin ever observed indefinite departure, and both knew of the counter-claims against it. Nonetheless, most biologists and all Darwinians since then have regarded indefinite departure from the original type as a given, without so much as asking whether it has been demonstrated experimentally.

So the question arises: Has it ever been demonstrated? If not, there may be no scientific reason to accept Darwinism as "a fact." Philosophical arguments in favor of an uninterrupted parent-offspring chain since the origin of life may be quoted, but the key evidence would still be missing.

It is usual at this point to make a distinction between microevolution and macroevolution, and to add that microevolution is obviously true. You differ from your parents, and you may do so in a thousand ways; we all differ from each other in small ways. Therefore, the argument goes, microevolution is a fact. But it is misleading, surely, to identify small individual differences as "evolutionary"—even if only in a "micro" way. Variations between generations were known to us long before Darwin, without ever being regarded as small steps in the direction of something completely new—incipient speciation, for example. They are a fact of life, not evolution in miniature.

Darwin, nonetheless, assumed that small changes do accumulate. It was central to his theory—virtually a restatement of it. It was based on extrapolation from the small variations that we see every day, and which animal breeders can to a small extent magnify. But was this extrapolation justified? A number of observations on this topic have been made over the years. A brief summary follows.

First, consider Thomas Robert Malthus (1766–1834). He died twenty-five years before *The Origin of Species* was written, but his famous (Malthusian) theory strongly influenced Darwin. Nonetheless, Malthus preemptively rejected "indefinite departure." (In the following, Malthus used the word "improvement" instead of "evolution," a word that was still not in general use.)

In his "Essay on the Principle of Population," Malthus wrote:

One of the most obvious features of the improvement is the increase of size. The flower has grown gradually larger by cultivation. If the progress were really unlimited it might be increased ad infinitum, but this is so gross an absurdity that we may be quite sure that among plants as well as among animals there is a limit to improve-ment, though we do not exactly know where it is.[3]

Francis Galton (1822–1911), Darwin's half-cousin—they shared a common grandparent—was an early eugenicist and statistician. He pub-lished "Regression towards mediocrity in hereditary stature" in 1886. Characteristics (e.g., height) in parents are not passed on completely to their offspring, he wrote. Rather, features in the offspring tend to regress towards a mediocre point (since referred to as the mean). Tall people usually have tall children, but maybe not as tall as their parents. Height, in other words, approaches a limit.

The very idea that there is what Galton identified as a mean fits un-comfortably with the idea of indefinite departure from the original type. At the least it challenges the idea.

In Chapter 1 of *The Origin*, Darwin brought up reversion to the mean. He referred to a statement often made by naturalists, "namely that our domestic varieties, when run wild, gradually but certainly revert in character to their aboriginal stocks. Hence it has been argued that no deductions can be drawn from domestic races to species in a state of nature."

But Darwin had no time for such negative thoughts. He countered that "in many cases we do not know what the aboriginal stock was, and so we could not tell whether or not nearly perfect reversion has occurred."

But it isn't necessary to observe "perfect reversion" to demonstrate that characters enhanced by domestic breeding are quickly lost in the wild. Darwin wanted to believe that he had discovered a process com-parable to a journey that could be extended indefinitely, not just one of a few steps which are then reversed.

Reversion to the mean suggests the metaphor of going for walk, or going to work, and then returning home, as opposed to wandering eter-nally. In fact, having no home epitomizes the Darwinian worldview. Fur-thermore, this wandering nature of evolution addresses a desire to es-cape tradition, stability, and home. It is "progressive" in the fullest sense of that word.

To alter the metaphor, reversion to the mean implies that species inhabit "plateaus" of limited space upon which variants are free to roam. Artificial selection can "push" varieties to the edge of the plateau, but they cannot be pushed off it or be made to invade the terrain of adjacent species. No experiment has shown us otherwise.

The Danish scientist Wilhelm Johannsen (1857–1927) was the first to introduce the term "gene" and to distinguish between genotype and phenotype—between the hereditary disposition of an organism and its bodily manifestation. In *Darwin's Century*, the author Loren Eiseley cited Johannsen as explicitly denying indefinite departure. The variations emphasized by Darwin in species change, wrote Eiseley, "cannot be selectively pushed beyond a certain point... such variability does not contain the secret of 'indefinite departure.'"[4]

The Columbia University geneticist and Nobelist Thomas H. Morgan (1866–1945), known for his experiments with fruit flies, spent a good deal of time investigating the Mendelian laws of inheritance. He also questioned the idea of indefinite departure. Selecting for extra bristles in fruit flies, he found that such selection "at first produces rapid effects, which soon slow down and then cease."[5]

Like others who followed him, Morgan assumed that Darwinism could be saved by positing that the appropriate mutations appear in sequence. But such sequential mutations have not been observed. Later, when Hermann J. Muller bombarded fruit flies with X-rays, in an attempt to "speed up" the mutation rate, the fruit flies that survived the onslaught stubbornly remained fruit flies; although some had bizarre shapes that were not transmitted to offspring.

Luther Burbank (1849–1926), a resident of Santa Rosa, California, funded by Andrew Carnegie, was called "the most competent breeder of all time." His standing as a scientist is questioned today because his record-keeping was supposedly hit or miss. He nonetheless formulated a law, "the Reversion to the Average." It is difficult to find Burbank's books today, but the following passage was quoted by Norman Macbeth in his book *Darwin Retried*:

I am willing to admit that that it is hopeless to try to get a plum the size of a small pea or one as big as a grapefruit. I have daisies on my farms little larger than my fingernail and some that measure six inches across, but I have none as big as a sunflower and never expect to have. I have roses that bloom pretty steadily for six months in the year, but I have none that will bloom twelve, and I will not have. In short there are limits to the development possible, and these limits follow a law.[6]

Julian Huxley, the grandson of Darwin's "bulldog," also found that breeders encounter limits:

In spite of intensive and long continued efforts, breeders have failed to give the world blue roses and black tulips. A bluish purple and a deep bronze in the tulip are the limits reached. True blue and jet black have proved impossible.[7]

Huxley attributed this limited variability to a "lack of modificational plasticity"—a polysyllabic restatement of the problem: variation can only go so far. Different species of plants differ greatly in this respect, Huxley added. Some remain "extremely constant" in a wide range of environments. As for animals, "we have less information on the subject."[8] When Huxley wrote that, the centennial of Darwin's 1844 Essay was approaching.

In 1980, the science writer Roger Lewin described a gathering of about 150 leading evolutionary theorists at the University of Chicago. Their conference was entitled "Macroevolution," and their task was "to consider the mechanisms that underlie the origin of species." Lewin wrote the following in *Science* magazine:

The central question of the Chicago conference was whether the mechanisms underlying microevolution can be extrapolated to explain the phenomenon of macroevolution. At the risk of doing violence to the positions of some of the people at the meeting, the answer can be given as a clear No.[9]

The French zoologist Pierre-Paul Grasse (1895–1985) spent a lot of time studying bacteria. A Lamarckian, Grasse remarked:

What is the use of their unceasing mutations if they do not change? In sum, the mutations of bacteria and viruses are merely hereditary fluctuations around a median position; a swing to the right, a swing to the left, but no final evolutionary effect.[10]

In *Darwinism: The Refutation of a Myth* (1987), the Swedish embryologist Søren Løvtrup said something similar. He wrote: "Neither in nature nor under experimental conditions have any substantial effects ever been obtained through the systematic accumulation of micro-mutations."[11]

Richard Dawkins, in his book *The Greatest Show on Earth* (2009), restated the conventional Darwinian position. The idea that there are limits to variation is "essentialist," he said—something that Plato would have embraced. Dawkins illustrated his argument by referring to rabbits, but he could have used any other animal.

"The Platonist regards any change in rabbits as a messy departure from the essential rabbit, and there will always be resistance to change," Dawkins wrote. "The evolutionary view of life is radically opposite. Descendants can depart indefinitely from the ancestral form, and each departure becomes a potential ancestor to future variants."[12]

The idea of a standard rabbit "denotes no more than the center of a bell-shaped distribution" of real rabbits, "and the distribution shifts with time." Dawkins then continued (my italics):

As generations go by, there *may gradually come* a point, not clearly defined, when the norm of what we call rabbits will have departed so far as to deserve a different name. There is no permanent rabbitiness, no essence of rabbit hanging in the sky… What was once part of the old distribution *may find itself* the center of a new distribution later in geological time.[13]

All is fluid, Dawkins wrote, recalling Heraclitus. Nothing is fixed. "After a hundred million years it *may* be hard to believe that the descendant animals ever had rabbits for ancestors."[14]

Dawkins gave no examples. What preceded the rabbit? He didn't say because he didn't know. He treated Darwinism as an established fact and deduced indefinite departure from it. He reverse-engineered his own conclusion. When Darwinism is treated as a fact (as it is in Dawkins's books), indefinite departure must be true. To cap it off, he used ridicule ("essence of rabbit hanging in the sky") to delegitimize the alternative.

Jerry Coyne made a related case, explicitly defending Darwinian extrapolation:

> When, after a Christmas visit, we watch grandma leave on the train to Miami, we assume that the rest of her journey will be an extrapolation of that first quarter-mile. A creationist unwilling to extrapolate from micro- to macroevolution is as irrational as an observer who assumes that, after grandma's train disappears around the bend, it is seized by divine forces and instantly transported to Florida.[15]

Like Dawkins, Coyne serves up his argument with a dose of sarcasm. Of course, the two cases are not remotely comparable. We know from thousands of observations and no counter-examples that trains have repeatedly traveled beyond that first quarter-mile—all the way to Miami. On the other hand, extrapolating from micro- to macroevolution asserts as true something that has not yet been observed.

Vincent Torley, a philosopher, responded to Coyne's example as follows: "It is really hard to know if grandma will ever arrive at Miami when she is laying the track, randomly directed, one rail at a time, as she goes."[16] When you rely on random variation and natural selection, as Coyne does in his metaphor, the track that he presupposes isn't even known to exist beyond what has been observed. Coyne himself is pleased to tell us in another context that natural selection is non-directional. So even if many such tracks could be created, they might lead anywhere, or nowhere.

Note also the real significance of Coyne's far-fetched defense of extrapolation. If the real thing had been observed, so that evolution could be extrapolated, Coyne wouldn't have needed to reach his desired conclusion by extrapolation.

In his rabbit example, Dawkins set forth the Platonic case for "essentialism." We are told that it is misguided, even though it is all that we ever see. Its denial assumes that an antecedent organism is slowly trans-formed into a rabbit, which generations hence will become something else. Therefore, no essence of rabbit exists. But no known facts compel us to accept such a claim. It is simply a deduction from the theory of common ancestry that was central to Darwin's theory.

John Stuart Mill, Darwin's well-known contemporary, was also opposed to the idea of essences in the non-biological realm. He wrote that there has always been a strong tendency to believe that whatever is given a name must be an entity, "having an independent existence of its own":

> [I]f no real entity answering to the name could be found, men did not for that reason suppose that none existed, but imagined that it was something particularly abstruse and mysterious.[17]

But it is precisely the Darwinians who live in Mill's "abstruse and mysterious" world. Theirs is one of "common ancestors"—theoretical beings that are never identified. (Stephen J. Gould once said that Darwinian trees of life identify organisms at tips and nodes; but the fact is that nodes are almost always left vacant because we don't know what organism should go there.) The fact is, we continue to live in a world of essences and yet at the same time we are expected to oppose essentialism.

Denying the reality of essences became the life-long campaign of Ernst Mayr (1904–2005), as ardent a Darwinian as you'll find. He devoted decades of his long life to obsessive assaults on essentialism, hoping to replace it with what he called "population thinking." He also said that, although he didn't realize it at the time, Darwin "invented the concept of biopopulation." This is the idea that "the living organisms in any assemblage are populations in which every individual is uniquely different…"[18]

In a late interview, Mayr claimed that Darwin "showed" that "essentialist typology was absolutely wrong."[19] Darwin did no such thing, although it arguably was wrong if his theory had been shown to be factual. But like Richard Dawkins, Ernst Mayr derived his "facts" from his antecedent faith that evolution has been established. As so often in evolutionist thinking, deduction from doubtful premises is substituted for scientific observation.

Elliott Sober, a well-known philosopher of science at the University of Wisconsin, addressed this topic in his 1980 article, "Evolution, Population Thinking, and Essentialism." He made an initial effort to defend essentialism. Chemistry, for example, is a field in which such thinking had been vindicated, as the periodic table of elements showed. The essence of each kind is its atomic number and it was "hardly irrational for chemists to search for this feature. Their assumption that such essences were out there, far from stifling inquiry, was a principle [sic] contributor to that inquiry's bearing fruit."[20] Therefore essentialism in chemistry is a legitimate "working hypothesis."[21]

But when he turned to biology, Sober's outlook was "congenial to many of Mayr's views." The gradual evolution of species must mean that "the boundaries of species are vague," he said. Yet, he added, essentialists hold that there are characteristics which all and only the members of a given species possess. So their views are not tenable.

Sober, in short, could not bring himself to question Darwinism, and in his deference to the dominant evolutionist culture of our time he aligned himself with Dawkins, Mayr and others.

The philosopher Marjorie Grene later defended essences, even though she supported evolution broadly construed. Mayr's "population thinking" turns out to be "ontologically impossible," she said. Types, kinds and sorts "are bound to crop up somewhere," for if they didn't, "we not only could not speak about nature; there would not be a nature to speak about."

Evolutionists impugn typology, she said, by saying that its advocates view types as eternal, whereas in reality the living world is constantly changing. To this Grene retorted:

> I have always found this argument very difficult to understand. Why, just because something does not last forever, should it lack a nature?... That animals are born and die doesn't mean you can't tell one from another while it lasts, or even after it is dead.... Why, equally, shouldn't we be able to talk about the nature of a certain collection of plants or animals, or better yet, a family, or lineage, of

plants or animals? There are no mammoths nowadays, but surely we can say something about the kind of ungulates mammoths were.[22]

One might put it this way: If there is no essence of human beings, why are we never in doubt as to whether the being that we see is human? We never have reason to say: "It's hard to say whether that organism is human or not." Nor do we live in a world in which we say, "Is that a cat or a dog? Could be one or the other." Small children can instantly recognize the difference, without any help from anatomists or systematists. On the other hand, we can encounter ambiguity when lions and tigers mate, as they sometimes do. Their offspring are not merely ambiguous but usually also barren, like mules.

Ernst Mayr's lengthy campaign against essences, also placed front and center by the textbook writer Douglas Futuyma, should be seen as a bid to disguise the shortcomings of Darwinism. As for unlimited variation, or indefinite departure, it has not yet been observed. If it had been, we would never stop hearing about it. It has been deduced by assuming the truth of the theory that it is meant to confirm. The continued advocacy of indefinite departure by biology departments amounts to the triumph of ideology over science; or perhaps, we might say, to the triumph of hope over experience.

Perhaps, then, the "original type" is something real that cannot be escaped. Ernst Mayr thought that "essentialist typology" was "absolutely wrong." But maybe it is absolutely right? Earlier, in *The Origin of Species*, Darwin inveighed against archetypes. Maybe archetypes are real, too. In biology, "essence" and "archetype" both convey the same idea.

An archetype is commonly understood as a Platonic ideal, not a physical thing. We are told that we never see a real circle, for example, only a close approximation of one. It may be, then, that what we are seeing anatomically, in succeeding generations, is the repeated attempt to reproduce the archetype or "essence" of a given species.

Darwin, on the other hand, expected to see (and his followers still expect to see) something quite different: a species or "type" that is constantly in the process of becoming something else. So the claims of Darwinism and essentialism are in direct conflict. The truth is that what we observe, year in, year out, decade after decade, is much closer to the latter than to the former.

# 9. HOMOLOGY AND ITS POSSIBLE CAUSES

SCIENCE DEALS WITH THE EMPIRICAL—WITH WHAT WE CAN SEE, touch, and measure. But Darwinism goes way beyond that, making claims that have not even remotely been observed. "Indefinite departure from the original type," is perhaps the best example. What the evidence shows us is not indefinite departure but oscillation about a mean.

With homology, on the other hand, we come to something that is really observed: the shared characters of organs all across the animal kingdoms. Humans, for example, resemble dogs, monkeys, and other mammals in having hair and other mammalian characters. And we resemble mammals in numerous other respects. At a more general level of classification, that of vertebrates, our limbs share bone structures and so do our digits: there are usually five digits on each limb. We also share two eyes, two ears, and so on.

Homologous organs that are shared by different groups are far too numerous to list. The underlying similarity between groups is not superficial, either. The homologous forelimbs of bats, horses, porpoises, and humans constitute one of the best-known icons in biology. They illustrate the artistic idea of variations on a theme. It is impossible to look at their structure without acknowledging that homology is a fact.

In *Evolution: A Theory in Crisis*, Michael Denton quoted the 1980 *Encyclopaedia Britannica* as giving the pride of place to homology in discussing the evidence for evolution. "The indirect evidence for evolution is based primarily on the significance of similarities found in different organisms," the *Britannica* wrote. "The similarity of plan is easily explicable if all descended with modification from a common ancestor."[1]

"If," please note. More recently, there has been a tendency to substitute "because" for "if." More cautiously, *Wikipedia* says that "evolutionary theory explains the existence of homologous structures adapted to different purposes as the result of descent with modification from a common ancestor."[2]

Homology was well-known to Darwin, who wrote in Chapter 13 of *The Origin*:

> We have seen that the members of the same class, independently of their habits of life, resemble each other in the general plan of their organisation. This resemblance is often expressed by the term "unity of type"; or by saying that the several parts and organs in the different species of the class are homologous... What can be more curious than that the hand of a man, formed for grasping, that of a mole for digging, the leg of the horse, the paddle of the porpoise, and the wing of the bat, should all be constructed on the same pattern, and should include the same bones, in the same relative positions?[3]

How did it happen? "On the ordinary view of the independent creation of each being," Darwin went on, it has "pleased the Creator to construct each animal and plant" in just that way. But Darwin thought that homology was better explained by appealing to common descent: to the existence of an "ancient progenitor" which embodied the underlying character. He continued:

> If we suppose that the ancient progenitor, the archetype as it may be called, of all mammals, had its limbs constructed on the existing general pattern, for whatever purpose they served, we can at once perceive the plain signification of the homologous construction of the limbs throughout the whole class.[4]

So heredity explained the similarity, and that was one part of Darwin's explanation. The other was natural selection: the selection of "slight modifications," each one profitable to the modified form. That explained the difference between the homologous organs of different species—the difference between the forelimbs of bats and porpoises, for example.

By such means, Darwin argued:

The bones of a limb might be shortened and widened to any extent, and become gradually enveloped in thick membrane, so as to serve as a fin; or a webbed foot might have all its bones, or certain bones, lengthened to any extent, and the membrane connecting them increased to any extent, so as to serve as a wing: yet in all this great amount of modification there will be no tendency to alter the framework of bones or the relative connection of the several parts.[5]

Without further evidence or argument, Darwin asserted that "in changes of this nature, there will be little or no tendency to modify the original pattern, or to transpose parts." But why not? Natural selection could transform anything, on his theory. One might expect that it could as easily make fundamental changes in organs as it could preserve them in outline. In fact one expects exactly that, if natural selection is to explain the transmutation of species.

But Darwin had found a formula that suited him. It could account for both underlying similarities between species and the differences between them. It could preserve the theme while introducing new variations. In fact, he could make it come out any way he wanted. A bone needed to be thickened or lengthened? Connecting membranes increased? But without modifying the original pattern? Coming right up, sir. Natural selection at your disposal.

To many of his contemporaries that seemed like good science; and his argument—that common ancestry and natural selection explain homology—is widely accepted today. So it is time to ask: Has our more recent knowledge of DNA, mutations, and embryology shed any further light? The whole topic needs a closer look.

## Homology before Darwin

HOMOLOGY WAS widely recognized before Darwin. The comparative anatomist Richard Owen used the term in the 1840s. The founder of the Natural History Museum in London, Owen was the leading critic of Darwinism in his day. He identified homologous parts as "the same organ in different animals under every variety of form or function."[6]

Owen also distinguished between homology and analogy. The wings of bats and birds for example, are analogous but not homologous. Both aid flight, but they are built quite differently. Feathers don't resemble the skin flaps that propel bats through the air, for example. Their design is quite different.

Furthermore, some characters are shared by many species but are admittedly not present in a common ancestor. The example most frequently given is that of human and octopus eyes. Those eyes are structured somewhat similarly, but on any understanding of the evolutionary tree they are remote from one another.

Evolutionists have labeled such structures as "homoplasies," but the label does not remove the difficulty that they pose for Darwin's theory. That such complex and similar structures could have come about separately, at widely different times, by chance mutations, would strain the credibility of Darwinism. In fact, the phenomenon of homoplasy closely resembles the phenomenon of "convergence," which has related problems (discussed in Chapter 10 below).

After Darwin argued that homology could be attributed to a common ancestor, subsequent evolutionists took charge of the idea and went to work. In its neo-Darwinian reincarnation, homologous characters are defined as ones that are inherited from a common ancestor. Ernst Mayr proclaimed in *The Growth in Biological Thought* (1982) that the "biologically most meaningful definition" of homology is this: "A feature in two or more taxa is homologous when it is derived from the same (or a corresponding) feature of their common ancestor."[7]

In *The Flamingo's Smile*, Stephen Jay Gould followed Mayr down the same path:

> We call parts of two organisms 'homologous' when they represent the same structure by a criterion of evolutionary descent from a common ancestor. No concept is more important in unraveling the pathways of evolution, for homologies record genealogy, and false

conclusions about homology invariably lead to incorrect evolution-ary trees.[8]

Ernst Mayr reiterated his earlier position in his last book, *What Evolution Is*. He claimed that Darwin "said that certain characteristics of two species were homologous if they were derived by evolution from an equivalent characteristic in the nearest common ancestor of the two species."[9]

But in 2009, Richard Dawkins, of all people, rebuked his late colleagues (although not by name) for this *faux pas*. (Gould died in 2002, Mayr in 2005.) "If we want to use homology as evidence for the fact of evolution, we can't use evolution to define it," he wrote.[10] We question Dawkins's phrase "the fact of," but that is a separate issue. Otherwise he was on target. He saw that what Darwin had proposed as an explanation for homology had more recently become its definition. One might even say that homology itself had evolved under Mayr's tutelage.

Mayr quietly assumed that common ancestry is something that can be ascertained independently of morphology—as though we already have at our finger-tips a vast family tree of branching varieties and species. If that were so, we could simply look up common ancestors, and determine which groups share homologous features. With Darwin, evolution is still a theory and homology is part of its evidence. With Mayr the assumption is that evolution has been independently established.

"The controversy has raged ever since," William Dembski and Jonathan Wells wrote in *The Design of Life*, adding:

Neo-Darwinists continue to defend their conjunction of homology with common ancestry, whereas critics object that it confuses definition with explanation and leads to circular reasoning. The philosopher of biology Ronald Brady, one of the more outspoken critics of neo-Darwinism in the last generation, observed, 'By making our explanation into the condition to be explained, we express not scientific hypothesis but belief ... Dogmatic endeavors of this kind must eventually leave the realm of science.'[11]

But the inference of common ancestry from homology had earlier run into an obstacle from an unexpected source—Gavin de Beer. A normally loyal Darwinian and embryologist, de Beer (1899–1971) was a Fellow of the Royal Society. In the 1950s he was the director of London's Natural History Museum—a successor to Richard Owen. In his 1971 book *Homology: An Unsolved Problem*, de Beer wrote:

> It is now clear that the pride with which it was assumed that the inheritance of homologous structures from a common ancestor explained homology was misplaced; for such inheritance cannot be ascribed to identity of genes. The attempt to find 'homologous' genes, except in closely related species, has been given up as hopeless.[12]

It's surprising to find so well-established a figure as Sir Gavin—he was knighted in 1955—accusing Darwin of pride. But de Beer had identified a serious problem. "Homologous structures need not be controlled by identical genes," he wrote. "And homology of phenotypes does not imply similarity of genotype."[13]

If inheritance is the key to homology, as Darwin maintained, and what is transmitted throughout the generations is DNA, or genes, then homology should be correlated with genes. But tracking the relationship between genes and bodily form, or morphology, has turned out to be difficult, as Harvard's R. C. Lewontin pointed out years ago. He wrote in *The Genetic Basis of Evolutionary Change* (1974) that we do not know how to incorporate gene changes into a theory of speciation, and that in large part that is because "*we know virtually nothing about the genetic changes that occur in species formation.*"[14] [His italics]

His comments were as illuminating as they were radical. Mayr had mentioned a "genetic revolution," Lewontin wrote, but all such talk had to be held in abeyance until we could characterize "the *genetic* differences between the populations at various stages of *phenotypic* divergence." [His italics.]

The whole concept of a genetic revolution was driven by the idea that every gene affects every character, Lewontin went on. "But it does not follow that every gene substitution really matters." It may be true that "thou canst not stir a flower without troubling of a star," but, he continued,

> the computer program for guiding a space capsule does not, in fact, have to take my gardening into account... The problem of making quantitative statements about the multiplication of species has been that we have been unable to connect the phenotypic differentiation between populations, races, semi-species and species with particular genetic changes.[15]

Put another way, evolution by the mutation of DNA is one thing and the development of new phenotypes is another. And we still don't know how the two are connected. What we do know is that they are not connected in the simple, straightforward way that Darwinism calls for.

It gets worse, because structures that are *not* homologous are sometimes produced by organisms with similar genes, while, as Michael Denton pointed out, "apparently homologous structures are specified by quite different genes in different organisms."[16]

## Homology and Embryology

EFFORTS TO correlate homology with embryonic pathways have been no more successful than they were with genes. Gavin de Beer went further and questioned whether embryology sheds any light on homology. But to re-examine the issue we must once again turn back to Charles Darwin. He introduced Ernst Haeckel into the story, writing in the sixth edition of *The Origin of Species* (1872):

> Professor Haeckel in his 'Generelle Morphologie' and in other works, has recently brought his great knowledge and abilities to bear on what he calls phylogeny, or the lines of descent of all organic beings. In drawing up the several series he trusts chiefly to embryological characters, but receives aid from homologous and rudimentary organs... He has thus boldly made a great beginning...[17]

A German biologist and a great Darwin admirer, Haeckel (1836–1919) for a while persuaded much of the biological fraternity that embryology was the key to understanding community of descent. He did so with his drawings of the embryos of different vertebrate classes. Critics today call the drawings deceptive or even faked, but his slogan nonetheless became famous: "Ontogeny recapitulates phylogeny."

"Ontogeny" was Haeckel's word for the development of an organism in an embryo. So what the slogan meant was that the successive stages of an embryo would retrace the evolutionary stages of its early ancestors. But Haeckel misled his viewers by omitting the early embryonic stages entirely (when the embryos of different groups look quite different) and then focusing on the middle stages, when they do become a little more similar. But he redrew them to make them look more similar than they really are, and that was where the deception came in. For this reason, his drawings have been discredited.

Nonetheless, he did persuade Darwin, who wrote that "the leading facts in embryology, which are second to none in importance, are explained on the principle of variations in the many descendants from some one ancient progenitor." He also wrote that early embryos "show us more or less completely, the condition of the progenitor of the whole group in its adult state."[18] In a letter written to Asa Gray in 1860, Darwin considered embryology to be "by far the strongest single class of facts in favour"[19] of his theory of descent with modification.

Haeckel's embryo drawings became a leading "icon of evolution" in Jonathan Wells's book of that name. Wells also pointed out that Douglas Futuyma's textbook *Evolutionary Biology* says that "early in development human embryos are almost indistinguishable from those of fishes," while Brown University biologist Kenneth Miller described the development of the human embryo as a "microscopic trip through evolutionary time."[20]

But the embryologist Gavin de Beer was highly critical of such claims. "It does not seem to matter where in the egg or the embryo the living substance out of which organisms are formed comes from," he wrote. "Correspondence between homologous structures cannot be pressed back to similarity of position of the cells of the embryo, or the parts of the egg out of which these structures are ultimately differentiated."

De Beer also asked what mechanism could result in the production of the same patterns, in spite of their not being controlled by the same genes. "I asked this question in 1938," he added, "and [as of 1971] it has not been answered."[21] It still has not been answered today.

## Automobiles in Embryo

A FUNDAMENTAL feature of the evolutionist approach to homology is that it cursorily dismisses all design-based explanations. Darwinists long ago abandoned any thought of such a solution to the problem of homology—or to anything else in biology. In fact, Darwinism from the outset was intended to supplant design. But we are under no obligation to follow that example. Today, surrounded as we are by designed objects, it is not hard to see that homology flourishes in the world of design.

The best known example of evolutionist confusion on this issue was provided by the biologist Tim Berra of Ohio State University. In his book *Evolution and the Myth of Creationism* (Stanford University Press, 1990) he wrote:

> If you look at a 1953 Corvette and compare it to the latest model, only the most general resemblances are evident, but if you compare a 1953 and a 1954 Corvette, side by side, then a 1954 and a 1955 model, and so on, the descent with modification is overwhelmingly obvious. This is what paleontologists do with fossils, and the evidence is so solid and comprehensive that it cannot be denied by reasonable people.[22]

Phillip E. Johnson of U.C. Berkeley referred to this as Berra's Blunder. Corvettes of whatever year were all designed and that indeed is "overwhelmingly obvious." Yet Berra was so much in thrall to Darwinism that he even referred to year-over-year design changes as "descent with modification." He had forgotten that a naturalistic explanation of homology must exclude design, not appeal to it.

We might pursue the automobile metaphor further and briefly consider an auto assembly line, which is analogous to embryo development in biology. The completed car emerges at the end of the line. What's interesting about real assembly lines—visitors can see one in operation at Ford's River Rouge plant in Dearborn, Michigan—is the complexity of the operation compared to the finished vehicle. Machines do the heavy lifting, but the line is monitored by humans. At the first sign of a glitch they can halt the whole operation.

The assembly line is repeatedly updated to incorporate new models. Its planning and the importation of various auto parts are all offstage and cannot be detected by studying the completed vehicle. Today, that vehicle is likely to incorporate parts that come from different parts of the world. Yet it is also replete with parts that are homologous with structures in vehicles made by different companies; some made in Germany, some in Japan, and so on. To cite only the most obvious homology, almost all such cars are "quadruped," or four-wheeled. But there are many other such homologies.

Michael Denton concluded:

> A convincing explanation for the mystifying 'unity of type', the phenomenon of homology that Darwin thought he had so adequately explained by descent from a common ancestor, is probably still a very long way away. With the demise of any sort of straightforward explanation of homology one of the major pillars of evolution theory has become so weakened that its value as evidence for evolution is greatly diminished.[23]

In *The Living Stream* (1965) the British biologist Sir Alister Hardy said that "the concept of homology is absolutely fundamental to what we are talking about when we speak of evolution—yet in truth we cannot explain it at all in terms of present day biological theory."[23]

One is inclined to say that if homology is the best evidence for Darwin's theory, as some have thought, then that theory doesn't have much to recommend it. Further, that evidence is plainly more compatible with design theory than with descent with modification.

In the next chapter I shall review the evidence for convergence, the undoubted similarity of traits in organisms that no one supposes to share a common ancestor.

# 10. THE CONUNDRUM
# OF CONVERGENCE

LIKE HOMOLOGY, CONVERGENCE IS A BIOLOGICAL REALITY, BUT IT doesn't fit into the accepted evolutionary scheme. It draws attention to the undoubted similarity of different organisms, or their traits. Yet many such organisms share these similarities even though they were not present in their supposed common ancestor. In the last chapter we saw that that was true of mammalian and octopus eyes. In such cases, these similarities are said to have evolved independently but nonetheless converged, despite their different lineages.

Convergence, therefore, undermines the assumption that similarity is the result of common ancestry. So Darwinists try to bolster their case by calling it "convergent evolution." In doing so, of course, they prejudge its cause. Jerry Coyne, for example, said that convergence was explained "by invoking a well known process called convergent evolution." How does that work? "It's really quite simple," he wrote. "Species that live in similar habitats will experience similar selection pressures from their environment."[1]

Here is a standard definition of convergence:

In evolutionary biology, convergent evolution is the process whereby organisms not closely related independently evolve similar traits as a result of having to adapt to similar environments or ecological niches.[2]

Darwin did not explicitly mention convergence in the first edition of *The Origin of Species*, but he was aware of the phenomenon. He was also ready with his old standby explanation. Just as two men sometimes hit on "the same invention" independently, he wrote, so natural selection, "taking advantage of analogous variations, has sometimes modified in very nearly the same manner two parts in two organic beings, which owe but little of their structure in common to inheritance from the same ancestor."[3]

So natural selection pulled it off once again. This time Darwin saw it as the equivalent of human invention. In the sixth edition of *The Origin* (1872), Darwin brought up convergence explicitly. He mentioned a Mr. H. C. Watson,

> who thinks that I have overrated the importance of divergence of character (in which, however, he apparently believes), and that convergence, as it may be called, has also played a part. If two species, belonging to two distinct though allied genera, had both produced a large number of new and divergent forms, it is conceivable that these might approach each other so closely that they would have all to be classed under the same genus.[4]

Darwin didn't reach the modern explanation of convergence, which attributes convergent structures to the similarity of their (separate) environments. (In fact, Darwin never used the word "environment" in *The Origin of Species*; it is a modern word. Instead he used such phrases as "the conditions of life.")

That most orthodox of Darwinians, Ernst Mayr, restated the conventional position on convergence: "The same ecological niche or adaptive zone is often filled on different continents by exceedingly similar but entirely unrelated organisms." He added: "Convergent evolution is a phenomenon that convincingly illustrates the power of natural selection."[5] In a glossary, Mayr defined convergence as: "Phenotypic similarity of two taxa that is independently acquired and is not produced by a genotype from a common ancestor."[6]

Richard Dawkins said much the same thing in *The Blind Watchmaker* (1986). In many cases, he said, "independent lines of evolution appear to have converged, from very different starting points, on what looks very like the same endpoint." Dawkins, who (like Darwin) sees random mutation and natural selection as underlying all biology, had little choice but to see convergence as "striking testimony to the power of natural selection."[7]

Convergence nonetheless creates problems for Darwinism, as the following analogy may show. Two people are randomly selected from all over the world and are asked where they live. One says "Washington D.C." and the other says "Chevy Chase" (a suburb of Washington). "Coincidence" is a strong possibility as long as fraud is ruled out. At the same time, one might legitimately wonder whether they really were chosen at random. Now imagine that such a coincidence keeps on recurring, and we can establish that there is no fraud. This time we would know that something odd was afoot. But it does happen again and again in biology. Organisms from quite different parts of the world often have very similar characters.

True, Dawkins added, when we look in detail we find that this convergence "is not total." It would be "worrying" if we did.[8] Still, he never quite explained why the relevant organs became so similar, other than by invoking the evolutionists' abracadabra: "natural selection."

So far, we have encountered the claims that natural selection can design things just as human inventors do; it can also cause organs to diverge, or to converge—whatever is needed. Natural selection is the evolutionist's obedient servant. But if two different "habitats" can be judged similar, then that will suffice to explain the observed convergence between the characters of species that do not share a common ancestor.

## Mammals: Placental and Marsupial

THE MAIN mammalian branches, placentals and marsupials, provide numerous examples of convergence. Following the break-up of large land-masses roughly 100 million years ago, mammalian branches followed separate pathways. Despite this long separation, marsupials in Australia and placentals in North America often resemble one another in overall shape and way of life. But these similarities are superimposed on two quite distinct methods of reproduction: in one, the internal placenta connects the fetus to the uterine wall; marsupials, on the other hand, "carry" an external pouch, or pocket, into which immature offspring promptly climb.

There are marsupial and placental mice, each split into numerous species. The flying (marsupial) possum resembles the flying (placental) squirrel, both with skin stretched between their limbs to allow gliding from tree to tree. Marsupial and placental moles both burrow through soil to find insects. The Australian wombat, like the North American groundhog, uses rodent-like teeth to eat roots and plants. Rabbit-eared bandicoots resemble rabbits in North America. Both have well-developed hind limbs and a hopping form of locomotion.

The Tasmanian wolf, a carnivorous marsupial now extinct, resembled the placental wolf. Its limbs were adapted for running, and its skull and teeth were adapted for tearing meat. Both marsupial and placental saber-toothed cats are now extinct, but they shared a strikingly similar skull structure. In *Evolution: A Theory in Crisis*, Michael Denton wrote:

> Anyone who has been privileged to handle, as I have, both a marsupial and a placental dog skull will attest to the almost eerie degree of convergence between the thylacine [marsupial] and the placental dog. Yet in terms of the soft anatomy of their reproductive systems there is an enormous difference between the two groups.[9]

Mammals managed to converge with even more distant groups. A remarkable example was reported by *Science* in 2012. It involves the close parallel between the mechanism of hearing in mammals and in katydids, an insect known as a bush cricket (which comes in over 6,000 species). In mammals, the eardrum, the ossicle in the middle ear, and the cochlea with its "piano keyboard" of frequency sensors supposedly evolved by chance (as everything did in the Darwin story). But evolutionists now claim that the katydid in the rainforest possesses a three-part hearing mechanism closely similar to that of mammals. If mammals ever did share a common ancestor with insects, it must have been way back in the Cambrian Period, perhaps 500 million years ago.

A website that keeps track of these things commented:

Detecting the mechanism of katydid hearing was never possible in such detail before. The cochlear analogue in the katydid, which they named the acoustic vesicle, is so small (600 millionths of a meter) that it required x-ray micro-tomography and other state-of-the-art techniques to elucidate its structure. Yet in a remarkable diagram in *Science*, the authors compared the three parts of a human ear and katydid ear side by side, showing how analogous the structures are.[10]

The writer Arthur Koestler was impressed by convergence, citing the "nearly identical skulls" of North American wolves and the Tasmanian wolf. "Even the evolution of a single species of wolf by random mutation plus selection presents insurmountable difficulties," Koestler wrote. "To duplicate this process independently on island and mainland would mean squaring a miracle. The puzzle remains why the Darwinians are not puzzled, or pretend not to be."[11]

Koestler was always skeptical of Darwinism. He wrote that "the Australian *Doppelgangers* [of their placental look-alikes] lend strong support to the hypothesis that there are unitary laws underlying evolutionary diversity." Such laws—which are anti-Darwinian—"permit virtually unlimited variations on a limited number of themes."[12] Recall that we also saw the idea of variations on a theme play out in the chapter on homology.

Flight is also said to show convergence, in that it has reappeared in widely separate lines, among them insects, birds, bats, and pterosaurs. Some of these extinct reptiles were as big as F-16 fighters, and some as small as paper airplanes, according to the American Museum of Natural History.[13] The paleontologist Stephen Jay Gould made the curious comment that in the case of flight "highly adaptive forms that are easy to evolve arise again and again."[14]

Flight is easy to evolve? By a series of accidental mutations? Someone should tell Boeing engineers how that was achieved.

Ichthyosaurs are often cited as the best illustration of convergence. They are marine reptiles with bodies that in external form greatly resemble fishes. They have become "the standard textbook example of convergence," said Gould:

> Ichthyosaurs are most celebrated for their convergence upon the external form of superior swimmers among fishes... for we know how the threefold combination of flippers, back-fin and tail fin work in efficient hydrodynamic coordination, and we are awed that two independent lineages [reptiles and fishes] evolved such uncanny resemblance for apparently similar function.[15]

Gould added that the dorsal and tail fins are particularly impressive:

> For the terrestrial ancestors of ichthyosaurs obviously possessed neither back nor tail fin, and ichthyosaurs therefore evolved these structures from scratch—yet they occupy the position, and maintain the form, that hydrodynamic engineers deem optimal for propulsion and balance.[16]

Optimal!

Gould liked to ask what would happen if we could go back in time and rewind the tape of life. He decided that random mutations and environmental accidents played such a big role the first time around that we could not expect to see the same result twice. Simon Conway Morris, a paleontologist at Cambridge University, commented on this in an article he wrote for the *New Scientist*:

> [W]hen you examine the tapestry of evolution you see the same patterns emerging over and over again. Gould's idea of rerunning the tape of life is not hypothetical, it's happening all around us. And the result is well known to biologists—evolutionary convergence... When convergence is the rule, you can rerun the tape of life as often as you like and the outcome will be much the same... Convergence means that life is not only predictable at a basic level, it also has direction.[17]

In arguing that life has "a direction," the sometimes heterodox Conway Morris was violating one of the house rules of Darwinism—rules laid down by Gould among others: Life is not supposed to have any kind of purpose or direction. Purpose, after all, implies a purposive agent;

it implies design. For that reason, the history of life is said (by Gould among others) to resemble a bush, not a tree.

Conway Morris also said, in his book *Life's Solution*:

During my time in the libraries I have been particularly struck by the adjectives that accompany descriptions of evolutionary convergence. Words like, 'remarkable', 'striking', 'extraordinary', or even 'astonishing' and 'uncanny' are commonplace... the frequency of adjectival surprise associated with descriptions of convergence suggests there is almost a feeling of unease in these similarities. Indeed, I strongly suspect that some of these biologists sense the ghost of teleology looking over their shoulders.[18]

Teleology is the idea—disallowed in Darwin's theory—that an activity is directed toward a goal. The philosopher Michael Ruse once joked that teleology in biology is like a man's mistress: he can't live without her, but he can't be seen in public with her either.

Gould himself defined convergence as "evolved similarity from two very different starting points." Like Jerry Coyne, he tried to explain it by saying that convergent critters respond similarly to a "common environment and mode of life."[19] Coyne, we may recall, said that species living in "similar habitats" will experience "similar selection pressures," so they "may evolve similar adaptations, or converge." They end up looking "remarkably alike," even though "they are unrelated."[20]

But it's a stretch, surely, to say that Australia and North America are "similar habitats." Furthermore, if a common environment really does cause organisms to converge, why do we encounter so diverse a variety of animals all living in the same neighborhood, at the same time?

More recently, genes have provided a further illustration of convergence. In particular, a gene involved in the construction of eyes has received a lot of attention. It is known as the *Pax-6* gene. Eyes independently developed at least forty times "during the evolution of animal diversity," Ernst Mayr claimed.[21] *Pax-6* is found in organisms as diverse as jellyfish, arthropods, mollusks, and vertebrates. All these groups possess different eye types.

So how can the same gene influence the development of eyes that are so varied? At first, it was believed that all eyes are derived from a single ancestral eye, all possessing the *Pax-6* gene. But when Ernst Mayr pursued that idea, it began to fall apart:

> The geneticist [who did the relevant study] also found *Pax 6* in species without eyes, and proposed that they must have descended from ancestors with eyes. However, this scenario [in which eyesight was first acquired, then lost, then recovered again] turned out to be quite improbable, and the wide distribution of *Pax 6* required a different explanation. It is now believed that *Pax 6*, even before the origin of eyes, had an unknown function in eyeless organisms, and was subsequently recruited for its role as an eye organizer.[22]

Mayr then tried to explain away genetic convergence by appealing to the "hidden potentials of the genotype." But that sounds more like a (verboten) goal-directed activity than the (obligatory) undirected process of neo-Darwinism. So the Darwinists have found no easy way of resolving the convergence conundrum.

## Convergence before Darwin

IT'S WORTH taking a brief look at the pre-Darwinian position. Well before *The Origin of Species* was published, convergence was understood and described by William Buckland (1784–1856). An early paleontologist and geologist at Oxford, he would be called a creationist today. He published the first full description of a fossil dinosaur, naming it *Megalosaurus*. He was also appointed dean of Westminster by his friend Robert Peel, the first British prime minister. In those days, science and theology could be intermingled without loss of prestige to either party—something that would be unimaginable today.

Buckland was well-informed about ichthyosaurs. He knew they were reptiles, but as ordinary reptiles, he also realized, they wouldn't survive at sea. By 1836, he saw their convergence with fishes as proof of God's goodness, arguing that the resemblance of ichthyosaurs to fishes had been bestowed by "divine fiat," or (as he went on) by "the one and the same eternal principle of Wisdom and Intelligence, presiding from first to last over the total fabric of the Creation."

Gould made a remarkable comment on this claim by Buckland: "Read 'endowed by natural selection' for a modern version of the same argument," he said.[23]

That deserves a closer look. In identifying natural selection with divine fiat, Gould's statement could be construed as surrendering, but looked at in another way, it reveals how orthodox Darwinians see natural selection. They believe it "explains" whatever exists in nature, however improbable it might be, just as divine fiat did in pre-Darwin times. Seeing natural selection as all-powerful, they do not take kindly to a dispassionate scrutiny of what it can achieve, or what it has been shown to achieve by experiment.

Evolutionists, of course, believe that they are appealing to science, in contrast to the religionists' reliance on faith. But the truth is that when they utter their two-word incantation, "natural selection," they are not being remotely scientific. Nor are they expected to provide any details. How could natural selection make two different and unrelated organisms more and more similar to one another? Evolutionists are never expected to answer that question. But if pressed they would say something like this:

First, some reptiles began to live part of the time in the water. Then one of them accidentally began to develop both a dorsal fin and a tail fin. So it survived better than the others. That happened again and again in many succeeding generations. Then one day the fin reached a point where modern hydrodynamic engineers would ultimately find its design to be "optimal."

To today's biologist, in short, natural selection operates as an omnipotent force, just as divine fiat once did. Gould said he was "awed" by convergence, but perhaps he was even more awed by the ease with which natural selection functions as a password at any number of "scientific" checkpoints, with the assurance that no further questions will be asked.

In the ichthyosaur case, for example, paleontologists are not expected to point to a sequence of fossils showing the bit-by-bit increase in perfection of reptile dorsal and tail fins. In a slightly different context, Dawkins once referred to the "gradual ramp of improvement" that natural selection needs to "climb up."[24] Such a series, or "ramp," is never found with ichthyosaurs, where all the fossils are in their perfected state. But loyal Darwinists would view any request to produce such a sequence as quarrelsome nit-picking, "science denial," and perhaps incipient creationism.

As they see it, the problem was already solved—and solved in strictly materialistic terms—by Darwin in 1859.

George Gaylord Simpson (1902–1984), the curator of paleontology at the American Museum of Natural History and later at Harvard, once drew attention to the all-embracing nature of Darwinism, but did so as though it were a point in its favor. Animals from different lines can either converge, or evolve in parallel, or diverge, he said. Whatever happens, it "usually has an adaptive basis."[25]

So evolutionism has all the bases covered. It is "opportunistic," Simpson reassured us. What could possibly falsify such a theory?

If one cannot measure the variables "or the parameters with which the theory is constructed," Harvard's Richard Lewontin once wrote, "the theory becomes a vacuous exercise in formal logic that has no points of contact with the contingent world. The theory explains nothing because it explains everything."[26]

More recently, advocates of intelligent design have suggested that biological similarity without common ancestry is the result of common design. "Designers regularly re-use parts, programs or components that work in different designs," said Casey Luskin.[27] He gave the examples of wheels re-used on both cars and airplanes, and keyboards found on both computers and cell-phones. Computer scientists have given us more technical examples, showing how very similar or identical sections of computer code are used in quite different applications.

Convergence, then, can be seen in one of two ways, either as a sign of the awkward corner that Darwinists force themselves into by their embrace of a materialist philosophy, or as a biological analogy to the re-use of human designs in different applications. Intelligent design predicts that such re-use will be found frequently in nature, as indeed it is.

# 11. THE FOSSIL RECORD

DARWIN SAID IN *THE ORIGIN* THAT HIS THEORY PREDICTED A "finely graduated organic chain," but he accepted that the fossil record didn't show that. It was the "gravest objection which can be urged against my theory."[1] Darwin also reminded his readers that only small differences between parent and offspring could be allowed. Natural selection could not accommodate leaps or jumps—later called "hopeful monsters" by the geneticist Richard Goldschmidt (1878–1958), who wrote *The Material Basis of Evolution*. Goldschmidt doubted that the small differences we do see between the generations would ever add up to anything.

Darwin insisted that, by his theory, all living species must have been linked to their predecessors "by differences not greater than we see between the varieties of the same species at the present day." It was a severe (and admirable) limit that he imposed on his own theory. Those ancestors, although "now generally extinct," he believed, were similarly connected with "much more ancient species; and so on backwards, always converging to the common ancestor of each great class." But if that were the case,

> the number of intermediate and transitional links between all living and extinct species, must have been inconceivably great. But assuredly, if this theory be true, such have lived upon this earth.[2]

In a letter to Darwin, written the day before *The Origin* was published, his ally Thomas H. Huxley saw a problem. "You have loaded yourself with an unnecessary difficulty in adopting *natura non facit saltum* [nature doesn't make jumps] so unreservedly," Huxley wrote.[3] He believed that nature does in fact "make small jumps," but he gave no details.

On his round-the-world voyage aboard *H.M.S. Beagle*, Darwin took Charles Lyell's *Principles of Geology* with him. The book convinced him that the earth was ancient, which was a requirement for his theory. But the fossil record didn't offer much in the way of support. Admittedly, only a small part of the earth had been explored, and some species are known from a single fossil. "Wholly soft" organisms could not be preserved (not so, as it turned out); and shells and bones on the sea floor soon decayed. Nonetheless, a profusion of finely graded fossils should be down there somewhere. Yet fossil hunters hadn't been able to find them.

His theory-saving solution became well-known. It was that the geological record was highly imperfect. Most of the intermediates were never preserved at all (he assumed). So more excavations were called for. Maybe they would turn up at least some of the missing intermediate forms.

Almost immediately, a 150-million-year-old *Archaeopteryx* fossil was discovered in Bavaria. That was in 1861, and since then several more specimens have been found. *Archaeopteryx*, with teeth, feathers and clawed wings, seemed to bridge the gap between dinosaurs and birds, giving Darwin's theory an immediate boost (though some modern birds, such as the hoatzin, also have clawed wings).

The digging has persisted around the world for 150 years since then, and about 250,000 fossil species have been identified. According to Michael Denton, "so vast has been the expansion of paleontological activity over the past 100 years that probably 99.9 percent of all paleontological work has been carried out since 1860."[4]

A spokesman for the American Association for the Advancement of Science said in the 1980s that 100 million fossils have been identified and that they "constitute 100 million facts that prove evolution beyond any doubt whatever."[5] But fossils, of course, do not make the case for Darwinism. Absent finely graded sequences, the fossil remains of organisms do not imply or disclose ancestor-descendant relationships. Yet

Harvard's Ernst Mayr, one of the leading Darwinians of the twentieth century, wrote in *What Evolution Is*:

> The most convincing evidence for the occurrence of evolution is the discovery of extinct organisms in older geological strata[6]... Eventually the evidence for the conclusion that the world is not constant but forever changing became so overwhelming that it could no longer be denied.[7]

The problem is that Mayr's indisputable but weak claim that the world is "forever changing" does nothing to establish ancestry and descent. Henry Gee, a senior editor of *Nature*, wrote in 1999:

> The attribution of ancestry does not come from the fossil; it can only come from us. Fossils are mute; their silence gives us unlimited license to tell their stories for them, which usually take the form of chains of ancestry and descent... It is effectively impossible to link fossils into chains of cause and effect in any valid way, whether we're talking about the extinction of the dinosaurs or chains of ancestry and descent. Everything we think we know about the causal relations of events in Deep Time has been invented by us, after the fact.[8]

We can measure our knowledge of the completeness of collections— not just of fossils, but of any artifact, postage stamps, for example—by plotting what are known as "collectors' curves." Scientists use them to measure the extent of many different types of collections.

When we start collecting anything, each new item or specimen is one we have not seen before. Then, as we keep finding more, we are likely to find that most are already familiar to us. At that point our collector's curve begins to "level off." Increasingly, our response is likely to be: "We've already seen one of those." Casey Luskin says that when paleontologists see this leveling off, their knowledge of the different types of specimens is "relatively complete."[9]

That's where we are today. A paper published in *Nature* in 2000 found that among the higher taxonomic categories (family and above), "the past 540 million years of the fossil record provide uniformly good documentation of the life of the past."[10]

Michael Foote, a professor of paleontology at the University of Chicago, asked in 1997: "We would like to know whether we have a representative sample of morphological diversity, and therefore can rely on patterns documented in the fossil record." He concluded: "Although we still have much to learn about the evolution of form, in many respects our view of the history of biological diversity is mature." He used the statistical method outlined above.[11]

Foote's paper was cited by Stephen Meyer in his book *Darwin's Doubt* (2013). As more and more fossils are discovered, Meyer wrote, and as they fail to document the great array of intermediate forms, it grows ever more improbable that their absence is an artifact of "either incomplete sampling or preservation."[12]

The broadest category of animal life is known as a phylum. The difference in morphology between a member of one phylum and another is vast. Think of the "distance" between chordates (which include vertebrates), arthropods (insects, beetles, spiders), annelids (worms) and mollusks (squids, snails). Yet to this day paleontologists have failed to find forms that fill up these chasms of "morphological space." Meyer wrote:

> Foote's statistical analysis of this pattern, documented by an ever increasing number of paleontological investigations, demonstrates just how improbable it is that there ever existed a myriad of as yet undiscovered intermediate forms of animal life—forms that could close the morphological distance between the Cambrian phyla one tiny evolutionary step at a time.[13]

In *The Design of Life* (2008), William A. Dembski and Jonathan Wells approached the same question from the opposite direction. We can count the types of organisms living today and then compare them with the number found in fossilized form. The percentage recovered as fossils gives us a good indication of the completeness of the fossil record. They gave this example:

> Among 43 living orders of terrestrial vertebrates (the level of classification just below classes and phyla), 42 have been found as fossils. [Carnivores are one such order.] Thus 98 percent of extant ter-

restrial vertebrates at that level of classification were fossilized. It is therefore a good bet that if there were other orders of terrestrial vertebrates, they too would have been fossilized.[14]

James W. Valentine, a paleontologist with the University of California, found that 76.8 percent of the marine mollusk species currently living along the southern California and Baja California coast are also found in the fossil record.[15]

Nonetheless, some of Darwin's most vocal supporters insist that the fossil record is radically incomplete. In his textbook *Evolution* (2005), Douglas J. Futuyma of SUNY Stony Brook said:

> The fossil record is extremely incomplete, for reasons that geologists understand well. Consequently the transitional stages that we postulate in the origin of many higher taxa have not (yet) been found. But there is absolutely no truth to the claim, made by many creationists, that the fossil record does not provide any intermediate forms.[16]

Futuyma's is one of the leading college textbooks in the field. There are many such intermediates, he said; animals called therapsids, for example, were intermediate between reptiles and mammals. He said it is the most "beautifully documented example of the evolution of a major taxon."[17]

One problem is that the morphological sequence of therapsids does not match the temporal sequence; the fossils expected to be the most reptile-like should come earlier, but there are several inconsistencies. Futuyma also said the reptile-to-mammal transition is "so abundantly documented" that it is "impossible to tell which therapsid species were the actual ancestors of mammals."

But as Dembski and Wells commented, if mammals arose from just one of those lineages, then the others were not ancestral. In that case, why should the similarity of characters be treated as evidence for ancestry?

> If the same mammal-like features of therapsids keep emerging without being related by common ancestry, then why should mammals be regarded as related to therapsids by common ancestry?[18]

As we saw in the previous chapter, a similar problem arises with convergence. Very similar (or convergent) characters appear in widely separated groups that no one thinks are related by ancestry.

An important point is that fossils cannot distinguish between Darwin's claim that nature needs no designer and the alternative argument that it shows strong signs of having been designed. It is not that such a distinction cannot be made but that fossils cannot make it. If it is reasonable to assume that a living organism needs no designer, then the same assumption equally applies to a fossil of that organism.

In *Science on Trial* (1983), Futuyma brought up another issue related to fossils—one that is often mentioned by Darwinians. Fossils tell us that there is an "orderly history" to life, he wrote. Different groups originated at different times. "It is inconceivable that flowering plants or horses could have existed for hundreds of millions of years without leaving a trace, and then left a rich record thereafter."[19]

Brown University biologist and evolution-crusader Kenneth Miller has made a similar argument. The appearance of life on earth has a "sequential character," and he cautioned that "any theory of intelligent design must take these sequences into account."

> To put it plainly, if design is the explanation for life, then the designer has chosen to work gradually, assembling a living world over the course of hundreds of millions of years.[20]

Miller's and Futuyma's claim that life is orderly and sequential can certainly be taken as evidence for "evolution" (depending on how that word is defined). But it is also acceptable to those who are more skeptical. In a world of human artifacts, such as automobiles, cameras and computers, design is always sequential. The Ford Mustang was designed thirty-six years after the Model A (two of the most successful Ford vehicles).

Miller and others who are impressed by the temporal sequence of fossils never explain why they think designers are expected to do everything at the same time. It is one more instance of the evolutionist tendency to stray into theology. Their not-quite-stated position is that

God, if he existed, should have been able to do everything at once. But if sequential design happens with human constructions, why should the sequential design of life itself be ruled out?

## Cambrian Explosion

AN IMPORTANT discovery of new fossils was made by the American paleontologist Charles Doolittle Walcott in 1909. The fossils were embedded within the Burgess Shale, in British Columbia. Dating to the Cambrian period, about 540 million years ago, they documented what became known as the Cambrian Explosion. They were extensively described by Harry B. Whittington (1916–2010), a paleontologist at Cambridge University, and by his assistant Simon Conway Morris, now also at Cambridge. Stephen Jay Gould discussed their findings at some length in his book *Wonderful Life: The Burgess Shale and the Nature of History* (1989).

Almost all the animal phyla appear abruptly in the fossil record of the Cambrian. "The Burgess Shale includes a range of disparity in anatomical design never again equaled, and not matched today, by all the creatures in all the world's oceans," Gould wrote. The large initial stock of animals was then "decimated" (Gould worried about that word, because it seemed the phyla were in fact reduced by more than a tenth), and since then the residue has dominated the history of multi-cellular life. Gould continued:

> The story of the last 500 million years has featured restriction followed by proliferation within a few stereotyped designs [sic], not general expansion of range and increase in complexity as our favored iconography, the cone of increasing diversity, implies.[21]

Gould felt free to criticize "our favored iconography," but he could well have gone a step further and added that the iconography was the brain-child of Charles Darwin himself.

Almost all the animal phyla appeared without known progenitors in the Cambrian era. The paleontologist James Valentine has estimated that at least sixty phyla appeared at that time and that more remain to be discovered. He also said this:

> We consider these estimates to be very conservative. If they are in the correct general order, then the evolutionary events near the pre-Cambrian–Cambrian boundary not only occurred with unexpected rapidity within lineages but involved so many higher taxa as to form an evolutionary explosion without precedent, both rapid in pace and broad in scope.[22]

This near-instant explosion of body plans is the opposite of what Darwin's theory predicts. As he visualized the "tree of life," the number of body plans or phyla should increase with time. Yet today, the number of phyla is estimated at about thirty—perhaps half the number found in the Cambrian.

Dembski and Wells wrote in *The Design of Life* that "the more fossils paleontologists have found, the clearer it has become that they form a pattern at odds with Darwin's theory." The pattern is not a gradually branching tree but a collection of clusters separated by gaps:

> Perhaps that should not be surprising—it is, after all, the same pattern we see among living organisms today... Any theory that attempts to account for the emergence of major taxonomic groups within the animal kingdom must explain how such a dramatic range of body plans appeared so abruptly.[23]

Eldredge and Gould's ideas about "punctuated equilibrium" also lent some support to these non-Darwinian views. A paleontologist with the American Museum of Natural History, Niles Eldredge became an expert on trilobites—extinct marine arthropods and the best-known of the Cambrian fossils. Well-preserved trilobites are among the earliest animals found in the Cambrian. They have lens-focusing eyes with a 360-degree field of vision. ("Not so primitive," as Stephen Meyer wrote.)

At first it bothered Eldredge that the trilobites were all so similar. Then he concluded that the absence of change was itself significant. Stasis is "data," as he put it. He was joined by Gould, and they theorized that animal body forms are static for long periods. Intermediate forms come and go so quickly that they leave little or no record.

As a theory, "punctuated equilibrium" was formulated in 1972. Paleontologists had long observed lengthy periods of stasis in the fossil record. That stability is then interrupted by new species that restore a new "equilibrium" at a different level. It's as though life's history resembles a series of sharp steps, instead of the gradual slope that Darwin had anticipated.

Gould wrote in *The Panda's Thumb* (1980):

> The extreme rarity of transitional forms in the fossil record persists as the trade secret of paleontology. The evolutionary trees that adorn our textbooks have data only at the tips and nodes of their branches; the rest is inference, however reasonable, not the evidence of fossils. All paleontologists know that the fossil record contains precious little in the way of intermediate forms; transitions between major groups are characteristically abrupt.[24]

Gould accepted that the intermediate forms once existed (though they were difficult to see in the fossil record), so neither he nor Eldredge should be confused with creationists. Still, they pointed to a real problem, which persists to this day.

Interviewed at the American Museum of Natural History in the early 1980s, Donn Rosen (1929–1986), formerly chairman of the museum's Department of Ichthyology, summarized the dilemma for Darwinists: "Darwin said that evolution happened too slowly for us to see it. Gould and Eldredge said that it happened too quickly for us to see it. Either way, we don't see it."[25]

Steven M. Stanley, a paleontologist who for most of his career taught geology at Johns Hopkins University, agreed with Eldredge and Gould. But he went even further when he said in 1979:

> The known fossil record fails to document a single example of phyletic evolution accomplishing a major morphological transition, and hence offers no evidence that the gradualistic model can be valid.[26]

Ernst Mayr complimented his junior colleagues when he said that evolutionary stasis had been "unexpected by most evolutionary biologists," and that punctuated equilibrium had had "a major impact on paleontology and evolutionary biology."[27] Futuyma agreed. Species delimited in shape "persist without appreciable change for millions of years," he said, and that "is not limited to specific characters, but marks all the detectable morphological features."[28] It is "organism-wide," in other words.

Fossils discovered in China in 1984 showed an even greater variety of Cambrian body plans, from layers of rock that were older than the Burgess Shale. They helped to establish that the Cambrian animals "appeared even more explosively than previously realized," said Stephen Meyer.[29]

The Chinese fossils showed that the new phyla—new in the sense that they had no predecessors in the fossil record—appeared within a 10 million-year period. No plausible ancestors have yet been found in lower strata, whether in British Columbia or in China.

What about the claim made by Darwin that forms lacking hard parts could not be expected to fossilize? The fact is that lots of pre-Cambrian soft-bodied organisms have been preserved, but they don't bring us closer to a solution. Others say that the explosive period took only five to six million years. How sudden is that? Compared with the reported three-billion year history of life on earth, the Cambrian explosion is the equivalent of one minute in a twenty-four-hour day. It happened in the twinkling of an eye.

Dembski and Wells commented:

The origin of new phyla represents evolution's greatest achievement in diversifying the forms of animal life. Yet, the origin of new animal phyla is crammed into the first one or two percent of the animal fossil record.[30]

When the Chinese paleontologist J. Y. Chen discussed some of these findings at the University of Washington in Seattle more than a decade ago, he went out of his way to express doubts about the adequacy of Darwinism in accounting for what we see. The paleontologists in the audience ignored his doubts, and afterwards he asked a visitor why. The visitor told him it was very unpopular to doubt Darwinism in the U.S. He laughed and said: "In China we can criticize Darwin, but not the government; in America, you can criticize the government, but not Darwin."[31]

Darwin knew about the Cambrian strata, which were originally discovered in Wales, not far from where he grew up in Shrewsbury. He also realized that unless closely related fossil sequences were found, his theory was in trouble:

> The difficulty of understanding the absence of vast piles of fossiliferous strata, which on my theory were no doubt somewhere accumulated before the Silurian epoch [now called the middle Cambrian], is very great. I allude to the manner in which numbers of species of the same group suddenly appear in the lowest known fossiliferous rocks.[32]

So the problem has been understood for 150 years. Others have recently drawn attention to it. Douglas Erwin's and James Valentine's *The Cambrian Explosion: the Construction of Animal Biodiversity* (2013) was published a few months before Stephen Meyer's book. They agree that no one has found the missing fossils or plausibly suggested how the new body plans arose so quickly.

Both Erwin and Valentine have questioned the ability of conventional evolutionary theory to explain what the fossils tell us. Erwin, at the Smithsonian, and another colleague, Eric Davidson of Caltech, "have now ruled out standard neo-Darwinian theory—vehemently in Davidson's case," Meyer wrote.[33] In spite of this, Erwin, Valentine, and Davidson remain Darwinians in the broader sense.

The paleontologist David Raup said in 1979 that although our knowledge of the fossil record has been greatly expanded since Darwin's time, "we have even fewer examples of evolutionary transitions" now than we did then. Some of the classic transitions in the fossil record, such as the evolution of the horse, "have had to be discarded or modified as a result of more detailed information."[34]

Fossil remains spread across the history of life confirm "evolution" if that is simply taken to mean "change over time." But a more detailed look shows the fossil record to be more of an obstacle than a confirmation of what is entailed by Darwin's theory.

# 12. Evolution and Systematics at the American Museum

THE SYSTEMATICS DISCUSSION GROUP USED TO MEET EVERY month at New York's American Museum of Natural History. A "systematics discussion" doesn't sound terribly interesting, but sometimes it is, and one evening, in the fall of 1981, it was. The speaker was Colin Patterson, a senior paleontologist at the Natural History Museum in London. Later he became a Fellow of the Royal Society. He was invited to the American Museum by Donn E. Rosen, who had recently been chairman of the Ichthyology Department there; both were strongly supported by Gareth Nelson, himself later a chairman of Ichthyology. Another supporter was Norman Platnick, an entomologist at the American Museum and one of the world's foremost experts on spiders.

Patterson's talk created a huge controversy. For that reason the written version of his speech was published in 2002 by *The Linnean*, which is the version quoted here.

Patterson died of a heart attack in 1998, as he bicycled to the British Museum in London. He was sixty-four years old. By then I had interviewed him several times. Phillip Johnson, the "godfather" of what later became the intelligent design movement, also interviewed Patterson in London, in 1988.[1]

First, an overview. "Systematics" is the study of the relationships between organisms. It is not quite the same thing as taxonomy, which identifies and names the various species and groups. According to the Book of Genesis, naming the animals was a task first assigned to Adam. God brought him the species "to see what he would call them; and whatsoever Adam called every living creature, that was the name thereof."[2]

Genesis notwithstanding, Patterson's views had nothing to do with the Bible or religious faith. He told me that he was an atheist, and once referred to the belief-system underlying the Church of England as a "pack of lies."

Discerning the difference between varieties, species, and families as a preliminary to naming them is a difficult exercise. So Adam had his work cut out for him. But determining the relationships between these groups is even more difficult. Since Darwin's time it has usually resolved itself into a search for ancestors. But Patterson, Nelson, Platnick, and others concluded that, in the absence of birth records and the like, ancestry is not something that can be determined.

"The concept of ancestry is not accessible by the tools that we have," Patterson once said.[3] People can get together for a family reunion on the basis of family records or immediate recollections. But in nature there are no such records or memories; there are only fossils.

In his book *Human Diversity* (1982) Harvard's Richard Lewontin lent support to this idea. "Despite the excited and optimistic claims that have been made by some paleontologists," he wrote, "no fossil hominid species can be established as our direct ancestor."[4]

When I discussed this with Lewontin, he brought up a little noted contradiction in the search for ancestors: "If it is different enough from humans to be interesting, then you don't know whether it's an ancestor or not," he said. "If it's similar enough to be human, then it's not interesting."[5] His argument, of course, applies to all fossils, not just to hominids.

## Systematics and Cladistics

COLIN PATTERSON, Gary Nelson, and others belonged to a group of systematists called cladists. True to form, cladists are themselves divided into different groups. The group we are interested in, sometimes called "transformed cladists," dispense with all assumptions about ancestry. They say that ancestry, and therefore phylogeny, cannot be determined until we first identify the characters of each group. So they study them without asking: Which came first? An analogy might be to say that it makes no sense to ask whether one word should precede another in an alphabetical dictionary until we know exactly how both words are spelled.

The founding father of what became known as cladistics was Willi Hennig (1913–1976), an entomologist who lived in East Germany. His best-known work, *Phylogenetic Systematics*, was reprinted by the University of Illinois in 1966. It's a difficult book with a lot of technical terms, most of which I shall try to avoid.

Cladists study patterns. They use a criterion of parsimony to decide which traits deserve more weight than others. It's not difficult to appreciate that all this quickly becomes complicated. At times Patterson's talk reflected that complexity, but I shall try to avoid the difficulties.[6]

Illustrating his point that characters make a difference to the way species are related, Patterson brought up "The Great Hippocampus Question," discussed in Charles Kingsley's children's book, *The Water Babies* (1863). "In fact, not in fiction,"[7] Patterson added, Kingsley had elaborated on a controversy pursued in 1861–1862 by Richard Owen and T. H. Huxley. Richard Owen, the creationist, insisted that man was quite distinct from the apes, and couldn't be related to them by descent, "because the brain of man contained a certain centre, the hippocampus, that was absent in apes."[8]

The row went on for two years, Patterson said, and "as usual, Huxley won." But more recently there had been a reversal. Another comment from Patterson:

> [H]ere we are 120 years later, and we have Mayr, the evolutionist, insisting that man is quite distinct from the apes—because the brain of man contains Broca's centre, that is absent in apes. Mayr goes on to cite J. Huxley... Sounds familiar, doesn't it. Yet notice how the roles have become reversed. The part of Owen, the creationist [with

the hippocampus], is now taken by Mayr, the evolutionist [with Broca's center].[9]

## Evolution and Creation

THE CONTROVERSY in Patterson's talk was initiated by Donn Rosen, who had suggested that it should be titled "Evolutionism and Creationism." That was why Patterson introduced those sharply opposing characters, Mayr and Owen. Most of Patterson's controversial remarks came early in his talk, and here is the part that set off the controversy:

> Usually, when I get up to speak on some subject, I've been confident of one thing—that I know more about it than anybody in the room. I don't have that confidence today: I'm tackling two subjects about which I feel I know nothing at all. One of the reasons I started taking a non-evolutionary view was my sudden realization that after working, as I thought, on evolution for 20 years, that I knew nothing whatever about it: It was quite a shock to learn that one could be so misled for so long. Either there was something wrong with me, or there was something wrong with evolution and naturally I suppose there is nothing wrong with me. Over the last few weeks, I've tried putting a question to various people and groups of people. The question is "Can you tell me anything you know about evolution—any one statement that seems to be true"? I tried that question on the Geology staff in the Field Museum [of Natural History], and got no answer. I tried it on the members of the evolutionary morphology seminar in the University of Chicago. After a long silence, one person said "I know it ought not to be taught in high school." I wonder if anyone here has a better answer? The only other answer I've got from anyone—and I've had this from several people like Ken Campbell and Jim Hopson—is "Convergence is rampant—it's everywhere". I'll come to convergence later: but the level of knowledge about evolution is pretty low—we know it ought not to be taught in high school and that's about all. What about creationism—I suppose we know the same fact about it—that it ought not to be taught in high school—and that's about the lot.

... I'm not interested in the controversy over high school teaching, and if any militant creationists have come here looking for political ammunition, I hope they will be disappointed.[10]

Patterson added that this was the Systematics Discussion Group, so he would try to concentrate on that. Then he brought up Neal Gillespie's book, *Charles Darwin and the Problem of Creation* (1979), which would provide the text for his talk. Gillespie's book tried to account for the amount of space that Darwin gave in *The Origin* to combating the creationist argument. Darwin was trying to substitute a view of the world "in which there was no need for final causes, and no room for them,"[11] a view of the world in which there was no purpose in nature. Patterson added that Gillespie took it for granted that Darwin and his disciples had succeeded in this task: in short, a rationalist view of nature has replaced an irrational one.

"I myself took that view for granted until about 18 months ago," Patterson went on. He continued as follows:

> I woke up, and realised that all my life I had been duped into thinking of evolution as revealed truth. From my new viewpoint, some of Gillespie's comments seem very apt, when I transpose them from the period he's talking about, the 1850s, to the 1970s and 1980s.[12]

Gillespie had said that from a materialistic perspective creationism is "an antitheory," something that "has the function of knowledge but conveys none." But what about evolution? Replying to his own question, Patterson said:

> [Evolution] has the function of knowledge, but does it actually convey any? Well, we're back to the question I've been putting to people—'Can you tell me one thing about evolution?' And the absence of answers seems to show that indeed no knowledge has been conveyed. Here we all are with all our shelves full of books on evolution, and yet we seem to have learned nothing from them, as I learned nothing from what I thought was over 20 years of work on evolution. Gillespie's comment—'a void that has the function of knowledge but conveys none,' seems very apt.[13]

# Paraphyletic Groups

PATTERSON THEN made what was surely his most important point—a critique of some well-known evolutionary claims. But his comments may have proceeded too quickly, and probably got buried amidst the general tumult and interruptions. First, in Patterson's words:

> In systematics, there are pieces of evolutionary knowledge that all our heads are stuffed with, from the most general—statements like "eukaryotes evolved from prokaryotes," or "vertebrates evolved from invertebrates," down to lower-level statements like "man evolved from apes". I imagine that by now you all appreciate that such statements exactly fit Gillespie's description—'voids that have the function of knowledge, but convey none.'[14]

His claim was not further discussed, and while "this group" may well have appreciated the weakness of those evolutionist claims, laymen today are likely to have missed the point. Why are such statements "voids," exactly? Patterson went on to explain—but again perhaps too hurriedly:

> Because when analysed, all such statements say that there is a group—a real group with characters—eukaryotes, vertebrates, Homo sapiens, whatever, opposed to a non-group—prokaryotes, invertebrates, apes, or whatever—abstractions that have no characters, no existence in nature, and convey [no] knowledge, although they appear to.[15]

Let me go over that again by asking another question: Why are such groups as invertebrates "non-groups"? Why do they "have no existence in nature"? The answer is that they are all misleadingly identified by the absence of characters. The point is best appreciated by considering the simple sentence:

"Vertebrates evolved from invertebrates."

The problem is that "from invertebrates" adds nothing new to what is already asserted as true in the first two words. The last two words seem to validate the claim that evolution has been observed by identifying the ancestral group. It's a veiled assertion that an instance of "evolution" has been identified. The claim is made more plausible by naming the ancestral group.

The problem is that when vertebrates evolved for the first time, the ancestral species must have been a non-vertebrate. Otherwise the newly evolved vertebrate wouldn't have been the first one. So what we are seeing is not a factual claim but a disguised truism. At the end of the day we still have no idea how to identify the species that the first vertebrate evolved from. We are told that it was not a vertebrate—that it was an invertebrate—but we knew that already.

The same problem arises when we claim that humans evolved from apes. First, there is a group consisting of humans, chimpanzees, gorillas, and orangutans—the *Hominidae*. If humans are excluded from that group, the remaining group is called "apes." If the question is then asked, "What did humans evolve from?" the logical answer is that they evolved from non-human *Hominidae*, otherwise known as apes. It's a disguised way of saying that humans evolved from non-humans—which again, on evolutionary assumptions, we knew already.

The same emptiness appears in the claim that mammals and birds evolved from reptiles. Reptiles are non-mammalian, non-avian amniotes, and so (logically enough) birds and mammals (also amniotes, and therefore requiring amniote ancestors) are said to have evolved from them—another truism that contains no real knowledge.

Willi Hennig invented the word "paraphyly" in 1962, to identify groups with absent characters; but, according to icthyologist Gary Nelson, it was Patterson who was the first to identify the ancestral groups of traditional evolutionary theory as paraphyletic, i.e., as lacking the characters that are said to have evolved in the descendant group.

Asked in a BBC interview what he thought of transformed cladistics, the British biologist Beverly Halstead replied:

> Well, I object to it! I mean, this is going back to Aristotle. It is not pre-Darwinian, it is Aristotelian. From Darwin's day to the present we've understood there's a time element; we've begun to understand evolution. What they are doing in transformed cladistics is to say,

'Let's forget about evolution, let's forget about process, let's simply consider pattern'.[16]

(In *On the Parts of Animals*, Aristotle wrote that "there can be no specific forms of what is non-existent, of Featherless, for instance or of Footless, as there are of Feathered or Footed."[17])

## Nelson and Platnick

I SPENT some time talking to Gareth Nelson and Norman Platnick. In Nelson's office, a table was covered with papers and jars stuffed with small, silvery fish—anchovies—preserved in alcohol. At that time Nelson was just about the world's expert on anchovies, although he told me that the number of people studying them (three or four) is a small fraction of the number of anchovy species (150 known species, and probably many more in reality). This disparity between the magnitude of the "problem" and the number of people working on it is surprisingly common in biology.

Most laymen think that the experts have exhaustively studied life on earth, when they have barely scratched the surface. What about the fossil record? In an automobile museum you can find the "ancestors" of contemporary cars lined up in sequence: Thunderbird back to Model T. Doesn't that apply to extinct animals, too?, I asked Nelson.

"Usually with fossils all you find are a few nuts and bolts," he said. "An odd piston ring, maybe, or different pieces of a carburetor that are spread out or piled on top of one another, but not in their correct arrangement."

Too much importance has been attached to fossils, he said. "And it's easy to understand why. You put in all this effort studying them, and you get out a little bit. Therefore you are persuaded that that little bit must be very important. I can get ten times more information per unit with recent fishes." He said it was common for paleontologists to go to the trouble of digging up fossils without realizing that the animals in question were still walking about.

"Say you dig up a 50-million-year-old beetle," he said. "It looks like it belongs to a certain family, but there may be 30,000 species in the family. What do you do? Go through all 30,000? No, you just give it an appropriate-sounding name, Eocoleoptera, say. If it is one that has been in existence for 50 million years, somebody else will have to find that out, because you don't have enough time. You're out digging in the rocks, not poking through beetle collections in museums."

When I asked about anchovy fossils, he said that a graduate student at the museum studied the question, and it turned out that "all the fossils previously described as anchovies are not anchovies at all." So the fossil record of anchovies was reduced to zero. But then they found one in the British Museum, maybe 10 million years old, from the Miocene in Cyprus. It turns out to be the only known anchovy fossil. "There is information suggesting it is the same kind of animal we find inhabiting the Mediterranean today," Nelson said.

Norman Platnick's office was on the fifth floor of the American Museum. Here, spiders (dead) were inside labeled bottles; journal articles were neatly stacked. Platnick told me that when he was an undergraduate at a small Appalachian college, he would go along with his wife when she collected millipedes. "But when we arrived home, all I would have in my jars would be spiders." So he studied them. Now he has a PhD from Harvard, and he and Nelson are co-authors of a difficult book, *Systematics and Biogeography: Cladistics and Vicariance.*

Spiders, which go back to the Devonian period, 400 million years ago, belong to the class *Arachnida.* They are among the "invertebrates," in other words, and they are not well-preserved in the fossil record. About 35,000 species of spiders have been identified, Platnick said, "but there may be three times that many in the world."

He thought there were perhaps four full-time systematists examining spiders in the United States. The American Arachnological Society had 475 members worldwide, some of them amateurs. They meet once a year and discuss scorpions and daddy-longlegs, as well as spiders.

"Most of the spiders I look at may have been looked at by two or three people in history," Platnick said, adding that he would most likely be dead before anyone looked at them again.

When I asked what was known about spider ancestry, he said "Very little. We still don't know a hill of beans about that." We certainly don't know what species was ancestral to the first spider. We don't even know of any links in the (presumed) 400-million-year chain of spider ancestry.

"I do not ever say that this spider is ancestral to that one," Platnick said. In fact, he didn't know of a single case in the modem literature "where it's claimed that one spider is the ancestor of another." Some spiders have been well-preserved in amber. Even so, Platnick said, "very few spider fossils have been so well-preserved that you can put a species name on them." Like Nelson, he said, "You don't learn much from fossils."

The point stressed by Platnick and Nelson is that unless we know the relationships between organisms—what makes each unique and different from others—we cannot possibly know their ancestral relationships. Things in nature here and now must be ranked according to their taxonomic relationship before they can be placed in a family tree.

Whether we will ever fill in those gaps is something that Platnick could not answer. One problem is the shortage of taxonomists. "Systematics," he said, "doesn't have the glamour to attract research funds." Grants have increasingly gone to molecular and biochemical studies; the result is that support for taxonomy at many institutions has "withered away."

He added: "I am fully prepared to resist any biologist who says evolutionary theory is more important, or more basic. But without the results of systematics there is nothing to be explained."

## A Theory Held Very Dear

A YEAR or two later I asked Patterson what he thought about his talk and the reaction to it. He answered:

I was all fired up, and I said what I thought. I went through merry hell for about a year. Almost everybody except the people at the

British Museum objected. Lots of academics wrote. Deluges of mail. 'Here we are trying to combat a political argument,' they said, 'and you give them ammunition!' One has to live with one's colleagues... They hold the theory very dear. I found out that what you say will be taken in 'political' rather than rational terms.

Patterson told me that he regarded the theory of evolution as "often unnecessary" in biology. "In fact," he said, "they could do perfectly well without it." Nevertheless, he said, it was presented in textbooks as though it were "the unified field theory of biology," holding the whole subject together—and binding the profession to it. "Once something has that status," he said, "it becomes like religion."

When I asked him if he "believed in" evolution himself, he replied: "Well, isn't it strange that this is what it comes to, that you have to ask me whether I believe it, as if it mattered whether I believe it or not. Yes, I do believe it. But in saying that, it is obvious that it is a faith."

The complex organisms that he studied certainly exist. And as an atheist he had little choice but to accept that they assembled themselves one small bit at a time. But the fossil record gives little or no support for this faith.

# 13. Intelligent Design and Information Theory

Intelligent design became an informal "movement" about twenty-five years ago. In 1990, the lawyer and Darwin-skeptic Norman Macbeth unexpectedly received in the mail a manuscript from the U. C. Berkeley law professor Phillip E. Johnson. He questioned Darwinism in much the same way that Macbeth had in his book *Darwin Retried*. Not long after that, Johnson's manuscript was published as *Darwin on Trial* (1991). It's convenient to think of the intelligent design [ID] movement as beginning with that book.

Some of ID's leading researchers soon joined Phillip Johnson and gave him their full support. Here are seven, in alphabetical order: Michael Behe, William Dembski, David Klinghoffer, Stephen Meyer, Paul A. Nelson, Richard Sternberg, and Jonathan Wells. Today, many more names could be added. Discovery Institute also opened its doors in 1991.

Others say that claims about intelligent design began earlier—in the 1980s. The (atheist) astronomer Fred Hoyle used the term in 1982, and in 1984, three scientists, Charles Thaxton, Walter Bradley, and Roger Olsen, published *The Mystery of Life's Origin*. They argued for an "intelligent cause" behind the origin of the information in DNA.

In 1861, Charles Darwin referred to intelligent design, but in a way that Richard Dawkins surely would have liked and admired. Here's Darwin:

One cannot look at this Universe with all living productions & man without believing that all has been intelligently designed; yet when I look to each individual organism, I can see no evidence of this.[1]

And here's Dawkins: "Biology is the study of complicated things that give the appearance of having been designed for a purpose."[2]

In *The Origin of Species*, Darwin did not address the problem of how life began, beyond saying that it was "breathed" into some primordial form. Later, in an 1871 letter to his friend J. D. Hooker, he said that life may have begun in a "warm little pond." Darwin's allies have basically accepted that because they don't have anything better to offer.

To this day, the origin of life remains a mystery. No one has been able to create life, whether in a warm little pond or in a test tube—but not for lack of trying. Nita Sahei, a professor at the University of Akron and an origin-of-life researcher, listed some of the types of molecules that would have to be coordinated to form life, including (as she put it) "four nucleotides, twenty amino acids, a few lipids... several clays and other minerals."[3]

In a 2014 lecture entitled "The Origins of Life: From Geochemistry to Biochemistry," she called the task of getting just the right components to form life in a lab "a combinatorial nightmare." Then she said: "We need to use intelligent—not intelligent design..."[4] Oops, she almost invoked the forbidden theory. She was quickly rescued by another professor who told her to say "careful selection." So she changed the wording: "We need to carefully select which nucleotides to start with, which amino acids and minerals..."[5]

As this intervention suggests, "intelligent design" has become unmentionable in biology departments, except as something to deny, disdain, or attack. I shall say more about biologists' hostility to the very idea of intelligent design later in this chapter.

Meanwhile, it is more than reasonable to maintain that the origin of life did indeed require "intelligent design." No one yet has been able to explain that origin without design. When Ben Stein asked Richard

Dawkins in the movie *Expelled: No Intelligence Allowed* how life began, Dawkins said that he had no idea, and neither did anyone else.

## Late in the Day

ONE MIGHT say that, for those who dispute Darwinism, intelligent design theory came along late in the day. One explanation is that an effective critique of Darwinism can be mounted without relying on intelligent design, just as Macbeth did in *Darwin Retried*. Furthermore, ID in its recent incarnation has largely depended on the discovery of DNA and its details, in the 1950s and 1960s.

Nonetheless, intelligent design adds considerably to the case against neo-Darwinism. It confronts the theory with huge improbabilities that Darwin himself could not have foreseen. Random DNA change is the only mechanism at the Darwinists' disposal, so they must either abandon their creed or accept that highly improbable events routinely occur within the cell.

Recall that Darwin and his contemporaries had no way of knowing just how complex a cell is. Today it is sometimes compared to a high-tech factory. But a cell is far more complex than that. For one thing, factories can't replicate themselves.

Meanwhile, we are repeatedly told that ID can't be right because Darwinian evolution "is a fact." But we can search in vain for facts that establish the truth of the theory. Natural selection? It cannot create new species. Instead, it works in the Darwinian mind as a magic wand that makes problems disappear as easily as a magician's props.

Further, natural selection is not available as a mechanism until the first replicating cell has appeared. Common descent is a deduction from Darwin's theory, but it has never been demonstrated. Homology is a fact of nature, but it is also common in human design. Organisms are observed to vary about a mean, but never to "depart indefinitely from the original type." And so it goes.

But one philosophy has attached itself like a limpet to Darwinism. That is the philosophy of materialism, or naturalism, and it does seem to support the theory. But it turns out that philosophical materialism severely restricts the possibilities of science. In fact, science was long promoted by Christians without any reliance on materialism. In *The Genesis of Science* (2011) James Hannam elaborates on his thesis that the Christian Middle Ages launched the scientific revolution. Later, Isaac Newton, a theist, saw that design was necessary in explaining the origin of the Solar System's planetary orbits.

## ID as an Inference

INTELLIGENT DESIGN is not a deduction from a philosophy but an inference from observed facts. In everyday life we make inferences to design all the time. The philosopher William Lane Craig put it this way: "A beachcomber who comes upon a sand castle recognizes that it's not the result of the action of the waves and the wind, but of intelligent design."[6] An archaeologist excavating a site can tell the difference between a human artifact, such as a statue, and an object misshaped due to erosion. Sometimes it can be difficult to make that distinction, as with an early hand axe, but the occasional difficulty does not render the distinction itself invalid.

Inferences to design are often made long after the designer has departed from the scene, or whose identity may never be known. Anyone who tried to argue that the image of four U.S. presidents on Mount Rushmore was a product of wind erosion would be judged insane. We know that they were designed, and we know that without necessarily knowing the name of the designer, the number of his assistants, or when or how the carving was done. Stonehenge? We know it was designed thousands of years ago, although we don't know by whom. As for its purpose, that is still uncertain and debated.

We have no problem, then, in inferring human design. After all, humans design things every day. But an inference to design in nature, and biology in particular, is contrary to the unwritten rules of contemporary science. Allowing that organisms are designed would take us into forbidden territory. That reminds us of the materialist philosophy that currently presides over science, even though its role is often inexplicit.

In a purely materialistic universe design is impossible. In such a world, all we have are colliding atoms and molecules. Matter, on a materialistic theory, creates mind. Phillip Johnson once allowed that "evolution is the most plausible explanation for life if you're using naturalistic terms," or materialistic philosophy.[7]

Why should our everyday judgments about design be suspended in the case of living organisms? Because admitting design in biology would immediately overthrow Darwin's theory. Its whole thrust from the beginning was to eliminate the need for a designer—to persuade us that nature could construct organisms without any "input" from a designer. That is precisely what natural selection was supposed to have achieved. But of course it didn't.

"In order to find out what or who its designer is," said Thomas Woodward, a historian of intelligent design, "one must go outside the narrow discipline of biology."[8]

## Irreducible Complexity

IN DARWIN'S BLACK BOX (1996), Lehigh University's Michael Behe drew attention to the "irreducible complexity" of the bacterial flagellum, a molecular machine that drives bacteria through fluids. The removal of a single segment of the flagellum immobilizes the whole thing. Behe's description of irreducible complexity was a key moment in the development (or should I say the evolution?) of the ID movement. Much has been made of the flagellum because of Behe's expert knowledge of the topic, but many other body parts have diverse components and are also irreducibly complex.

Darwinism requires that bodies be built one small step at a time. But Behe argued that the flagellum could not have been constructed that way. He used a mousetrap to explain why not. It will not catch any mice until all its parts are connected correctly. A solitary spring that is part of a mousetrap will not catch a single mouse. Analogously, the bacterial flagellum will not work until all of its parts are properly in place. Part of a flagellum will not propel a bacterium slowly. It won't propel it at all.

But Darwin's theory obliges us to accept that complex structures are assembled piecemeal, each piece conferring an advantage over its predecessor. In the Darwinian scheme, the organism also must be capable of surviving at each incremental stage. It's as though General Motors was obliged to construct automobiles in such a way that they could be driven both before and after each major component was added on an assembly line.

Loyal Darwinians, such as Kenneth Miller of Brown University, have tried to hold the line. "By the logic of irreducible complexity," he wrote, the component parts of the flagellum "should have no function" until all those parts "are put into place."[9] (Which is not what Behe claimed.) Miller pointed to one part in particular, the "type III secretory system," which exists both inside the flagellum and separately outside it. Therefore it didn't depend on the flagellum to work.[10]

In his response, Behe pointed out that Miller wasn't thinking clearly. To simplify: a number of functioning parts have to be inside a box if it is to work. Miller then found a part inside the box that also existed outside the box. In his criticism, Behe compared the secretory system to a pump:

> Suppose I said that a car was irreducibly complex because it needed wheels, a motor, and chassis. Later, it was discovered that a car also has a fuel pump. Miller's position is like saying the car is not irreducibly complex because the fuel pump can exist outside the car and work as a stand-alone pump. But that doesn't say how a functioning car can be put together without a fuel pump. The car still requires all those parts. Miller's argument doesn't even say where the fuel pump came from.[11]

In short, the flagellum resists the standard, Darwin-variety explanation. As it cannot function with a part missing, it is reasonable to infer that it was assembled all at once. And that implies design.

Notice this is not the same as claiming that God created the flagellum, or any other part. Such a conclusion is derived from a theistic premise, where the designer is posited at the outset. Intelligent design theory, then, does not identify a designer, any more than we can identify the designer of Stonehenge.

## Complex Specified Information

"It is unexceptionable that intelligent causes can do things which unintelligent causes cannot," said the mathematician and philosopher William Dembski, at the time a Senior Fellow at Discovery Institute.[12] In 1996 he published his "explanatory filter," yielding an inference to design.

The explanatory filter proceeds by eliminating events or structures that cannot be regarded as designed, because they are products either of chance or necessity.

It's true that "necessary" or law-like events are not designed. Consider a stone that is washed off a cliff. Its landing place can be predicted and its path described mathematically. But its landing place cannot be considered to be "intelligently designed." It is law-like—a product of gravity and Newton's laws of motion.

(Some might say that the law of gravity was itself designed by the creator of the universe but that introduces an unnecessary complication that can for our purpose here be ignored.)

Next in the filter we turn to chance. Chance events are obviously not designed. A randomly chosen sequence of say twenty (or more) letters of the alphabet is highly complex, and improbable. It would take a very long time to reproduce it by a random method—by throwing down Scrabble pieces, for example.

But the problem here is that any sequence of twenty letters is as improbable as any other. Improbability alone does not entail design. Every bridge hand ever dealt is improbable, and it would take a dealer a long time to replicate a given hand. But it is erroneous to see something as "designed" merely because reproducing it by random means would be time-consuming.

A random sequence of twenty or so letters or numbers does contain a high level of "information"—but that refers to information as measured by the MIT theorist Claude Shannon. The problem is that Shannon's theory "cannot distinguish functional or message-bearing sequences from random or useless ones," as Stephen Meyer said in *Signature in the Cell*.[13] Message-bearing does not appear until a particular sequence is specified. What does that mean? Consider a well-known sequence of letters:

"In the beginning was the word."

That series of letters and spaces is neither a product of law nor random. It corresponds to a sentence found independently of any procedure for randomly aligning letters. So it is specified. It is also complex. It would take a long time to reach that sequence from St. John's Gospel by throwing down letters randomly. So it is both complex and specified. From that we can infer that it was designed. Generalizing from this, William Dembski formulated the Law of Small Probability: Specified events of small probability do not occur by chance.

Going from the sublime to the mundane, an argument reminiscent of Dembski's was made by Ian Fleming in his James Bond book *Goldfinger*. At one point the villain said, "Once is happenstance. Twice is coincidence. Three times is enemy action."[14] Goldfinger understood that someone (James Bond!) was targeting him. His inference to enemy action was also an inference to design.

## Intelligent Design in the Body

Complex specified information is what is conveyed or represented by a particular arrangement or sequence of things. In biology it can be thought of as analogous to software code—instructions for a new computer program. "DNA is like a computer program but far, far more advanced than any software ever created," Bill Gates once said.[15] In the same way, DNA contains a set of instructions used in the assembly of proteins.

Darwin's geologist friend Charles Lyell said that in trying to understand events in the remote past, we should look for causes now in operation. Mind satisfies that requirement. In fact, mind is the only known cause of the kind of sequence-specific code that we see in biology.

Improbabilities, questionable in bridge hands, really do arise when sequences are specified. Along the DNA molecule we find a long string of nucleotides, signified by the four letters A, C, G, and T. Their sequence along the DNA backbone at first may seem to be random, just as the sequence of letters in an English sentence might appear random to someone who knows nothing about the English language.

But we now know that nucleotides form sequences that the genetic code uses to construct proteins. Proteins in turn are highly specified complex structures found all over the animal kingdom. Nucleotides convey information by virtue of their sequence, not their chemical properties. In other words the desired sequence is specific. DNA is like written language in that respect. Both s-a-l-t and l-a-s-t contain the same four letters, but convey different meanings based on their sequence alone.

The sequence hypothesis was first proposed in 1958 by Francis Crick, the co-discoverer of the structure of DNA. The hypothesis states that the sequence of bases in the genetic material determines the sequence of amino acids for which that segment of DNA codes. Crick also thought that the amino acid sequence in turn determines the three-dimensional structure into which proteins fold.

How rare are the functional sequences among those that are possible in an amino acid chain of a given length? Even by 1966 (eight years after Crick's proposal), not enough was known about molecular biology to answer that question. But a post-doctoral researcher at Cambridge named Douglas Axe was able to find some answers. If we are talking about sequences of 150 amino acids capable of folding into "function-ready" structures, compared to all possible sequences of that length, Axe determined the ratio to be 1 to $10^{74}$. Axe told Steve Meyer that the odds of finding a functional protein by random mutation are far lower than the odds of finding a given atom out of all the atoms in our galaxy.[16]

The underlying problem is that the twenty relevant amino acids can be assembled in trillions of ways, yet the vast majority of those sequences will not cause proteins to fold correctly; and proteins which do not fold correctly will not function.

Many necessary proteins in cells require numerous amino acids linked in sequence. "Most genes—sections of DNA that code for a specific protein—consist of at least 1000 nucleotide bases," Meyer wrote. That corresponds to $4^{1000}$ "possible base sequences of that length"—an unimaginably large number. Further, "proteins typically require hundreds of amino acids in order to perform their functions."[17]

Participants at the Wistar Institute conference in Philadelphia saw this as a problem as long ago as 1966. They understood "the immensity of the combinatorial space" associated with proteins of merely average length.

> They realized [Meyer continued] that if the mutations themselves were truly random—that is, if they were neither directed by an intelligence nor influenced by the functional needs of the organism (as neo-Darwinism stipulates)—then the probability of the mutation and selection mechanism ever producing a new gene or protein could well be vanishingly small.[18]

Discovery Institute's Jonathan Wells points out that the improbability problem is not confined to the first cell. "New protein folds would have to originate throughout the history of life, not just with the first cell," said Wells. "Even in the early history of bacteria, many new proteins would have been needed. Yet the origin of even one functional protein by a Darwinian mechanism is so unlikely that the odds are effectively zero."[19]

So the question is: if chance is the only permissible agent of change, how did the specified sequences appear in the DNA in the first place? The answer is that the cell, and along with it the DNA molecule, must have been intelligently designed.

No known undirected chemical process can produce the information necessary to account for the origin of the first living cell or any later cell or system. A professor of microbiology at the University of Chicago, James Shapiro, wrote in 1996 that "there are presently no detailed Darwinian accounts of the evolution of any biochemical or cellular system, only a variety of wishful speculations."[20]

Just as computer code comes from programmers, so functional information in the cell comes from intelligence. It comes from mind, not from matter.

## Entrenched Hostility to ID

IN PREFERRING intelligent to mechanistic cause, intelligent design theory is in direct competition with the dominant evolutionary theory of biological origins—neo-Darwinism. So it has faced much opposition. A good example is found in *Wikipedia*'s lengthy article on ID. It begins:

> Intelligent design (ID) is the pseudoscientific view that 'certain features of the universe and of living things are best explained by an intelligent cause, not an undirected process such as natural selection.'[21]

Numerous attempts have been made to change such derogatory comments, but all such changes are promptly reversed on *Wikipedia*—sometimes within minutes.

Leonard Krishtalka, a biologist and director of the University of Kansas Museum of Natural History, has said that design can't be measured. Therefore it is "a religious belief, and science has no comment on that."[22] He might have added that complex specified information can be measured, and has been found to be wildly improbable, absent design. He might also have said that macro-evolution has not yet been measured, or so much as observed. The pretense that it has depends on extrapolation, from which valid scientific conclusions can be drawn only tentatively and with numerous caveats.

In 2005, on the front page of the *Washington Post*, Barry Lynn, the director of Americans United for Separation of Church and State, said that intelligent design is merely "a veneer over a certain theological message," thus falsely identifying ID with religion.[23]

When he was at Baylor University, Dembski formed the Polanyi Institute to debate these issues, with Darwinians and ID opponents included on the board. But the Institute was shut down after vehement protests from Baylor's biology faculty. They did not want ID to be so much as discussed.

Darwinians today are eager to stick their own labels onto ID: "Intelligent design creationism" is one favorite. It's as though an unseen collective voice had cried out: "Give us back our preferred enemy! Bring back creationism! That, we knew how to respond to." But so far, no intelligent rebuttal of intelligent design has appeared.

## A Privileged Planet

INTELLIGENT DESIGN also arose as a contentious issue after publication of *The Privileged Planet: How Our Place in the Cosmos Is Designed for Discovery*. The book, by Guillermo Gonzalez and Jay W. Richards (Regnery Books, 2004), challenged the Copernican Principle—the idea that there is nothing special about Earth or its place in the universe. The authors replaced the Copernican principle with the Anthropic Principle—the claim that had the physical parameters of the universe been slightly different, we wouldn't be here to observe it.

"The implication is that intelligent life requires the existence of a cosmos of quite a specific level of complexity," said Steve Fuller, and that level of complexity "borders on the miraculous—unless, of course, it was somehow 'purpose-made.'"[24] A faculty member at the University of Warwick, Steve Fuller was appointed to a chair in Social Epistemology in 2011.

The presence of essential elements on Earth—particularly carbon, oxygen, and water in the right proportions—led to the claim by Gonzalez and Richards that the planet was designed for multicellular organic life. One reviewer of the book pointed out that "bringing together the conditions for life as we know it is so complex that advanced life may be exceedingly rare."

Extraterrestrial life remains elusive, despite a great deal of searching. So the idea that ours is a privileged planet still has not been refuted.

Gonzalez and Richards went further and said that the universe itself—not just our place in it—was "designed for discovery." They maintain, for example, that Earth and the Moon work together to sustain earthly life as one intricate system, producing the best solar eclipses available to earthly observers. They also claimed that Jupiter and Saturn protect Earth from cataclysmic destruction.

What happened next was perhaps more interesting than the claims in the book. Gonzalez, an assistant research professor of astronomy at Iowa State University, and the author of over sixty peer-reviewed scientific articles, including articles in *Nature* and *Science*, and a *Scientific American* cover story, was refused tenure in 2007.

The problem was that he had invoked intelligent design. This was too much for faculty members, and not just at Iowa State University. Over 400 professors across the state signed various statements, opposing "all attempts to represent Intelligent Design as a scientific endeavor." Both on and outside the planet, whether in astronomy or biology, the professors insisted, the philosophy of naturalism is expected to enjoy a monopoly. Any alternative claim was rejected as unscientific.

William H. Jefferys, a Professor of Astronomy at the University of Texas at Austin, spoke for many in the academy. He said in a review of *The Privileged Planet* that "[what is] new in this book isn't interesting, and what is old is just old-hat creationism in a new, modern-looking astronomical costume."[25]

In 2013, Guillermo Gonzalez joined the Department of Physics and Astronomy at Ball State University in Indiana. He told members of the department that he would continue his research on astrobiology and stellar astrophysics. "I will not be discussing intelligent design (ID) in my classes (I didn't discuss ID at Iowa State University either)." He reiterated his view that evidence of design in cosmology "is not out of the mainstream" and "a number of cosmologists and physicists hold to this view." He also said that he was denied tenure at Iowa State "not because of poor academics on my part, but for ideological and political reasons."[26]

# 14. Darwin and the Philosophy of Materialism

STEPHEN JAY GOULD ONCE POINTED OUT THAT DARWIN HAD worked out his theory of evolution by 1837, but didn't go public with it until 1858. What caused the delay? It wasn't that he was incapacitated. During that time he wrote a four-volume treatise on barnacles. (In his *Autobiography*, he doubted whether barnacles had been worth the time he spent on them.)

Gould argued that two of Darwin's notebooks, written in 1838 and 1839, contain the answer. Evolution itself wasn't the problem. Earlier in the nineteenth century, it was "a very common heresy,"[1] widely and openly discussed. Darwin's own grandfather had broached the subject. The problem was that Darwin's theory was distinguished from all the others by its unremitting materialism—then considered to be a greater heresy than evolution itself.

Previous essays on evolution were softened by a reliance on vital forces, organic striving, teleology and the like. In contrast, Darwin's theory conformed to full-blown materialism, encompassing what he termed "the citadel itself."[2] That was the human mind. He argued that the mind was nothing but a special configuration of matter.

Gould defined materialism as the claim that:

matter is the stuff of all existence and the claim that all mental and spiritual phenomena are its by-products. No notion could be more upsetting to the deepest traditions of Western thought than the statement that mind—however complex and powerful—is simply a product of brain.[3]

To be acceptable to his contemporaries, then, Darwin's theory needed a climate of opinion more favorable to materialism. That did not quite exist in the 1830s. But by 1860 the required liberalization had occurred.

Earlier in the nineteenth century, materialism had been actively repressed. Lectures were proscribed, publication hampered, professorships denied, and, according to the editor of the early Darwin notebooks, "fierce invective and ridicule [of materialism] appeared in the press. Scholars and scientists learned the lesson and responded to the pressures on them."[4] Sometimes they recanted and sometimes they published anonymously or "delayed publication for many years."[5]

In one of those notebooks, Darwin reminded himself to "avoid stating how far, I believe, in Materialism," (the redundant commas are Darwin's), and to say only that emotions, instincts and so on "are so because brain of child resembles parent stock." In another notebook Darwin mocked himself: "Love of the deity effect of organization, oh you materialist!..."[6]

Stephen C. Dilley, a philosopher at St. Edwards University in Texas and a student of Darwin's writings, showed that Darwin did not deploy materialism—sometimes called naturalism—consistently in *The Origin*. Instead, he "strategically and progressively" invoked it in the six editions of *The Origin*, "in order to enhance the persuasiveness of his theory, and to marginalize special creation from the scientific discussion."[7]

Alex Rosenberg, head of the philosophy department at Duke University and a committed naturalist, described his position this way:

> What is the world really like? It's fermions and bosons [atomic particles], and everything that can be made up of them, and nothing that can't be made up of them. All the facts about fermions and bosons determine or 'fix' all the other facts about reality and what exists in this universe or any other if, as physics may end up showing, there are other ones.[8]

Kai Nielsen, a professor emeritus of philosophy at the University of Calgary, reinforced Rosenberg: "Naturalism denies that there are any spiritual or supernatural realities."[9] But the U. C. Berkeley philosopher John Searle viewed the subject more critically:

> There is a sense in which materialism is the religion of our time, at least among most of the professional experts in the fields of philosophy, psychology, cognitive science, and other disciplines that study the mind. Like more traditional religions, it is accepted without question and it provides the framework within which other questions can be posed, addressed and answered.[10]

Notice that if full-blown materialism is true, then Darwin's theory of common descent must also be true. Complex organisms do exist, after all, so atoms and molecules in motion must have somehow whirled themselves into the far more complex structures that we see around us, whether bacterial or human. That also necessitates a finely graded series of structures that gradually and progressively evolve themselves from bits and pieces of molecules into life, bacteria, and so on. We don't need to bring natural selection into the discussion.

Armed with his creed, the true-believing materialist no longer needs to study evolution in any detail: Phylogeny, fossils, cell structure? Who needs them? The materialist can simply retort: "We have the starting point (molecules in motion); we have the end point (us). And given that only physical matter exists, how else could such a progression have happened, except by a protracted series of parent-offspring stages?"

At that point Darwinism becomes little more than a deduction from a philosophy. The science is redundant. There is no need to bother with information theory, enumerate mutations, whether favorable or unfavorable, or fuss about fossils. Darwin's theory is embedded in its underlying materialism. Natural selection meanwhile resembles gears disconnected from the engine. It operates as a convenient cover story, seeming to dissolve all the intervening improbabilities.

As we already saw (in Chapter 5) the best statement of the commitment to materialism was made by Harvard's Richard Lewontin in the *New York Review of Books* (1997):

> We take the side of science *in spite of* the patent absurdity of some of its constructs, *in spite of* its failure to fulfill many of its extravagant promises of health and life, *in spite of* the tolerance of the scientific community for unsubstantiated just-so stories, because we have a prior commitment, a commitment to materialism... Moreover, that materialism is absolute, for we cannot allow a Divine Foot in the door.[11]

Phillip E. Johnson, the founder of the intelligent design movement, commented:

> Lewontin is telling us that scientific materialists like himself ("we") don't believe in materialism because they are convinced by the broad claims of evolution. Rather, it is the other way around. They believe that the entire history of life can be explained by materialistic processes (evolution) because of their prior commitment to materialism.[12]

Most academics today share that commitment. A leading example is Tufts University's Daniel Dennett. In *Consciousness Explained* (1991) he wrote:

> The prevailing wisdom, variously expressed and argued for, is materialism: there is only one sort of stuff, namely matter—the physical stuff of physics, chemistry, and physiology—and the mind is somehow nothing but a physical phenomenon.[13]

In *Darwin's Dangerous Idea* (1995) he derided any alternative to this philosophy as relying on "sky hooks," or a source of design that does not build on lower, simpler layers. Darwinism, on the other hand, relies on "cranes," said Dennett, and cranes build from the bottom up.

Avowed materialists such as Dennett embrace an ideology. They are the atheistic counterparts to Christians who openly say: "I believe in the Bible and therefore I don't believe in Darwinism." Creationists are easy for materialists to rebut because they can reply: "That is just your belief. We don't accept that because we don't believe in the Bible."

In the same way, skeptics can say to the materialists: "That is just your belief. We don't have to accept your philosophy. Furthermore, it is the real basis of your faith in Darwinism."

The difference is the premise of what can be accepted as knowledge. Someone who accepts only what can be called scientific evidence must a priori reject everything else. The National Committee of Science Education identified non-natural explanations with miracles and said "whether or not miracles occur, they cannot be part of a scientific explanation."[14] They were right, but failed to demonstrate that miracles cannot occur and so begged the question.

## Denial of Free Will

IF MIND is just a special configuration of brain cells, then mind is nothing but matter. How can neurons "decide" to do one thing rather than another? They can't. With the mind reduced to matter, we can't decide to do something different; nerve cells can't make decisions. Therefore materialism repudiates the freedom of the will. The consistent materialist sees this, denies free will, and dismisses consciousness as a delusion. The best known Darwinians follow that path, and should be commended for their consistency.

"Our sense of self is a neuronal illusion,"[15] said Jerry Coyne, a fully paid-up materialist and the author of *Why Evolution Is True*. The molecular biologist Francis Crick said the same thing:

> [Y]our joys and your sorrows, your memories and your ambitions, your sense of personal identity and free will, are in fact no more than the behavior of a vast assembly of nerve cells and their associated molecules... You're nothing but a pack of neurons.[16]

Michael Egnor, a neurosurgeon and professor in the Department of Pediatrics at Stony Brook University, replied that certain aspects of the mind—intelligence and will—are inherently immaterial. Therefore they "cannot be yoked to matter deterministically."[17] Thereupon a defender of the Jerry Coyne position said that such an argument implies that "computers can't even work":

For example [wrote the Coyne defender], how does a computer know that a particular binary string is an ASCII character versus a binary number... For anybody who knows how computers do work, the answer lies in the design of the computer chips, base instruction sets, and how more complex concepts are built from simpler ones.[18]

To which Egnor responded:

Your computer doesn't know a binary string from a ham sandwich. Your math book doesn't know algebra. Your Rolodex doesn't know your cousin's address. Your watch doesn't know what time it is. Your car doesn't know where you're driving. Your television doesn't know who won the football game last night. Your cell phone doesn't know what you said to your girlfriend this morning.

People know things. Devices like computers and books and Rolodexes and watches and cars and televisions and cell phones don't know anything. They don't have minds. They are artifacts—paper and plastic and silicon things designed and manufactured by people—and they provide people with the means to leverage their human knowledge.[19]

The materialist philosophy puts its advocates at odds with the great majority of mankind, alerting the rest of us to the implausibility of what we are expected to believe. Being told that "evolution is a fact" can be intimidating because many laymen won't know how to respond. But to be told, "Your will is not free, even though you think it is," or "You're an automaton and you don't even know it," is likely to get people's backs up.

Richard Dawkins has aroused people in this way, and Phil Johnson respects him (and Daniel Dennett) for doing so. The same applies to the late Cornell biologist William B. Provine (1943–2015). He and Johnson would debate these issues on nation-wide tours. Johnson disagreed with Provine intellectually but respected his consistency and enjoyed his company. Provine outdid everyone in his bluntness. Here is one of his better-known sallies:

Let me summarize my views on what modern evolutionary biology tells us loud and clear. There are no gods, no purposes, no goal-directed forces of any kind. There is no life after death. When I die, I am absolutely certain that I am going to be dead. That's the end for me. There is no ultimate foundation for ethics, no ultimate meaning to life, and no free will for humans, either.[20]

Richard Dawkins made the same claim: "Religion teaches the dangerous nonsense that death is not the end."[21] It's interesting to reflect that Dawkins, Provine, and some others may in the end cause more trouble for evolutionism than the "theistic" evolutionists whose goal in life is to have it both ways.

The best-known group of theistic evolutionists is BioLogos, founded by Francis Collins, now the director of the National Institutes of Health. He and others, notably Brown University's Kenneth Miller, embrace both Christianity and Darwinism and see no incompatibility between them.

## Methodological Naturalism

WE COME now to a distinction, contrasting "methodological naturalism" (MN) with "philosophical naturalism" (PN). The term "methodological naturalism" was invented by the Christian philosopher Paul de Vries in the mid 1980s when he was teaching at a Christian institution, Wheaton College. Methodological naturalists argue that Christians don't need to accept full-blown materialism, or PN. The methodological naturalist proceeds "as if" naturalism is true—when doing natural science—without actually believing that naturalism is true. Here is the reasoning: Scientists work only with nature (not with God, souls, etc.) and therefore in their work, for all practical purposes, nature can be treated as if it is all that exists, but religious life, ethics, etc. do not have to assume that nature is all that exists. So, if the MN/PN distinction is valid, a Christian scientist can be a methodological naturalist all week long in the laboratory, while remaining philosophically non-naturalist outside of the laboratory, at church on Sunday, etc. Thus, theistic evolutionists can be as naturalistic as Darwinians when doing science, while being anti-Darwinian in religion and ethics, due to their non-naturalistic beliefs about God, immortality, etc.

Methodological naturalism is supported by the National Center for Science Education, the AAAS, the National Academy of Sciences, and by other groups populated mainly by materialists. They "don't want to be seen as strident atheists or as bullying their theistic fellow citizens," says Discovery Institute's Paul Nelson. Full-blown materialism invites confrontation and arguments over evidence—arguments which they might lose.

Nelson is critical of the MN/PN distinction. He says that methodological naturalism is "the polite, apparently inoffensive, seemingly religiously neutral version" of materialism. It looks modest, merely promoting observation and testability. It seems to claim "we're all good empiricists here," ruling out "spooks or occult causes." And that makes it easy to sell to theists who are eager to be seen as reasonable and on-board with the science of Darwinism. But its practical consequences, Nelson added, "are identical to those of full-blown naturalism."

In his book *Darwin's Doubt*, Stephen Meyer argues that inferences to intelligent causation, while fully warranted by the evidence of the Cambrian explosion, run afoul of methodological naturalism. Its working assumption, Meyer said, is that "all features of the natural world can be explained by material causes without recourse to purposive intelligence, mind, or conscious agency."[22] But its fatal defect is easily seen: "if researchers refuse as a matter of principle [namely, MN] to consider the design hypothesis, they will obviously miss any evidence that happens to support it."[23]

One cannot evaluate the evidence for or against any hypothesis that has been ruled out a priori. For this and other reasons, intelligent design theorists regard MN as an obstacle to knowledge and a rule that should be dispensed with.

On the other side, Robert Bishop of BioLogos thinks that MN requires phenomena to be explained solely by material or physical causes. "Agency" should be restricted to human activities only. An intelligent agent is a presupposition "external to cellular and evolutionary biology," and so is "brought in from the outside." Intelligent design—which does indeed countenance non-material causation—therefore "violates the well-defined boundaries of natural science." At that point "biologists rightly object," Bishop said.[24]

But mind itself imports causation from the outside, because it cannot be reduced to matter. This is the argument that Thomas Nagel has eloquently made.

## Why Materialism Is Almost Certainly False

THE MOST prominent recent criticism of materialism has come from Thomas Nagel, a philosopher at New York University. His essay, "What Is it Like to be a Bat?," received a lot of attention and was later reprinted in his *Mortal Questions* (1979). His more recent book, *Mind and Cosmos: Why the Materialist Neo-Darwinian Conception of Nature Is Almost Certainly False* (2012), may turn out to be a game-changer.

Nagel also expressed support for various scholars associated with the intelligent design movement, including Steve Meyer, Michael Behe, and David Berlinski. It is difficult for diehard materialists to call him a creationist, because he is an atheist. Nagel received a lot of support, a turn of events suggesting that we may moving back to the pre-materialist intellectual climate of the 1830s.

Inadvertently, the philosopher Michael Ruse aided that idea. Initially a Baptist, Ruse spent half his life writing books defending Darwinism and along the way became an atheist. He once told Daniel Dennett that he (Dennett) could be more effective with his materialism if only he were more tactful. Then he compared Thomas Nagel to Sam Wilberforce, the Bishop of Oxford who debated T. H. Huxley in 1860. (Huxley, incidentally, was not a materialist, believing "materialism to involve grave philosophical error."[25])

In a review of Nagel's book in 2013, the evolutionary geneticist H. Allen Orr wrote:

> Consciousness is the most conspicuous obstacle to a comprehensive naturalism that relies only on the resources of physical science. The existence of consciousness seems to imply that the physical descrip-

tion of the universe, in spite of its richness and explanatory power, is only part of the truth, and that the natural order is far less austere than it would be if physics and chemistry accounted for everything.[26]

Nagel made the following objection to materialism, or naturalism: "Evolutionary naturalism provides an account of our capacities that undermines their reliability, and in doing so undermines itself."[27] Put another way, if our minds are simply the accidental products of a blind process, what reason do we have for accepting materialistic claims as true?

Years ago, C. S. Lewis made the same case in his book *Miracles*. "[A] strict materialism refutes itself for the reason long ago given by Professor Haldane,"[28] Lewis said, continuing as follows:

> If my mental processes are determined wholly by the motions of atoms in my brain, I have no reason to suppose that my beliefs are true… and hence I have no reason for supposing my brain to be composed of atoms.[29]

Lewis added:

> A theory which explained everything else in the whole universe but which made it impossible to believe that our thinking was valid would be utterly out of court. For that theory would itself have been reached by thinking, and if thinking is not valid that theory would, of course, be demolished. It would have destroyed its own credentials. It would be an argument which proved that no argument was sound—a proof that there are no such things as proofs.[30]

Nagel also said that minds convey subjective experiences that are outside the objective world of space and time. So the physical sciences cannot describe such experiences or tell us how the world appears to individuals. Does my "red" look like your red? How can we know?

Nagel:

> There can be a purely physical description of the neurophysiological processes that give rise to an experience, and also of the physical behavior that is typically associated with it, but such a description, however complete, will leave out the subjective essence of the experience—how it is from the point of view of its subject—without which it would not be a conscious experience at all.[31]

In short, the physical sciences "necessarily leave an important aspect of nature unexplained."

That it was even necessary for an eminent philosopher to make such common-sense claims shows how deeply embedded materialism has become in our time. Nagel went on to offer criticism of evolutionism, while at the same time distancing himself from creationism:

> [S]ince the long process of biological evolution is responsible for the existence of conscious organisms, and since a purely physical process cannot explain their existence, it follows that biological evolution must be more than just a physical process, and the theory of evolution, if it is to explain the existence of conscious life, must become more than just a physical theory.[32]

In the end the most sensible position may be to substitute the dualism of René Descartes for the materialism of Darwinism and his followers. Dualism holds that the mind is a nonphysical substance, evident to all of us in our conscious experience.

Materialism is surely false, to amend Nagel only slightly. But it's a false philosophy with side benefits. It serves to remind us that Darwinism itself is mostly a philosophy dressed up as science. And once the philosophy of materialism is rejected, can Darwinism itself be far behind? Dislodged from its bed of materialism, what is left?

## Darwin's Atheism

DARWIN HIMSELF was antagonistic to religion and became ever more so as he aged. In his autobiography he wrote:

> Thus disbelief crept over me at a very slow rate, but was at last complete. The rate was so slow that I felt no distress, and have never since doubted even for a single second that my conclusion was correct. I can indeed hardly see how anyone ought to wish Christianity to be true; for if so, the plain language of the text seems to show that the men who do not believe, and this would include my Father, Brother, and almost all my best friends, will be everlastingly punished. And this is a damnable doctrine.[33]

I shall look more closely at his religious views in Chapter 20.

# 15. DNA: God is in the Details

For almost a hundred years after *The Origin* was published, living things were studied at the level of limbs or whole organisms. Evolutionists knew little or nothing about the cellular or molecular details. But once they were understood, Darwin's theory ran into difficulties. In this chapter I shall try to explain why.

If an organ could not be formed by "numerous, successive, slight modifications," Darwin wrote in *The Origin*, his theory "would absolutely break down."[1] Natural selection must either work by "slight modifications," or not at all; jumps or leaps were not allowed. Then, in *Darwin's Black Box*, the biochemist Michael Behe made a case for the "irreducible complexity" of a particular organ: the bacterial flagellum. That met Darwin's condition: an irreducibly complex organ is one that cannot be formed by successive, slight modifications. If so, evolution has been falsified by Darwin's own criterion. Later in this chapter I shall take a closer look at Behe's flagellum argument.

What is undeniable is that in the last half-century our understanding of molecular complexities has greatly increased—and with it the challenges to evolution. Behe has compared the problem to looking down at the ground from 30,000 feet. From that height, he said, the terrain's details are invisible. It's hard to see the difficulties that creeks and ravines presented to American pioneers traveling in covered wagons. In much the same way, evolutionist ideas are comparable to looking down from an airplane and imagining that a trek from one large feature to another wouldn't be difficult:

> As science probes ever deeper into the molecular details of life, serious evolutionary thought has been forced to descend from 30,000 feet to ground level, and grave obstacles to undirected evolution have become manifest.[2]

Ever more powerful microscopes, instead of illuminating Darwin's theory, have pointed to numerous obstacles in its path.

## The Cell

NOT SURPRISINGLY, nineteenth-century naturalists conceived of life in an over-simplified way. Consider the cell. First seen in a strip of cork by Robert Hooke in 1685, it resembled monastic cells, hence the name. But its interior was not remotely understood; Darwin knew nothing of what went on inside a cell. At one point in *The Origin* he used the phrase "merely of cellular tissue,"[3] seemingly confident that the cells themselves wouldn't pose any great difficulties.

Some have claimed that Darwin did understand cellular complexity, citing a letter in which he quoted G. H. Lewes, the novelist George Eliot's friend. But Lewes, no wiser than any scientist of his time, was a poor source. He said the cell was a structure of "exaggerated importance" with "mysterious powers," surrounded by a "microscopic lump of jelly-like substance" called "protoplasm." And the protoplasm lacked any "trace of organization."[4]

At the same time, the German biologist and Darwin admirer Ernst Haeckel believed that the cell was a "homogenous lump of protoplasm." He went to see Darwin in England and promoted his theory. He also met T. H. Huxley, who said that "protoplasm is the physical basis of all life; It is the clay of the potter."[5]

Today, we know that a cell performs many functions: absorbing nutrients, metabolizing them, manufacturing proteins, dividing itself into two cells, operating in a complex cycle, communicating with other cells, and excreting wastes. The cell contains numerous raw ingredients, including water, carbohydrates, ions, and fats. But organelles constructed of proteins do most of the work. By one account, a typical bacterium—a prokaryote, with no nucleus—requires more than 4,000 proteins to function.

Biologists have addressed the complexity of the cellular world with various metaphors. Some have compared its activity to that of a town full of people, with its own micro-factories and transportation systems. The British ethologist W. H. Thorpe said in the 1960s that "the most elementary type of cell constitutes a mechanism unimaginably more complex than any machine yet thought up, let alone constructed, by man."[6]

There may be 50 trillion cells in the human body—or double that number (they have never been counted). Cells (except for cancer cells) also know when to replicate. Within the human body, cells are divided into perhaps 200 types: skin cells, kidney cells, and so on; but others say that 200 is an undercount.

Oddly enough, classical genetics began in a monastery, with the work of the Augustinian friar, Gregor Mendel. In 1866 he proposed the existence of independent "factors," thought of as abstract particles, which determine the traits carried by pea plants. The Danish botanist Wilhelm Johannsen was the first to call them genes; that was in 1909. He also distinguished between genotype and phenotype. But Mendel's work was not widely noticed until 1900, and Darwin didn't know about it.

Later, genes were assumed to be contiguous sequences of DNA and were thought to "construct" identifiable body parts or traits. But the Harvard geneticist Richard Lewontin criticized that idea, saying "we don't have genes for noses."[7] Genes "for" parts of the body, or for height, size, or traits like intelligence, have never been found. The British geneticist Steve Jones said in 2011 that "we know of more than 50 different genes associated with height." Most human traits are influenced by so many genes, Jones said, that there is no likely systematic cause and effect.[8]

In fact, the gene itself has become ever more difficult to define. Today genes are defined less in terms of what they are and more in terms of what they do: they help construct proteins.

## The Molecular Revolution

WITH ELECTRON microscopes opening up a whole new world, biology departments soon embraced the molecular revolution. After all, a closer look at DNA was far more likely to turn up something new and interesting than one more look at old fossils. In addition, molecular structures haven't changed—at least not since Darwin's time. If the molecular folk need more information, nothing stops them from peering anew into their microscopes.

Francis Crick discussed the transition to molecular biology in his memoir, *What Mad Pursuit* (1988). "The classical period of molecular biology," he wrote,

> stretched from the discovery of the DNA double helix in 1953 till about 1966, when the genetic code—the dictionary relating the nucleic acid language to the protein language—was finally elucidated.[9]

Also in 1966, as it happened, participants in a symposium at the Wistar Institute challenged Darwinism using molecular data. The skeptics argued that it is extremely difficult to assemble a new protein by chance—as Darwinism requires—because of its huge improbability. Billions of amino-acid sequences are possible in constructing a protein, but few are chosen. A wrong sequence means that the protein won't work.

The Wistar event was titled "Mathematical Challenges to the Neo-Darwinian Interpretation of Evolution." It was something that Darwinism had not encountered before.

As we saw in Chapter 13, Bill Gates said that DNA "is like a computer program but far, far more advanced than any software ever created."[10] So what created DNA—bearing in mind that Darwinism only permits accidental events? Furthermore, natural selection cannot play a role until self-replicating organisms come into existence.

# Francis Crick (1916–2004)

"BIOLOGISTS MUST constantly keep in mind that what they see was not designed, but rather evolved," Francis Crick said, reminding us of Richard Dawkins. An atheist, Crick signed the "Humanist Manifesto" and called for humanism to replace religion "as a guiding force for humanity." Once rid of Christian beliefs, "we could get down to the serious problem of trying to find out what the world is all about."[11] Crick accepted an honorary fellowship from the newly founded Churchill College at Cambridge, but then resigned in protest when it accepted a donation to build a chapel.

Like Julian Huxley and Darwin himself, Crick was sympathetic to eugenics. He viewed infanticide as acceptable and argued that rich people should have more children. In 1977 he moved to the Salk Institute in San Diego and took up neuroscience in a (forlorn) attempt to "explain" consciousness.

In Crick's "sequence hypothesis," the nucleotide bases of DNA function like letters in a written language, or symbols in a computer code. But, as in spelling tests, the letter-sequence is important. In the following quotation, Crick discusses the improbability of these events. To generate "this miracle of molecular construction," he wrote,

> all the cell need do is to string together the amino acids (which make up the polypeptide chain) in the *correct order*. [Crick's italics] This is a complicated biochemical process, a molecular assembly line, using instructions in the form of a nucleic acid tape (the so-called messenger RNA)… Here we need only ask, how many possible proteins are there. If a particular amino acid sequence was selected by chance, how rare an event would that be?

> This is an easy exercise in combinatorials. Suppose the chain is about two hundred amino acids long; this is, if anything, rather less than the average length of proteins of all types. Since we have just twenty possibilities at each place, the number of possibilities is twenty multiplied by itself some two hundred times. This is conveniently written $20^{200}$ and is approximately equal to $10^{260}$, that is, a one followed

by 260 zeros! This number is quite beyond our everyday comprehension.[12]

Richard Lewontin then pointed out the chicken-and-egg problem. "The proteins of the cell are made from other proteins, and without that protein-forming machinery, nothing can be made. There is an appearance here of infinite regress (What makes the proteins that are necessary to make the protein?)"[13]

That, said David Goodsell, the author of *The Machinery of Life*, "is one of the unanswered riddles of biochemistry: which came first: proteins or protein synthesis? If proteins are needed to make proteins, how did the whole thing get started?"[14]

Crick understood that something as complex as a protein evolving by chance was highly improbable. So he became interested in "directed panspermia." Once self-replicating bacteria originated somewhere in the universe, they could be spread by intelligent life-forms using space ships to propel the minute critters through interstellar space. Crick used the word "directed" to imply that someone had deliberately sent bacteria to other planets. His theory was "obviously very speculative,"[15] he allowed.

So he had quietly relocated the problem to another planet. One is tempted to comment: Anything was preferable to bringing God back into the details!

## Fred Hoyle (1915–2001)

THE ASTRONOMER Fred Hoyle was the same age as Crick and also did most of his work at Cambridge. But temperamentally they were quite different. In his later years Hoyle threw up his hands when confronted by the molecular improbabilities and became an open skeptic. He learned something about cladistics from Colin Patterson at London's Natural History Museum and understood the weakness of the case for Darwinism.

Hoyle became critical of the belief that life evolved from non-life here on Earth. The odds were too long. Like Crick, he promoted the idea that life on Earth originated in space, spreading through the universe via "panspermia." Evolution, he believed, was given a head start on Earth by an influx of viruses arriving (accidentally) via comets or meteorites.

In 1982, Hoyle presented *Evolution from Space* for the Royal Institution's Omni Lecture. In his calculation, the odds of obtaining the required set of bio-molecules for even the simplest living cell without panspermia were even smaller than Crick's.

"The difference between an intelligent ordering, whether of words, fruit boxes, amino acids, or the Rubik cube, and merely random shufflings can be fantastically large," Hoyle wrote.[16] He compared it to the probability that a large number of blind men would correctly align a scrambled Rubik's cube and all come up with the right solution at the same moment. More from Hoyle:

> So if one proceeds directly and straightforwardly in this matter, without being deflected by a fear of incurring the wrath of scientific opinion, one arrives at the conclusion that biomaterials with their amazing measure of order must be the outcome of intelligent design. No other possibility I have been able to think of in pondering this issue over quite a long time seems to me to have anything like as high a possibility of being true.[17]

Hoyle also published a book called *The Intelligent Universe* in 1983. So he can be seen as an early proponent of what a decade later became the intelligent design movement. He regarded the notion that "the operating program of a living cell could be arrived at by chance in a primordial organic soup here on the Earth [as] nonsense of a high order."[18] Hoyle re-emphasized the point with his famous comment about a tornado in a junkyard:

> The chance that higher life forms might have emerged in this way [by random events] is comparable to the chance that a tornado sweeping through a junkyard might assemble a Boeing 747 from the materials therein.[19]

The evolutionary biologist John Maynard Smith responded to Hoyle in *The Problems of Biology* (1986): "What is wrong with it?" he asked. "Essentially, it is that no biologist imagines that complex structures arise in a single step."[20] But his reply would have been more convincing if he had pointed to cases where organisms had been observed to assemble themselves bit by bit. That has never been seen.

Maynard Smith also said that "even proteins formed as a random sequence of amino acids have some slight catalytic activity."[21] But that is now questioned. Just getting the slightest activity requires a protein with stable, functional folds, which is highly improbable. As David Goodsell said in *The Machinery of Life*:

> [O]nly a small fraction of the possible combinations of amino acids will fold spontaneously into a stable structure. If you make a protein with a random sequence of amino acids, chances are that it will only form a gooey tangle when placed in water.[22]

After Fred Hoyle's death in 2001, his assistant Chandra Wickramasinghe, a Sri Lankan-born astronomer and astrobiologist, said that in the "highly polarized polemic between Darwinism and creationism, our position is unique. Although we do not align ourselves with either side, both sides treat us as opponents."[23]

## Junk DNA

THE DNA molecule, with its three billion "letters" or nucleotides, is conventionally divided into stretches called "exons," which carry sequence information for proteins, and (in the higher animals) much longer stretches called "introns." These are interposed between the exons and, when they are spliced out, leave exons in connected segments. The exons are then transcribed into RNA chains that participate in protein synthesis. In 1988, Crick boldly called exons "the sense bits," while the excised introns he called "the nonsense sequences."[24]

"The existence of introns came as almost a complete surprise," Crick allowed. "Nobody had clearly postulated their existence before experimenters stumbled on them by accident."[25] Classical genetics gave us no hint of them. In *What Mad Pursuit*, Crick elaborated on the exon-intron distinction:

Much of our DNA, perhaps as much as 90%, appeared at first sight to be unnecessary junk. Even if it had some use its function probably did not depend on the exact details of its sequence. Leslie Orgel and I wrote an article suggesting that much of it was "selfish DNA"—a better term might be 'parasitic DNA.'[26]

The concept of "junk DNA" strongly appealed to Darwinists, who thought that nonsense sequences were to be expected if DNA was constructed by random mutation. Crick put it just that way: "The possible existence of such selfish DNA [or "junk"] is exactly what might be expected from the theory of natural selection."[27] But this prediction of evolution, like many others, has been dashed by recent research.

## Human Genome Project

AT THE start of the Human Genome Project, funded by the National Institutes of Health and promoted by James Watson among others, the number of human genes was estimated at 100,000 to 150,000. Thus, *Scientific American* began one story: "Now that all the 100,000 or so genes that make up the human genome have been deciphered…"[28] Many of these (non-existent) genes were even patented. Craig Venter and Francis Collins of the National Institutes of Health then brought everyone down to Earth with a very different count: maybe only 30,000 genes.

"We have only twice as many genes as a fruit fly, or a lowly nematode worm," said Eric Lander, a biology professor at MIT and a fellow traveler aboard the Human Genome Project.[29] Today there are thought to be 19,000 human genes—actually fewer than are found in worms. One obvious conclusion is that the concept of a gene is of questionable value.

*Nature* pursued that idea in 2006, in an article titled "What Is a Gene?" The magazine's summary: "The idea of genes as beads on a string is fast fading." The one-gene, one-protein idea was also coming under assault. "We've come to the realization that the genome is full of overlapping transcripts," one researcher said.[30]

With the publication of the Encyclopedia of DNA Elements (ENCODE) project in 2012, the idea that most DNA was "junk" (as Crick had thought) was shown to be wrong. More than thirty papers in various journals, including *Nature*, *Science*, and *Cell*, reported that many of the vast stretches of seeming "junk," comprising maybe ninety-five percent of the DNA, are the seat of crucial, functional activity. ENCODE showed that as much as eighty percent of the human genome is biochemically active. "Junk DNA," once welcomed by Darwinists as proof that evolution proceeds by random meandering, turned out to be another disappointment.

## Irreducible Complexity

MICHAEL BEHE made a case for the irreducible complexity of molecular structures in *Darwin's Black Box* (1996). He had in mind the bacterial flagellum—a tiny rotary engine attached to certain bacteria and functioning as a propeller, like an outboard motor.

The flagellum is composed of numerous parts. Behe's essential point was that every one of these parts must be operational before the flagellum can function. Possessing just some of those parts wouldn't do. Also, the flagellum can't expect the *deus ex machina* of natural selection to develop the organ bit by bit.

One expert who has agreed with Behe is microbiologist James Shapiro. In a review of Behe's book he wrote: "There are no detailed Darwinian accounts for the evolution of any fundamental biochemical or cellular system, only a variety of wishful speculations."[31] It would seem to be safe to assume that the great majority of molecular machines, not just the flagellum, are also irreducibly complex.

## Conflict between Molecular and Anatomical Trees

WE CAN construct "a tree of life based solely on the basis of similarities of... DNA sequences," said Francis Collins in *The Language of God: A Scientist Presents Evidence for Belief* (2006). The tree "does not utilize... anatomic observations of current life forms." Yet, he said, "its similarity to conclusions drawn from studies of comparative anatomy... is striking."[32]

This claim is "simply false," says Jonathan Wells. First, DNA-based trees are often in conflict with each other, and they also differ from those derived from comparative anatomy. Here is an example of a conflict between DNA trees: Francis Collins's results showed flying lemurs as closely related to tree shrews, with rabbits and monkeys on more distant branches; yet a separate study published in 2002 showed flying lemurs as more closely related to monkeys, with tree shrews closely related to rabbits.

Jonathan Wells wrote that conflicts based on different DNA-based trees "are a major headache for evolutionary biologists, some of whom spend their entire careers attempting to resolve them."[33]

Furthermore, phylogenies constructed with DNA often conflict with those based on anatomy. Consider whales. In the 1960s the evolutionary biologist Leigh Van Valen proposed on anatomical grounds that whales "Are descended from an extinct group of hyena like animals."[34] But in the 1990s "molecular comparisons suggested that whales are more closely related to hippopotamuses."[35]

Discovery Institute's Ann Gauger (PhD in developmental biology, University of Washington) makes the same point. She explained that while baboons and mandrills were once placed together due to morphology, modern phylogenetics based on DNA separates them.[36] Morphology and DNA give different patterns, and groupings based on morphology can be overturned by DNA similarities.

There is an additional problem, and to understand it we must return to Darwin's theory, in which natural selection acts on variations. The source of variation was not known, but differences between the generations could readily be observed. Natural selection then went to work and only "the fittest" variation survived. That was how evolution unfolded, as Darwin saw it.

Then, with the discovery of DNA and its three billion nucleotides, the source of variation was more precisely identified. It was mutation; some of the nucleotides periodically mutated, and mutations were (quite reasonably) construed as "errors." They could be compared to "typos" made by a typist in copying a manuscript, which is then passed on to the next generation. Then more typos are added. Analogously, Darwinians believe that when enough errors or "mutations" are added, a new species emerges from the old. But that's like believing that if there are enough typos, a poem by Shakespeare will eventually be transformed into one by Wordsworth. David Berlinski made just such a criticism of Darwinism in his book *The Devil's Delusion*.

Recently, however, we have learned that to preserve the information encoded in the genome, organisms go to great lengths to prevent such errors from appearing. Cells have error-correcting mechanisms built into them. If such "proof-reading" was absent, an organism would soon become little more than a mass of mutations, and not long for this world.

At the molecular level, then, we see that what had once been thought of as the source of variation and "fitness" became instead a source of errors, ultimately leading to speciation.[37]

## Darwin of the Gaps

KENNETH MILLER, a committed Darwin defender and professor of biology, said that cells are filled with structures "whose detailed evolutionary origins are not known." Therefore, those who argue against evolution

> might pick nearly any cellular structure—the ribosome for example —and claim correctly, that its origin has not been explained in detail by evolution.
>
> Such arguments are easy to make, of course, but the nature of scientific progress renders them far from compelling. The lack of a detailed current explanation for a structure, organ, or process does not mean that science will never come up with one. [38]

In his 1999 book, *Finding Darwin's God*, Miller made the familiar "God of the gaps" argument. "Creationists," he said, like to plug God into whatever Darwin didn't explain. But "as humans began to find material explanations for ordinary events," he added, "the gods broke into retreat."[39]

But notice that Miller introduces his own "gap" argument in discussing the origin of cellular structures. We might call it "Darwin of the gaps": we haven't found a material explanation for these molecular details yet, but (he adds in a touching appeal to faith), given "scientific progress," we shouldn't assume "that science will never come up with one."

## A Work in Progress

MOLECULAR BIOLOGY is still a work in progress, and little that we read today should be regarded as final. Consider the recent and destabilizing claims made on behalf of epigenetics, and then on behalf of horizontal gene transfer.

Epigenetics is the study of small chemical markers placed on top of the four DNA letters that constitute the genome. Environmental factors help determine where these markers are placed, and they in turn influence whether or not a gene is turned "on" or "off." In other words, what is in the environment can influence gene expression.

*Nature* reported in 2013 that in some organisms these markers are passed on to the next generation. If so, environmental factors affect gene expression not only in the present generation, but also in the next, and maybe the one after that. In 2014, *Science* magazine writer Jocelyn Kaiser called epigenetics researcher Michael Skinner a "heretic"[40] for maintaining that chemicals can cause changes in gene expression that persist across generations. But Skinner thought that epigenetics may become "the biggest paradigm shift in science in recent history."[41]

Some biomedical and epidemiological research has suggested, for example, that a susceptibility to diabetes and heart disease can be passed on by factors picked up environmentally and then passed on to later generations.

All this potentially puts us back into Lamarckian territory. We may recall that Darwin resorted to Lamarckism when his original theory was challenged by the Scottish engineer Fleeming Jenkin in 1867. Jenkin said that helpful variations occurring accidentally would soon be swamped by unhelpful variations in later generations. Darwin's appeal to a Lamarckian mechanism ran up against the "refutation" that the offspring of mice whose tails are cut off still have tails, but, as we have just seen, epigenetics shows that this "refutation" of the inheritance of acquired characteristics may no longer be decisive.

In Lateral (or Horizontal) Gene Transfer (LGT/HGT), organisms of different species living in the same environment transfer genes from one to the other. LGT, which has attracted attention in science journals recently, is common in bacteria and is thought to explain how they can generate resistance to antibiotics. It's as though immune bacteria are able to come to the rescue of vulnerable ones.

According to Alastair Crisp, a researcher at Cambridge University, "It appears that horizontal gene transfer has contributed to the evolution of many, perhaps all animals, including humans, giving rise to tens or hundreds of active 'foreign' genes." Crisp went on to say: "[T]he process is ongoing, meaning that we may need to re-evaluate how we think about evolution."[42]

Casey Luskin essentially agreed with Crisp, adding that gene transfers show that biologists have uncovered genetic data sharply at variance with universal common descent. Common descent implies that genes are inherited from parental generations and not from neighbors. Laterally transferred genes don't fit the standard evolutionary phylogeny, suggesting that the Darwinian tree of life may have to be rethought.

Michael Behe said that "it's a reasonable deduction to think that some genes were transferred between bacteria by viruses." Viruses seem able to do so by "engulfing the cellular debris" of bacteria, or by other means. Behe also said that he doesn't think the horizontal transfer

> explains the origin of a new use for the gene in the new bacterium. One can swap parts between a tool shop that works in the metric system with a tool shop that works with English measurements, but that won't tell you how new complex machinery is put together in the first place.[43]

In light of what we know about recent developments, Michael Behe commented that "the cell's known complexity has increased immeasurably in recent years, and points ever more insistently to an intelligent designer as its cause."[44]

In summary, the tendency of genomics has been to undermine the old Darwinian verities in a way that organismal biology never could. In particular, we have seen the huge improbability of finding the DNA sequences that generate correct protein folding. All the indications are that as "scientific progress" continues, with more and more complexities likely to appear, the molecular headaches for Darwin's theory will only increase.

# 16. LENSKI'S EVOLVING BACTERIA

SINGLE-CELLED ORGANISMS CALLED *ESCHERICHIA COLI* EXIST IN THE billions in the guts of animals, including humans. They are usually helpful, sometimes neutral, and occasionally harmful. But in his lab at Michigan State, Richard Lenski has been observing *E. coli* without any medical goal in mind. And he has observed them continuously, since February 1988.

Bacteria divide, much as cells of the body divide. As they can replicate (asexually) every forty minutes, Lenski and his lab assistants have seen a lot of bacterial divisions. The 60,000-generation mark was reached in April 2014. (Today it is closer to 65,000.) The experiment is supported by a grant from the National Science Foundation. Lenski calls it his Long-Term Evolution Experiment.

His underlying argument is that even in the absence of selection pressure, *E. coli* will evolve on their own, given enough time, or bacterial divisions.

A member of the National Academy of Sciences and the Hannah Distinguished Professor of Microbial Ecology at Michigan State University, Lenski has focused on genetic mechanisms "that drive evolutionary change" (his lab reported).[1] Twenty-five years of *E. coli* divisions are said to be the equivalent of one million years for humans. (Others say it is closer to 1.5 million years.)

Well-known science journals soon became Lenski's greatest admirers. Elizabeth Pennisi's article about him in *Science*, published in 2013, covered four full pages of the magazine. It was headlined "The Man Who Bottled Evolution," with this subhead: *"Richard Lenski's 25-year experiment in bacterial evolution shows no signs of running out of surprises about how mutation and selection shape living things."*[2]

Lenski and assistants grow bacteria in a dozen nutrient-filled flasks. Then, every day, one percent of the population of each flask is transferred to a new flask of fresh growth medium. Under these conditions, each population experiences 6.6 generations, or doublings, per day. The flasks are kept separate from each other so that the twelve different lines of descent don't get intermingled. (Richard Dawkins has called the separate flasks "tribes."[3])

After every 500 generations—taking about eight weeks—Lenski and his helpers deposit bacteria from each flask into a freezer. These become the "ancestors." They can be thawed whenever needed and then compared to their most recent descendants. In this way, Lenski has created a "fossil record" of his bacteria.

The experiment continued along these lines for over twenty-five years. Carl Zimmer, a journalist and the author of *Evolution: The Triumph of an Idea* (2001), reported in *Discover* magazine that the bacteria "have been evolving in all sorts of interesting ways," and the freezing and thawing has allowed Lenski "to reconstruct the history of that evolution in great detail."[4]

The experiment is "an absolutely magnificent achievement," said Douglas Futuyma, an evolutionary biologist and textbook writer at Stony Brook University. Richard Dawkins said that it is "a beautiful demonstration of evolution in action, something it is hard to laugh off, even when your motivation to do so is very strong." And for creationists, Dawkins added, that motivation "is very strong indeed."[5]

But before we get carried away, now may be the time to mention what is easy to lose sight of: that after so many generations and so much evolving, the bacteria remain bacteria to this day. It seems likely that they will stay that way for as long as the experiment lasts. It has no defined endpoint, says Lenski, but he wants others to keep it going after he retires.

He would like to see his experiment continue for another twenty-five years.

The biochemist Michael Behe told me that the experiment "can show you what can happen in long-term evolution." In his 2010 article on Lenski's experiment in the *Quarterly Review of Biology*, Behe pointed out that when trillions of bacteria replicate over 60,000 generations, numerous mutations are to be expected. Yet the most important "evolutionary" changes observed so far have involved the loss of old genetic functions rather than the acquisition of new ones.[6]

Behe said that he disagreed with Lenski's interpretations, but nonetheless he is a "big fan" of his work. He explained why:

> Although Lenski is decidedly not an intelligent design proponent, his work enables us to see what evolution actually does when it has the resources of a large number of organisms over a substantial number of generations. Rather than speculate, Lenski and his coworkers have observed the workings of mutation and selection. For this, we intelligent design proponents should be very grateful.[7]

In his 2007 book *The Edge of Evolution*, Behe said that unlike other micro-organisms, which have to fend for themselves and contend with the human immune system, Lenski's bacteria have been "coddled." One might say that they are on welfare. They have food, a stable environment, and no predators. "But doesn't evolution need a change in the environment to spur it on?" Behe asked. And, he further asked: "Shouldn't we expect little evolution of *E. coli* in the lab, where its environment is totally controlled?"

Behe answered both questions: No and no.

> One of the most important factors in an organism's environment is the presence of other organisms. Even in a controlled lab culture where bacteria are warm and well fed, the bug that reproduces fastest or outcompetes others will dominate the population. Like gravity, Darwinian evolution never stops.[8]

So Behe would concur, at least in part, when Lenski said in a National Science Foundation press release:

Most of us think about evolution in the past tense. After all, we were first exposed to the concept of evolution when we saw dinosaurs and other fossils at museums. But evolution has not stopped; it is an on-going process. Charles Darwin emphasized this point when he closed *On the Origin of Species* by saying: '... from so simple a beginning endless forms most beautiful and most wonderful have been, and are being evolved.'[9]

Behe agrees that evolution can be thought of in the present tense. But of course the big difference between Darwin's theory and Lenski's experiment is that Lenski began with *E. coli* in his flasks, and that is what he still has over a quarter of a century later.

Yes, there have been some changes. A year or two after the experiment began, something happened within the flasks, making the bacteria reproduce faster and take over the flask they were growing in. So there was a mutation, and it conferred a survival advantage on the bacteria.

Lenski would say that was just what Darwin would predict. Then later on, here comes another mutation and that helped even more. That was true enough, and it attracted headlines in the newspapers.[10]

But what changed, exactly? The problem initially was that Lenski had no way of knowing the molecular details of those changes. All he knew was that the bacteria would grow faster. (Also, the average size of the *E. coli* increased.) Then, in about 2005, new genome-sequencing technology made it possible to "read" the DNA, letter by letter. Today, the entire genome of *E. coli* has been sequenced, and the "frozen record" of Lenski's ancestral bacteria has allowed comparisons to be made between the bacterial old-timers and their most recent descendants. (Unlike humans, bacteria don't mind being frozen, then thawed and studied all over again.)

But once Lenski's lab did identify the mutations at the DNA level, many of the "beneficial" mutations turned out to be degradative ones. They were breaking or deleting pre-existing genes or regulatory elements, meaning that those genes or elements no longer worked. This is something that Lenski's enthusiasts, including Richard Dawkins and

Jerry Coyne (the latter in *Why Evolution Is True*) have failed to point out. Lenski himself is inclined to emphasize the positive in his experiment and to downplay the degrading of genes.

Sometimes a broken gene can actually help an organism "under the conditions in which it was grown," Behe pointed out. He gave this example:

> One change that helped the bacteria grow faster was that they lost their ability to make flagella. So the bacterial flagellum was essentially thrown out. The reason was that in his flasks the bacteria were shaken while they were growing. So no bacterium had to swim. Why spend energy on something when you can get a free ride? But that does not explain where the flagella came from in the first place.[11]

From this Behe formulated his "First Rule of Adaptive Evolution":

*Break or blunt any functional coded element whose loss would yield a net fitness gain.*[12]

He also emphasized the huge difference between constructing something and demolishing it. "Blowing up a bridge is not the opposite of making one," he said. In fact, knowing how to demolish something tells you little or nothing about what was needed to build it in the first place.

> That was one of the very interesting things. And it wasn't just the flagella. A number of other genes were not needed anymore because all the nutrients that the bacteria needed were supplied in the flask. So the ones that were needed in a normal environment were broken and thrown away.[13]

In a paper in the *Proceedings of the National Academy of Sciences*, Lenski gave another example. One of the mutations removed the ability of bacteria to proof-read their own DNA. Normally, "mistakes" get incorporated into DNA, but, as we saw in the previous chapter, cells have mechanisms to "spell-check" a "text" and fix them where the mistakes are made, as a typist corrects a typo. But the bacteria in Lenski's flasks lost the ability to do this.

However, the cells that had the mutation causing the loss of proof-reading ability were growing just as fast as the previous cells that had the original proofreading ability. The question, then, was why the loss of proofreading ability didn't hamper the growth of the cells. When Lenski looked more closely to see what had caused this, it turned out that yet another protein had been lost, by another mutation, and this loss had a compensating effect. Behe summarized the outcome this way:

> The initial mutation was the loss of one kind of protein, the kind that helped proofread it. And the second one, compensating for the loss of the first one, was the loss of a second protein. And that serendipitously helped. But you're going to run out of proteins to lose in a fairly short order if you keep on going like that.[14]

The most important claim, reported by Elizabeth Pennisi and others, was that the bacteria had "evolved a new way to feed themselves. Instead of relying on glucose they drew on a different energy source in their medium, citrate, which enabled them to reach much higher densities than in other flasks."[15]

"This was the biggest event in the entire *E. coli* experiment," said Lenski's assistant, Christoph Adami. "To have a complex new function develop seemingly from scratch is a big deal and quite remarkable."[16]

There was a lot of citrate in the medium, and in the absence of oxygen the *E. coli* have no problem consuming citrate. But when oxygen is present—as it is in Lenski's experiment—the bacteria can't "digest" citrate. Later, however, they found that a fairly simple change made its digestion possible. Citrate then became the new food supply. And that allowed the mutated (citrate-consuming) bacterium to "outcompete its relatives," Behe wrote.[17]

The ability to consume citrate became visually conspicuous in one flask at about the mid-point of the experiment (after about 33,000 generations). The normally clear flask became cloudy with the profusion of bacteria on citrate. But "at the molecular level nothing novel occurred," for, as Behe explained:

> The change was relatively simple. A piece of DNA close to the citrate gene got duplicated by accident. That put a 'control element' next to the citrate gene which allowed it to be active in the presence of oxy-

gen. Nothing novel occurred, because the control element already existed beforehand. All that happened was a duplication of what was already there and a rearrangement of the positions of the gene and control element.[18]

The analogy of a single-lane highway becoming a two-lane highway has been used to account for the ability of the bacteria to consume citrate. And yet, I asked Behe, doesn't the building of a whole new highway lane seem like a fairly complex change?

In response, he developed the analogy further. It is as though the highway lane were already there, he said, but blocked by a sawhorse barrier. The mutation essentially knocked the barrier away and traffic could then use the pre-existing lane.

Behe said that the Lenski experiment had failed to show beneficial mutations that resulted from building what he called new "Functional Coded elemenTs" ("FCTs"). Roughly, that is a sequence of DNA that helps in the production or processing of a gene or a gene product. "Improvements" had been made by breaking existing genes, or fiddling with them in minor ways. But new genes or regulatory elements still had not shown up.

Richard Lenski was interviewed by National Public Radio for its Morning Edition in 2013, celebrating the 60,000th birthday of the bacteria. Random mutations had allowed the bacteria to improve their fitness, meaning to reproduce faster. "In evolutionary biology," Lenski told NPR, "fitness is this representation of the ability of an organism to survive and reproduce." All else being equal, organisms that reproduce more quickly will have an advantage when competing with those that reproduce more slowly.[19]

Readers may recall that Lenski brings us back to the same problem I began with at the beginning of this book. What does "fitness" mean? Lenski defines it in terms of faster reproduction. But the problem is that surviving even as you reproduce faster is not quite what Darwin had in mind when he talked about the mechanism—natural selection—that is said to explain the origin of species.

In 1966, the geneticist C. H. Waddington said that some of the statements of neo-Darwinism are "vacuous." Darwin's understanding of fitness was later turned into "a lot of mathematics," Waddington added, and then it was redefined (by Ernst Mayr among others) "simply in terms of leaving more offspring."[20] Therefore Lenski leaves us in the same place that Waddington criticized. Some *E. coli*, if left to their own devices, leave more offspring than others in a given time period, and that is all there is to it. The idea is "smuggled in" (to echo Waddington) that the bacteria leaving the most offspring are going to be the best, "but nothing like this [is] explicit in the theory." Similarly, all Lenski has shown is that some organisms leave more offspring than others.

Michael Behe summarized the experiment this way:

Lenski's lab did an immense amount of careful work and deserves much praise. Yet the entirely separate, $64,000 question is, what do the results show about the power of the Darwinian mechanism? The answer is, they do not show it to be capable of anything more than what was already known.[21]

# 17. THE SOCIOBIOLOGY WARS

AT THE OUTSET, HARVARD'S EDWARD O. WILSON, THE WORLD'S leading expert on ants, was the villain. In 1975 he published the book that started the war: *Sociobiology: The New Synthesis*, with sociobiology defined as "the systematic study of the biological basis of all social behavior."[1] His early chapters dealing with insects were well-received, but the final chapter, on human behavior, "ignited the most tumultuous academic controversy of the 1970s," as Wilson himself wrote.[2]

Boyce Rensberger wrote a page-one article for the *New York Times* headlined "Updating Darwin on Behavior." Earlier, insect societies were seen as "evidence for the remarkable variety of nature," Rensberger wrote. But now there was something new. Beneath that variety were "common behavioral patterns governed by the genes, and shaped by Darwinian evolution."[3]

Behavior "governed by the genes"—that was the contentious issue.

In 1963, the geneticist Theodosius Dobzhansky had summarized the older view: "Culture is not inherited through genes, it is acquired by learning from other human beings."[4] But Wilson's sociobiology tended to put the genes back in charge. One might say that he revived the old nature vs. nurture debate.

Richard Dawkins was one of many biologists who at first agreed with Wilson. But the storyline kept changing and Dawkins took offense when Wilson sharply dissented from Dawkins's book, *The Selfish Gene*. Wilson also accused Dawkins of being a "journalist." But all that came later.

## Wilson as Philosopher and Naturalist

WILSON ONCE called himself a "Roosevelt liberal turned pragmatic centrist."[5] He grew up as a Baptist in Alabama and read the Bible through twice. Then, after studying science, he lost his faith. But unlike others in that position, he had "no desire to purge religious feelings."[6] So he tried to fortify the bleak philosophy of materialism by rethinking it as a "consilient" whole. "Preferring a search for objective reality over revelation is another way of satisfying religious hunger," he wrote.[7]

He presented his "dream of a unifying theory" in *Consilience* (1998). Ever-wider fields of knowledge were united in single "Ionian Enchantment." Everything can be reduced to the laws of physics. Everything evolved. Mind is matter.

One day I went to see Wilson at his Harvard office. He showed me the ants patrolling about behind clear glass without paying us any mind. He talked most interestingly about them for an hour or more. Ants come in maybe 12,000 species but there may be twice that number; the vast majority have never been studied by anyone. Ants are rarely fossilized, but sometimes they are trapped in amber. What did ants evolve *from?* We don't know, but wasps are one possibility.

Like many other visitors, I left wanting to know more. When he is describing his ants, discovering their pheromones, or writing about olfactory communication among animals, Wilson is being what he calls himself, a naturalist, and an impressive one. But "consilience," in which everything is interconnected, was questionable. It was fluid enough that almost anything under the sun could be explained.

## Genes versus Instincts

IN THE pre-gene decades, animal behavior was often attributed to instinct. In *The Origin*, Darwin attributed to "the hive-bee making its cells" an instinct so wonderful that some might see it as "sufficient to overthrow my whole theory."[8] Later, however, instinct fell out of favor as an explanatory term. It glossed over mechanisms that are not remotely understood. The history of science has often shown this tendency. A new concept creates the illusion of explanation—for a while. Then it wears thin, and philosophers must invent something new.

So instinct was replaced by genes, thought of as the material cause of a vast range of human traits and maladies. The powers imputed to genes reached a peak with the "decoding" of the human genome at the turn of the new century.

Gene-driven animals did whatever was needed to find food, avoid predators, make nests, reproduce, and so on. They didn't have to learn— "only obey," as Wilson put it.[9] Ants are "hard wired." Once born, they march off and do their thing without trial or error. When Konrad Lorenz allowed that all these marvels must have developed through material evolution by natural selection, the youthful Wilson was well-pleased. "He secured my allegiance."[10]

## Ideological Conflicts

It's worth noting that the sociobiology conflict divided scientists whose shared beliefs were otherwise quite fundamental. Those who quarreled over sociobiology all accepted materialism as a given: Mind and consciousness "emerged" from matter. And for all parties to the dispute, reliance on a creator or an intelligent agent was excluded *ab initio*. Yet despite these agreements, sociobiology pitted scientist against scientist.

One might think that an expanded version of Darwinism that explained the behavior of both humans and ants in materialistic terms would win the universal acclaim of materialists, and would offend only the religious. Yet the cry of indignation against genetically induced human behavior arose not from Christians (few of whom noticed), but from a handful of leftists, mostly based in Cambridge, Massachusetts. A well-known opponent was Richard Lewontin (like Wilson born in 1929), whose office was one floor below Wilson's. Paradoxically, Wilson the naturalist was on the side of the genes, while Lewontin the geneticist was on the side of culture (to oversimplify). His best-known ally was Stephen Jay Gould (1941–2002).

For the Left, the argument, framed in terms of genes, was too deterministic. How could a "new society" appear if our tiny masters (i.e., our genes) held us (as Wilson said) "on a leash"?[11] Such a vision could only discourage revolutionary change. So the "Study Group of Science for the People" led a counterattack.

The Left's critique was often irresponsible, its wild accusations contrasting sharply with Wilson's moderate views. The low point came in 1978. At a meeting in Washington, a protestor dumped a jug of water over Wilson's head while others denounced his supposed encouragement of genocide and racism. Even as ice cubes were sliding down his back, Wilson had the presence of mind to note that Garland Allen, a science historian in the audience, had taken the floor to say why the attack had been justified.

"He said it was all of a piece," Wilson recalled. "Since the nineteenth century there had been a strong bias toward genetic determinism, the claim being that human beings are fixed in their destiny by their genes, therefore there was nothing we could do about it. Therefore the existing order is the best possible order, validating the ruling class in their position. It was all a part of the continuing conspiracy by scientists in the ruling class."[12]

The Left was just as extreme on paper. Co-signers of a statement in the *New York Review of Books* dismissed Wilson's book as an attempt to revive theories which had "provided an important basis for the enactment of sterilization laws and... eugenics policies which led to the establishment of gas chambers in Nazi Germany."[13]

By the time Wilson deplored "this ugly, irresponsible and totally false accusation,"[14] he had the vast majority of scientists on his side. Nowhere had he said that human behavior is *determined* by the genes. "In rough terms," Wilson said, "I see maybe 10 percent of human behavior as genetic and 90 percent as environmental."[15]

But such statements don't get us far if the effective cause (whether genetic or environmental) can only be established by observing the resulting behavior. If one thing happens, the genes dominate; if another, it's the environment. No outcome can falsify the theory. Meanwhile, the genes that are said to cause the behavior (or to cause it sometimes) have not been identified in a single instance.

Lewontin and his allies did make such criticisms. But the science was often buried beneath comments so ill-advised that the *New York Times*, normally sympathetic to left-wing opinion, didn't hesitate to take Wilson's side.

## Hamilton's Contribution

A KEY contribution to sociobiology was made by the evolutionary biologist William D. Hamilton. He would migrate from his chilly graduate-student digs to the (somewhat warmer) waiting room at Waterloo railway station, where he was rewarded with a key insight. Darwin's theory had implied that natural selection would generate a selfish world. It was "the fittest" that survived, after all. Yet undeniably there was a lot of altruism out there. Hamilton's explanation, published in 1964, took time to sink in. But once it did, the evolutionists sang their hosannas. Kin selection—of course!

A particular gene exists not just in one organism, Hamilton argued, but also in others, closely related. Siblings share half their genes, first cousins one-eighth of theirs, and so on. These ratios were not arrived at by comparing actual DNA sequences, but deduced mathematically. Therefore, Hamilton argued, an action that endangers an individual but promotes the survival of more than two siblings, or more than eight first cousins, would be advantageous: It would promote the spread of the gene that triggered the seemingly ill-advised behavior.

Hamilton's argument became central to Dawkins's *The Selfish Gene* (1976), a book intended "to examine the biology of selfishness and altruism."[16] Wilson also embraced kin selection. Darwinism was now shown to be consistent with altruism, by taking this more "inclusive" view of fitness.

The sociobiologist Robert Trivers wanted to expand the analysis to more distantly related animals, positing genes for "reciprocal altruism."

That was thought less successful, but with the costs and benefits appropriately assigned, it could be invested with an air of plausibility. While at Harvard, Trivers instructed Huey Newton in jail and even joined the Black Panthers. MIT's Steven Pinker called Trivers "one of the great thinkers in the history of Western thought."[17]

Hamilton's kin selection theory, published in the *Journal of Theoretical Biology*, was highly mathematical, but that was one of its triumphs. It seemed so obscure, yet also up-to-date. When Hamilton (1936–2000) died of malaria in the course of a research expedition to Africa, his funeral oration in the chapel of New College, Oxford, was delivered by the atheist Dawkins. "Those of us who wish we had met Charles Darwin can console ourselves," Dawkins began his eulogy. "We met W. D. Hamilton."[18]

Hamilton, Wilson, Dawkins, & Co. had scored a great victory. Henceforth, if you wanted to explain anything, whether physical or behavioral, you could assert that there were genes "for" those qualities. Darwinism could then be invoked to say that natural selection had "acted on" those genes. After all the rancor and theatrics, that seemed sufficiently scientific. In due course genes were supplemented by other units of selection: "memes"— replicators of cultural behavior, invented by Dawkins, and "modules"—traits evolving independently, the notion of Pinker. "Probably," Pinker wrote in *How the Mind Works* (1997), modules "look like roadkill, sprawling messily over the bulges and crevasses of the brain."[19]

A recalcitrant Lewontin said in one of his essays that we still hadn't found the genes for skin color.[20] (We still haven't, but their existence is assumed because the trait is hereditary.) Furthermore, you didn't have to know anything about the environment in which a given gene was said to have been "selected." You could make up your own story. Lewontin and Gould dismissed such scenarios as Just-So stories.

How did the leopard get its spots, for example? Well, one leopard accidentally had a "spots" mutation (call it a gene from now on) and it survived better, because camouflage helped. So spotted leopards survived better than plain vanilla ones, and eventually displaced them. So that was how the leopard got its spots.

The same argument could be applied to any trait, whether animal or human. "The method consists essentially of contemplating the trait and then making an imaginative reconstruction of human history that would have made the trait adaptive," Lewontin and his co-authors wrote in *Not in Our Genes* (1984).[21]

A related problem arose with kin selection. In a plain language section of his famous article, William Hamilton wrote:

> The alarm call of a bird probably involves a small extra risk to the individual making it by rendering it more noticeable to the approaching predator, but the consequent reduction of risk to a nearby bird previously unaware of danger *must* be much greater. [italics added][22]

The relevant costs and benefits are never actually measured, notice. In fact, there is no way of measuring them other than by observing the behavior they are said to shape. The fact that one bird emits the alarm call itself demonstrates (to Hamilton's satisfaction) that the benefits (to the species) must exceed the costs. The problem is that the theory never gets off the page and into the real world.

## Explanatory Power of Sociobiology

SOCIOBIOLOGY PURPORTED to explain many aspects of human behavior, including territoriality, entrepreneurship, faith, xenophobia, aggression, and warfare. Later, in deference to the fact of altruism, sympathy, kindness, and selflessness were added. Some behavior does seem ill-suited to the theory: masturbation, adoption, homosexuality, contraception, and celibacy of the clergy.

Another argument was that evolution happened aeons ago, so that we are "adapted to the Stone Age."[23] Genes evolved in one environment, and we live in another. This gives sociobiology a defense against facts that don't fit. If the facts correspond to a given adaptation story, the theory is confirmed. If not, it's because the environment is now different. Robert Wright said in *The Moral Animal* (1994) that Darwinian selection had reached a point where "one no longer entertains the possibility of encountering some fact that would call the whole theory into question."[24] But a field that smoothly "explains" whatever exists is no longer a part of science. As Karl Popper said, irrefutability is not a virtue of a theory (as people often think) but a vice.

Omitted from the sociobiologists' categories was the faculty of reason. Stephen Jay Gould drew attention to this shortcoming when he criticized the claim that Eskimo behavior validates altruist genes. When food is scarce and an Eskimo family must move, grandparents sometimes stay behind to die rather than slow down the entire family. But altruistic genes are redundant, Gould pointed out. Elderly Eskimos can figure it out for themselves, and have an incentive to stay behind in families where "sacrifice is celebrated in song and story; aged grandparents who stay behind become the greatest heroes of the clan."[25]

Once reason is admitted as a human characteristic—and in truth it may be the most important characteristic of all—it can be shown to preempt many or perhaps all so-called behavioral genes.

Nonetheless, in the biology departments, at least, the debate was won by Wilson and allies. The claim that sociobiology would take over the field of sociology was not borne out, but it had some success in psychology, where it advanced under the rubric of evolutionary psychology.

## Enter: Evo-psych

THE SEMINAL work of evolutionary psychology was *The Adapted Mind* (1992), edited by the husband-and-wife team from U. C. Santa Barbara, Leda Cosmides and John Tooby. A prominent addition to the evolutionary psychology genre was *A Natural History of Rape: The Biological Bases of Sexual Coercion* (2000), by Randy Thornhill and Craig Palmer.

In 1975, it's safe to say, Cambridge collectives would have been on the march at the mere suggestion of a book about rape-specific "adaptations." The authors had wisely skirted the gene word, but by then the field was so lax that almost anything was waved through. "Adaptations" are vaguely said to be "in" bodies, but Thornhill and Palmer never said where. (How would they locate them?)

Explaining something by saying that (unidentified) genes for it exist, and were "selected for" is little more than a reassertion of the facts whose explanation we are seeking. Analogously, if the stock market drops, investors looking for an explanation may find the headline: "Selling Pressure Causes Stocks to Drop." But that doesn't help—it merely re-describes the phenomenon. Unobserved genes for behavior have the same defect.

In a critical review of the rape book, the loyal Darwinian Jerry Coyne pointed out in *The New Republic* that the authors' evidence is so adverse to their thesis that it is consistent with a more obvious hypothesis: that rape is not "adaptive" at all. "As with most sociobiological arguments," he added, "only some level of concordance with prediction need be found to brand an act as an adaptation."[26] (Some rapes do cause pregnancy, in other words.)

Coyne was right, but the critics of evolutionary psychology were disarmed by the materialist worldview they shared with their opponents. As Thornhill and Palmer wrote: "When one considers any feature of living things, *whether* evolution applies is never a question. The only legitimate question is how to apply evolutionary principles."[27] For good materialists, "Darwinian processes" must explain everything.

When sociobiology is seen in a political light, the leftist animus against it is understandable. Sociobiology "explains" (in a very weak sense of that word) whatever exists. Existing qualities of human nature are accounted for by the usual, unfalsifiable formula: the trait first arose by accident; then it was selected for. But as Marx said, socialists want to change the world, not explain it. The world that exists must be replaced by something better: a world without inequality, for example. The *raison d'être* of the Left is to champion states that do not exist. The sociobiologists' retort—that these things don't exist either because the requisite genes aren't there or were *not* selected for—put the Left on the defensive.

The whole field of sociobiology suffers from this defect, and in that sense it really does have a "conservative" bias.

Fashionable for a while, "Evo-psych" in due course faded, and today it is rarely discussed.

## Wilson's Latter-Day Rebellion

A SURPRISING twist to the story came in 2010. Along with two mathematicians from Harvard, Martin Nowak and Corina Tarnita, Wilson published an article in *Nature*, "The Evolution of Eusociality." Its math was obscure but its message was plain—and unexpected. Now Wilson had given up on kin selection! He had replaced it with an updated form of group selection.

Eusociality? Wilson and his pair of math-helpers said it meant that "some individuals reduce their own lifetime reproductive potential to raise the offspring of others" who are not necessarily closely related. It was said to underlie "the most advanced forms of social organization and the ecologically dominant role of social insects and humans."[28]

Dawkins called this development a "poorly defined and incoherent view, that evolution is driven by the differential survival of whole groups of organisms."[29] Later he said in *Prospect* magazine that Wilson's article had provoked "very strong criticism" from 137 evolutionary biologists, "including a majority of the most distinguished workers in the field."[30] That included Coyne, Pinker, Trivers, Cosmides, and Tooby—all mentioned above. (By then, Gould and Hamilton were dead, and Lewontin had retired to Vermont.)

Dawkins further complained of "the patrician hauteur with which Wilson ignores the very serious drubbing his *Nature* paper... received":

> He doesn't even mention those many critics: not a single, solitary sentence. Does he think his authority justifies going over the heads of experts and appealing directly to a popular audience, as if the professional controversy didn't exist—as if acceptance of his (tiny) minority view were a done deal?[31]

WILSON: "The beautiful theory [kin selection, which he had earlier championed] never worked well anyway, and now it has collapsed."[32]

DAWKINS: "Yes it did and does work, and no, it hasn't collapsed. For Wilson not to acknowledge that he speaks for himself against the great majority of his professional colleagues is—it pains me to say this of a lifelong hero—an act of wanton arrogance."[33]

Jerry Coyne, on Wilson's new position: "If you're a famous biologist you can get away with publishing *dreck*."[34]

The war may not be over yet. Interviewed by the BBC in 2014, Wilson was asked to explain his *contretemps* with Dawkins. He replied:

> There is no dispute between me and Richard Dawkins and there never has been, because he's a journalist, and journalists are people that report what the scientists have found and the arguments I've had have actually been with scientists doing research.[35]

In effect, Wilson had enraged Dawkins by questioning the basis of Dawkins's book, *The Selfish Gene*. By then, those old adversaries, Wilson and Lewontin, had almost become allies.

Wilson relied on "standard natural selection theory in the context of precise models of population structures." Somehow, it represented a "simpler and superior approach."[36] Yet Wilson was candid enough to tell *The New Yorker* that he couldn't understand the all-important math contributed by his co-authors.[37]

## Damaging the Darwinian Enterprise

PHILLIP JOHNSON of U. C. Berkeley pointed out that the critics of sociobiology had threatened Darwinism itself. Sociobiology's "obviously pseudoscientific methodology" had undermined "the credibility of the whole Darwinian enterprise" Johnson said. Its critics may have "burned down the Darwinist house in order to roast the sociobiological pig."[38]

The same critical scrutiny could have "far-reaching consequences" if it were applied to the generally accepted Darwinian theory. For Darwinism, too, claimed that complex adaptive organs came into existence through the accumulation of micro-mutations by natural selection. And like sociobiology, it assumed "that stories of adaptive evolution require no confirmation from genetics, or paleontology, or anything else except the adaptationist community's prevailing sense of plausibility."[39]

Some of Wilson's later books—there were several—were praised by various environmentalists, among them Al Gore, Bill McKibben, and Jeffrey Sachs. In *The Future of Life* (2002) one of Wilson's chapters was titled "The Century of the Environment." By then Wilson had emerged as a fashionable crusader for "sustainable development," deploring human-caused species extinctions. We humans were too numerous, should "change our destructive ways" and "settle down before we wreck the planet."[40]

One has to hand it to Wilson: having started out as the villain of the piece, he became the hero in the end. And today we hear little more of sociobiology or evolutionary psychology.

# 18. HUMAN EXCEPTIONALISM AND ITS ENEMIES

As far as we know, the claim that humans are unexceptional—and arrogant for thinking otherwise—was first made by Darwin. He asked in a notebook over twenty years before *The Origin* was published: "Why is thought[,] being a secretion of brain, more wonderful than gravity[,] a property of matter? It is our arrogance, it [is] our admiration of ourselves."[1]

And in the same notebook: "Man in his arrogance thinks himself a great work, worthy [of] the interposition of a deity. More humble & I believe truer to consider him created from animals."[2]

He speculated that grinning began with baboons baring their "great canine teeth," and that "Laughing [was] modified barking, smiling modified laughing." Barking itself may have started out as a way of signaling the "discovery of prey." Darwin allowed that "crying is a puzzler."[3]

He never changed his opinion. In *The Descent of Man* (1871) he said that his object was "to shew that there is no fundamental difference between man and the higher mammals in their mental faculties."[4] What about language? "With respect to animals," he said, "I have already endeavoured to show that they have this power, at least in a rude and incipient degree."[5]

Darwin repeatedly adopted this strategy of minimizing the difference between the mental powers of humans and animals. In another variation on this theme, he claimed that some humans are mere "savages" or "barbarians." The Fuegians at the tip of South America, for example, "rank amongst the lowest barbarians."[6] They and other such are little re-moved from the "higher animals." Any remaining gap could then easily be bridged by Darwin's all-purpose mechanism, natural selection.

For his followers, the alleged ordinariness of human beings was little more than a deduction from common descent. His supporter Thomas Huxley wrote in 1863:

> Is man a peculiar organism? Does he originate in a wholly differ-ent way from a dog, bird, frog, or fish? And does he thereby justify those who assert that he has no place in nature, and no real relation-ship with the lower world of animal life? Or does he develop from a similar embryo, and undergo the same slow and gradual progressive modifications?

> The answer is not for an instant doubtful, and has not been doubt-ful for the last thirty years. The mode of man's origin and the earlier stages of his development are undoubtedly identical with those of the animals standing directly below him in the scale; without the slightest doubt, he stands in this respect nearer the ape than the ape does to the dog.[7]

It didn't seem to occur to Huxley that even though human develop-ment in the womb may resemble that of other animals, the end-product is quite different.

Darwin's accusation of "arrogance" was changed to a charge of "van-ity" by Huxley, for whom ridicule was the preferred weapon: "It is not I who seek to base Man's dignity upon his great toe, or insinuate that we are lost if an Ape has a hippocampus minor."

> On the contrary [Huxley added], I have done my best to sweep away this vanity. I have endeavored to show that no absolute structural line of demarcation, wider than that between the animals which im-mediately succeed us in the scale, can be drawn between the animal world and ourselves.[8]

To be sure, in *The Uniqueness of Man* (1951), Thomas Huxley's grandson Julian did acknowledge uniquely human features, among them language, conceptual thought, and the transmission of knowledge by writing. But the theme of "arrogance" took hold, and has been regularly repeated since. Here is Stephen Jay Gould in *Ever Since Darwin* (1977):

> Chimps and gorillas have long been the battleground of our search for uniqueness; for if we could establish an unambiguous distinction—of kind rather than of degree—between ourselves and our closest relatives, we might gain the justification long-sought for our cosmic arrogance. The battle shifted long ago from a simple debate about evolution: educated people now accept the evolutionary continuity between humans and apes.
>
> But we are so tied to our philosophical and religious heritage that we still seek a criterion for strict division between our abilities and those of chimpanzees. For as the Psalmist sang: 'what is man, that thou art mindful of him? For thou hast made him a little lower than the angels, and has crowned him with glory and honor.'[9]

The accusation of arrogance is self-defeating on its face. Only humans are capable of arrogance or of seeing themselves as superior to other animals. Animals cannot rise to that level of abstraction. Do cats or dogs think themselves superior to humans? (Well, dogs don't, but I'm not so sure about cats.) The criticism of arrogance itself rests on human exceptionalism. Meanwhile Gould, who lost his own faith—as Darwin did his—saw himself as someone who had lost nothing but his arrogance.

The University of Washington biologist and liberal activist David P. Barash introduced a variation on the same theme. In the *New York Times* he denied the uniqueness of human moral values:

> Before Darwin, one could believe that human beings were distinct from other life-forms, chips off the old divine block. No more. The most potent take-home message of evolution is the not-so-simple fact that, even though species are identifiable (just as individuals generally are), there is an underlying linkage among them—literally and phylogenetically, via traceable historical connectedness.[10]

He added that "no literally supernatural trait has ever been found in Homo sapiens; we are perfectly good animals, natural as can be and indistinguishable from the rest of the living world at the level of structure."

But at the level of structure, what would a good materialist like Barash expect to find? Seraphic wings? Looking for supernatural traits at the natural level is as illogical as hunting for the mind in brain cells.

## Human Exceptionalism versus Darwinism

SENTIMENT FOR human exceptionalism is inversely related to Darwinism. If we regard humans as exceptional, we are likely to reject Darwin's theory. In his book *Created from Animals* (1990), James Rachels (1941–2003) claimed that after Darwin, "we can no longer think of ourselves as occupying a special place in creation—instead, we must realize that we are products of the same evolutionary forces, working blindly and without purpose, that shaped the rest of the animal kingdom."[11] An animal rights activist, Rachels was also a supporter of "active" euthanasia.

Here's a conventional-wisdom update from *New Scientist*:

For much of our existence on Earth, we humans thought of ourselves as a pretty big deal. Then along came science and taught us how utterly insignificant we are. We aren't the center of the universe. We aren't special. We are just a species of ape living on a smallish planet orbiting an unremarkable star in one galaxy among billions in a universe that had been around for 13.8 billion years without us.[12]

But wait; there was a correction. "Maybe we were too hasty to write ourselves off," the editorial continued:

There is a sense in which we are still the center of the universe. Science also teaches us that the laws of physics are ridiculously, almost unbelievably 'fine-tuned' for you and me. Take the electromagnetic force. It has a value that is perfectly set for getting stars to bind protons and neutrons to create carbon—the building block of life as we know it. Or the strong nuclear force, which binds the insides of protons and neutrons. If it were even a tiny bit stronger, the whole world would be made of hydrogen; if it were weaker, there would be no hydrogen at all. In either case, life as we know it wouldn't be possible.[13]

A more elaborate version of that revisionist argument was made by Guillermo Gonzalez and Jay Richards in *The Privileged Planet* (2004).

The ancient (and modern) claim that humans display a unique intelligence has been met with a search for it elsewhere: within the solar system or outside it; in our machines, in the form of artificial intelligence; or in other animals—most commonly chimpanzees.

The search for extraterrestrial intelligence, artificial intelligence, or chimp-talk thus constitutes a three-pronged search for what humans possess by the age of four. They are looking for something that evolutionists are convinced should be there, so they keep on looking. The unstated goal is to justify Darwinism by denying human uniqueness.

## Chimp Talk

THE ASPECT of human uniqueness that Darwin might have examined more closely is language. We can talk to one another; animals can't. We can put words on paper and others can read them. Darwin did discuss "articulate language" in *The Descent of Man*, and he allowed that it is "peculiar to man"—but with his own reservations. Humans, "like the lower animals," make inarticulate cries "to express their meaning, aided by gestures," he said.[14] Darwin used such observations to convince himself that the gap between animals and humans is not so great after all.

He also noted "the tendency in our nearest allies, the monkeys, to imitate what they hear." And "monkeys certainly understand much that is said to them by man." (Not really, of course.) So it's possible that "some unusually wise ape-like animal should have thought of imitating the growl of a beast of prey, so as to indicate to his fellow monkeys the nature of the expected danger." This "would have been a first step in the formation of a language."[15] And at that point Darwin seemed to imagine that his problem was all but solved.

Earnest attempts to get chimpanzees—not monkeys—to communicate did not begin for about another 100 years. In the 1970s and later we heard about Lana, Moja, Kanzi, Washoe, Panbanisha, and maybe a dozen other chimpanzees. The most celebrated was Nim Chimpsky, a pun on Noam Chomsky. MIT's Chomsky had earlier poured cold water on the project, saying that the ability to use language is an innately

and uniquely human development. Nonetheless, Gould became so convinced by the chimp reports that he thought the only honest alternative
to human exceptionalism was to admit

> strict continuity in kind between ourselves and chimpanzees. And
> what do we lose thereby? Only an antiquated concept of soul to gain
> a more humble, even exalting vision of our oneness with nature...
> We are more nearly akin to the chimpanzee than even Huxley dared
> to think.[16]

Language was "the last bastion for potential differences in kind,"
Gould wrote. True, "early experiments on teaching chimps to talk were
notably unsuccessful." But there was a simple explanation. "The vocal
cords of chimpanzees are constructed in such a way that large reper-
tories of articulated sounds cannot be produced."[17] But as the linguist
Noel Rude, an expert on Native American languages, has pointed out,
parrots can accurately reproduce words with only a beak.[18]

Next, Gould promoted sign language. When "Lana" of the Yerkes
laboratory began to ask for the names of objects she had not previously
seen, "can we any longer deny to chimps the capacity to conceptualize
and to abstract?" Gould asked. "This is no mere Pavlovian condition-
ing."[19]

Baby chimps began making recognizable signs, and their progress "is
no slower than that of a human child," Gould said. In short, we have seen
"a striking demonstration of how we have underestimated our closest
biological relatives."[20] Likewise, primatologist Sue Savage-Rumbaugh,
formerly with the Iowa Primate Learning Sanctuary, promoted a grada-
tion of linguistic skills, from primates to humans.

But animal language research fell into disrepute when "talking"
chimps like Washoe and Nim Chimpsky were exposed as unintention-
al frauds. Scientists found strong evidence that the chimps had simply
learned to please their teachers by contorting their hands in various ways.
The trainers, straining to find examples of linguistic communication,
thought they saw words, "like children seeing pictures in the clouds."[21]

Mark Seidenberg, a graduate student at Columbia during the Nim project, doubted whether chimp signing and human language were ever related. Animal rights activist Peter Singer cited results using the most generous possible interpretations. In deciding what Washoe or Koko meant when they signed "banana," for example, researchers relied on what is called "rich interpretation." They assumed that the ape possesses whatever knowledge a child possesses in using the same word. The real challenge—to determine whether ape and child do possess the same knowledge—was sidestepped. Seidenberg and others with no personal investment in particular outcomes challenged Singer's account. Eventually much of the research funding was withdrawn because the science was not credible.

"In my mind, this kind of research is more analogous to the bears in the Moscow circus who are trained to ride unicycles," said Dr. Steven Pinker, a cognitive scientist at MIT (later Harvard) who has studied language acquisition in children. "You can train animals to do all kinds of amazing things." He doubted that the chimps learned anything more than how to press the right buttons in order to get humans "to cough up M & M's, bananas and other tidbits of food."[22]

Linguists have also noted how quickly children (but not chimps) can go from cobbling together two-word utterances to spinning out complex sentences with phrases embedded within phrases. Children can easily put together sentences that they never heard before and will never use again.

In the journal *Science*, Nim Chimpsky's trainer Dr. Herbert Terrace, a Columbia University psychologist, asked: "Can an ape create a sentence?" He "reluctantly" concluded that the answer was no. There was no evidence that chimps had acquired a generative grammar—the ability to string words together into sentences of arbitrary length and complexity. Like Pinker, Terrace said that Kanzi, another trained chimp, was simply "going through a bag of tricks in order to get things."[23]

Terrace rejected comparisons to human children. "If a child did exactly what the best chimpanzee did, the child would be thought of as disturbed."[24]

Helene Guldberg, editor of the *Spiked Review of Books*, wrote that, despite the dedication of a number of primatologists, "the cognitive and linguistic abilities of the great apes have never surpassed those of a two-year-old child."[25]

## From Chimps to the Stars

FIRST, I'LL briefly mention the mundane explanation for the ongoing search for intelligent life at the extraterrestrial level: funding. NASA keeps looking for extraterrestrial intelligence because it will greatly increase the agency's popularity on Capitol Hill. Congress is far more likely to fund sorties to outposts of life than to barren rocks. Expeditions to planets outside the solar system are not remotely plausible, but maybe distant civilizations can be detected using short-wave radio receptors.

But the Copernican Principle, sometimes called the Mediocrity Principle, claiming that there was nothing special about the Earth, soon gave way to the Fermi Paradox. In 1950, at Los Alamos, the nuclear physicists Enrico Fermi, Edward Teller, and others were discussing the latest ideas about the universe: it was much larger and older than had earlier been thought; it contained billions of stars evolving over billions of years, probably accompanied by more planets than stars; and the physical laws that apply here also applied out there.

So, "where is everybody?" Fermi famously asked. It became known as the Fermi Paradox.

Enter Frank Drake, a Cornell astronomer who responded in 1959. Using radio telescopes, scientists could listen for signals from aliens. Drake cobbled together the Drake Equation, hoping to estimate how many intelligent, communicating civilizations there are in our galaxy. The novelist Michael Crichton rightly complained that the equation was vacuous because it included no data. Cosmologists and evolutionists plugged in their own numbers anyway, and in their math, the probability

of life—possibly intelligent, communicating life turned out to be a near
certainty. All you needed was enough habitable platforms—planets—to
work with. They are now finding some of those planets. But no extraterrestrial life—let alone intelligence—has yet been discovered.

Darwin speculated that life may have first appeared in a "warm little
pond."[26] No experiment has been able to generate life from non-life, and
today life on Earth is the only life that we know. But Darwinians have
theorized that given enough warm little ponds, life surely must have appeared somewhere else in the universe.

## From Exceptionalism to Misanthropy

IN THE late twentieth century, a new element entered into our philosophy—disapproval of the human race. Misanthropy became fashionable,
as it still is today. Gould jeered at our "need to see ourselves as separate
and superior."[27] "Exceptionalism" was now admitted, but in a different
form: Human beings were exceptionally bad. For one thing, we were
too numerous for our own or anything else's good. And we did harmful
things, exploding nuclear weapons and so on.

In The Panda's Thumb, reflecting on the extinction of the dodo,
Gould wrote that "we who revel in nature's diversity and feel instructed
by every animal tend to brand Homo sapiens as the greatest catastrophe
since the Cretaceous extinction."[28] Environmentalists today see humans
as doing harm and little else. Meanwhile, they worry that nothing could
be more exceptional than being alone in the Cosmos. So they keep looking for life somewhere else.

## Religious Implications of Extraterrestrial Life

GOULD ONCE argued that "a positive result [finding extraterrestrial intel-
ligence] would be the most cataclysmic event in our entire intellectual
history."[29] But why cataclysmic? He didn't say. Maybe what he meant
was that it would be cataclysmic not to find it.

The physicist Lawrence Krauss—like Gould an atheist—said that
the discovery of extraterrestrial life would be "jolting" to "orthodox

Christians." Earlier, the "revelation that the Earth is not the center of the solar system" had delivered a similar jolt, he believed.[30] (Actually, it didn't.)

Here is the columnist Charles Krauthammer on the same topic:

As the romance of manned space exploration has waned, the drive today is to find our living, thinking counterparts in the universe. For all the excitement, however, the search betrays a profound melancholy—a lonely species in a merciless universe anxiously awaits an answering voice amid utter silence. That silence is maddening. Not just because it compounds our feeling of cosmic isolation. But because it makes no sense. As we inevitably find more and more exo-planets where intelligent life can exist, why have we found no evidence—no signals, no radio waves—that intelligent life does exist?"[31]

Maddening? Jolting? Cataclysmic? Maybe they sense that Darwin's philosophy is at stake.

What lies beyond the solar system? Probably we'll never know, unless extraterrestrials transmit that sequence of prime numbers that Carl Sagan and others hoped to see transmitted. Until then, a good case can be made for the uniqueness of life on Earth. And that would entail the uniqueness of intelligent, human life. The thought that life on Earth might in fact be unique is unpopular with materialists, because it raises the discomforting possibility that God was responsible for the origin of life and everything else.

The Nobel Prize-winning physicist Steven Weinberg said in *The First Three Minutes* that humans are "just a more or less farcical outcome of a chain of accidents reaching back to the first three minutes…"[32] He has also argued that if—if—"calculations showed" that the odds of a planet having the right gravity, temperature, and chemical composition were very small and "the earth on which we live were the only planet in the universe" then a "benevolent designer" might indeed "make sense." For it would be difficult "without supposing divine intervention to understand our great good fortune in having come into being."[33]

But, Weinberg added, we now know that "a good fraction of stars have planets." So, "we need not be surprised that chance events governed by impersonal natural laws have produced intelligent life on at least one of the planets."[34] Let's just say that Weinberg was eager to avoid finding in favor of a Designer. He simply assumed that the probabilities support the case he wanted to make—that life arose accidentally and has no meaning. He has also called religion "an insult to human dignity."[35]

Carl Sagan, one of the leading promoters of extraterrestrial intelligence, "believed in superior beings in space, creatures so intelligent, so powerful, as to resemble gods."[36] Sagan had proposed that a new civilization is formed just in our galaxy every ten years. If so, Sagan concluded, "there are a million technical civilizations in the [Milky Way] galaxy."[37]

Surprisingly, Richard Dawkins has shown similar inclinations. He was quoted in the *New York Times* as saying, "It's highly plausible that in the universe there are God-like creatures." He was careful to stipulate that "these Gods came into being by an explicable scientific progression of incremental evolution."[38]

But even if we do assume the existence of a "Goldilocks" planet—one that has the right size, temperature, and atmosphere to encourage the appearance of life—we still have no idea how likely it is that life will appear spontaneously, because we don't know how to create life ourselves. Nor do we have any idea how likely it is that such life will evolve to the point where it can build radio telescopes.

Sagan's faith in the widespread emergence of civilizations arose "because he believed uncritically in Progress," said his biographer Keay Davidson.[39] It was the Enlightenment that had inculcated this faith. Darwin also embraced it. So did Huxley, Herbert Spencer, and a hundred other thinkers. But even as our modern-day misanthropy has been embraced, our assumption of progress has been discarded. And that puts our modern philosophy directly at odds with the evolutionist faith. I will take a closer look at this conflict in Chapter 21. Meanwhile, in the next chapter I shall examine the attempts to locate artificial intelligence within computers.

# 19. The Search for Artificial Intelligence

T HE FIRST CONFERENCE ON ARTIFICIAL INTELLIGENCE WAS HELD at Dartmouth College in 1956. It explored "the conjecture that every aspect of learning or any other feature of intelligence can in principle be so precisely described that a machine can be made to simulate it."[1]

In short, maybe those new machines called computers could rival the human mind. The grant proposal expressed the (optimistic) hope that "a significant advance" could be made in this direction if a select group of scientists were to work on the problem "for a summer."

There was an oft-cited precedent. The English mathematician Alan Turing thought in the 1930s that thinking machines could be constructed, and by the end of the twentieth century, he believed, "one will be able to speak of machines thinking without expecting to be contradicted."[2] In 1950, he devised the Turing test: If someone behind a screen could not distinguish between human and machine responses, the machine could be considered intelligent.

Sixty years after the Dartmouth conference, computers have still not passed the Turing test. Advances have been made in related areas, but there has been no sign of machines that can "think" or form abstractions. In fact, we still don't know how to describe human intelligence in such a way that machines can simulate it.

The principal organizers of the Dartmouth conference were two mathematicians, John McCarthy and Marvin Minsky. McCarthy was also the first to use the term *artificial intelligence* (AI). After a few years he moved to Stanford and Minsky to MIT.

At a fiftieth-anniversary event celebrating the Dartmouth conference, Max Lungarella and colleagues said:

> [I]t is clear that the original goals set by the first generation of AI visionaries have not been reached. Not only is natural intelligence far from being understood and artificial forms of intelligence so much more primitive than natural ones, but seemingly simple tasks like object manipulation and recognition—which a 3-year-old can do—have not yet been realized artificially.[3]

The writers went on to say that "the cultural and social processes that have helped to shape human intelligence" remain mysterious. They also noted that current robots "fall far short of even very simple animals" in intelligence. That was in 2006.[4]

A survey of the years 1956–2006 shows conflicting results. IBM's Deep Blue beat the world chess champion in 1997. But at the same time, programmers couldn't get robots to do simple things such as stack up children's bricks. Robots would try to put the top brick in place first, not understanding that other bricks must be beneath it.

Maybe that's because computers really don't "understand" anything.

That was the opinion of Lord Byron's daughter Ada, the Countess of Lovelace, who has been admired by AI researchers ever since. As a debutante in London in the 1830s, she was introduced to Charles Babbage, sometimes called the father of the computer. The Lucasian professor of Mathematics at Cambridge, Babbage hoped to build an "analytical engine." A precocious student of mathematics herself, Ada Lovelace wrote up her notes describing Babbage's ideas even though the "engine" still had not been built. Feminists understandably have put Lovelace on a pedestal, but AI programmers have worried because she also wrote this: "The Analytical Engine has no pretensions whatever to originate anything. It can do whatever we know how to order it to perform."[5]

She was probably in her twenties when she wrote that plain statement, relegating computers to the status of slaves. Over 180 years later, despite much effort by PhDs from Stanford, MIT, Carnegie-Mellon, and elsewhere, nothing has yet shown her comment to be out of date.

## AI: Strong and Applied

IN THE past half-century, an important distinction has emerged between computers that actually "know" something (i.e., exhibit the still-unattained goal of "strong" AI), and computers that can run a programmed sequence of tasks in order to achieve a well-defined goal (i.e., exhibit "applied" AI).

Applied AI has been a success. Robots can perform on assembly lines, and they don't need tea breaks or pensions. Computers can decipher voices over the phone and diagnose diseases. Another success has been the use of driverless vehicles. In 2005, vehicles without drivers completed a 130-mile course in the Mojave Desert and Stanford's entry, "Stanley," was one of only five vehicles to finish. Carrying radar, stereo cameras, five lasers and GPS on board, it traveled at an average speed of nineteen mph and won the DARPA prize.

I interviewed John McCarthy at Stanford at about the time of the Mojave contest. While on the campus at night I caught a glimpse of a very different kind of navigation. A swift blur crossed my path. It was a fox going at about twenty miles an hour, with utter self-assurance and little light to steer by. No GPS, lasers or computers onboard either. So how did it acquire that "software"? On a related theme, George Gilder wrote in *The Silicon Eye*:

> [A fly] can do flawless flip landings on the edge of a glass or on a glass ceiling while scarcely slowing down. [Caltech computers] could not even scratch the surface of the evident superiority and continuing inscrutability of the eye, brain and nervous system of the fly... No obvious quantitative measure explained it.[6]

I asked McCarthy about the fox on the campus. How did its internal "computer" get programmed?

"Well, it has had trillions of trials, over many millions of years," he said. "It would be very interesting to know how good the first mammals were," which might be ascertainable. "The past is turning out to be less impenetrable than we imagined." He mentioned intelligent design, but he found Discovery Institute's website disappointing because "all of its links were to polemics against evolution, rather than taking their own ideas seriously." (ID theory has advanced since then.)

He considered it possible that the actions of a designer, or "intervenor" as he put it, could be investigated using the methods of science. He also allowed that almost all who work on AI are materialists. Everything is assumed to be physical, the mind included. A physical description of the brain can yield a complete account of mental states, he thought. McCarthy told me he is a materialist himself.

In 2003 the *Washington Post* columnist Charles Krauthammer elaborated on the materialist case. It seemed obvious to him that machines will achieve consciousness:

> After all, we did, and with very humble beginnings. In biology, neurons started firing millions of years ago, allowing tiny mindless organisms to move about, avoid noxious stimuli, etc. But when enough of those neurons were put together with enough complexity, all of a sudden you got… us. A cartoon balloon pops up above that mass of individually unconscious neurons and says, 'I exist.' In principle, why should that not eventually occur with silicon? The number of chips and complexity of their interaction will no doubt be staggering and may require centuries to construct. But I do not see why silicon cannot make the same transition from unconsciousness to consciousness that carbon did.[7]

I asked McCarthy how he thought artificial intelligence had fared, fifty years after the Dartmouth conference.

"I have to say that I was over-optimistic," he said. "In my proposals in the 1960s, I expected to accomplish things within three years that haven't been done to this day." Another Dartmouth participant, Herbert Simon, predicted—as long ago as 1965— that within twenty years machines would be doing anything "that a man can do."[8]

This pattern of unwarranted optimism has persisted. Arthur Clarke, writer of the sci-fi novel *2001: A Space Odyssey*, also thought that AI would reach human levels. In 1999, however, he postponed that development until "after 2020." By then, he thought, there would be "two intelligent species on Planet Earth, one evolving far more rapidly than biology would ever permit."[9] It hasn't happened yet.

By the time he wrote *The Society of Mind* in 1985, Minsky still shared the materialistic outlook that almost all of the founding AI generation accept. "Minds are simply what brains do," he said.[10]

## The Singularity

THE LEADING enthusiast for "strong" AI has been the utopian futurist Ray Kurzweil, now with Google. A student of Minsky's, he developed voice-recognition software, and made the good prediction that a computer would beat the world chess champion in 1998 (it did so a year earlier).

In *The Age of Spiritual Machines* (1999) Kurzweil declared that "the emergence of machines that exceed human intelligence in all of its broad diversity is inevitable."[11] This would happen by 2029. Kurzweil referred to this emergence as "the Singularity." In a later book, *The Singularity is Near* (2005) he postponed the Singularity's arrival to 2045. Post-Singularity, having evolved minds of their own, computers would make far more rapid progress. Human and computer minds would merge—a development known today as transhumanism. Thoughts would be downloadable, and an age of freaks would commence. Furthermore, humans would become immortal.

*Forbes Magazine* reported in 2009 that Kurzweil, who was born in 1948, consumed between 180 and 250 pills a day so that he would live to see the Singularity. He has relied on Moore's Law—computing power doubles every eighteen months. His book *How to Create a Mind: The Secret of Human Thought Revealed*, was published in 2012. Yet we still don't begin to know how to create a mind. Kurzweil's basic error was to assume that quantitative additions will bring about qualitative changes; he thought we could expect a growth in complexity to transform itself into an entirely new kind of substance.

In 2000, Bill Joy, then with Sun Microsystems, put a pessimistic spin onto Kurzweil's message. His anti-technology diatribe, "Why the Future Doesn't Need Us," was a seven-day marvel, praised by technologists who should have known better. Joy declared that robotics, nanotechnology, and genetic engineering would gang up on us. "It is no exaggeration to say that we are on the cusp of the further perfection of extreme evil," he wrote.[12]

John McCarthy ignored that Joy-less message but told me that he rejected Kurzweil's vision. "He imagines that there is a Moore's Law of artificial intelligence. Everything doubles in 18 months? I don't see that—either as a characteristic of the past or of the future."[13]

Then again, "some expert systems have been a great success," McCarthy added. "Many companies now support AI departments." (The Google search engine, when it prompts us with "Did you mean…" demonstrates applied AI.) A more plausible worry is not that computers will start telling us what to do, but that they will cause unemployment. But others are confident that new technology creates more jobs than it sheds.

I asked McCarthy about the difficulty of stacking bricks. Robots can easily do that today, he said. Nonetheless, the method employed "doesn't correspond to human common sense knowledge about objects." Picking up bricks—yes. "Picking up cats—no." Robots can't do that. "Not even dead cats."

## Common Sense, Uncommon Difficulty

IN THE gulf separating strong and applied AI, there is a paradox. Computers can easily and quickly do things that humans can do only slowly—multiply two large numbers, for example. In contrast, computers cannot do things that humans (and sometimes animals, too) can do easily, and often without thinking at all.

Small children know millions of things they learned in the first three years of life, without anyone having to teach them. We call it common sense. But it has turned out to be one of the great unsolved problems for AI. Feeding it into computers is extraordinarily difficult.

Since 1984, Cycorp CEO Douglas Lenat and his assistants have been encoding common-sense knowledge—the literally millions of things that small children know but that are normally too obvious to spell out. Two examples: people who die stay dead; and nothing can be in two places at once. Lenat gave this example: "If you are carrying a container that's open on one side, you should carry it with the open end up."[14] (Especially if it contains water.)

The idea is to represent such a basic understanding of life in formal logic as opposed to English sentences. Machines are supposed to crank through the deductions from these logical statements.

By 2002, Lenat told Computerworld, Cycorp had put in "600 person-years of effort, and we've assembled a knowledge base containing three million rules of thumb that the average person knows about the world, plus about 300,000 terms or concepts."[15] But there was still a long way to go. The Cycorp project (Cyc) then contained only about two percent of the information its designers thought necessary to operate with something like human intelligence.

Lenat, funded by Microsoft billionaire Paul Allen, said (in Daniel Crevier's book *AI: The Tumultuous History of the Search for Artificial Intelligence*) that "no one in 2015 would dream of buying a machine without common sense."[16] Well, 2015 has come and gone, and we still have to use our own intelligence and common sense to use the latest computers. But they still only do what they are told—if we are lucky, and nothing crashes.

By 2001 Marvin Minsky had become almost as disillusioned as McCarthy:

> As far as I know [Minsky said] no computer knows that you can use a string to pull an object, but not to push it. You probably shouldn't eat string and [if you tie a box with it], you should have put the stuff in it before… the point is, there are a whole lot of things you know about string. There's been only one large project to do something [about the common-sense problem], and that's the famous Cyc project of Douglas Lenat… He's coming along, but if you look at Cyc, it

still can't do any extensive amount of 5-year-old type common-sense reasoning.[17]

## The Frame Problem

A RELATED difficulty is called the frame problem. If an intelligent program is to work, it must be able to infer that certain events will follow from a given action. But computerized inferences tend to be extremely literal. Therefore the relevant consequences of a specified action must be spelled out and the irrelevant ones ignored. McCarthy found, for example, that in proving that one person could talk to another after looking up his phone number, "we were obliged to add the hypothesis that if a person has a telephone, he still has it after looking up a number in the telephone book."[18]

To get this right, computer-programmed AI must know the context of an action. When we do one thing in the real world, many external things change, but most of those changes are irrelevant. Knowing which are relevant and which are not has turned out to be difficult. And if all changes have to be spelled out, the problem becomes insoluble. It raises basic questions about the applicability of formal logic to everyday life. A parallel problem arises with Natural Selection (see my Chapter 5). A changed environment may be advantageous to an organism, or it may not.

Robotics encounters another difficulty. A robot can "compute" its new location when it moves, but if there is any wheel spinning, a discrepancy will open up between its real and its calculated position. After a few such displacements an early robot called Shakey soon lost track of its location and would bump into walls. Yet, in an exaggeration that has characterized almost all reporting on AI, *Life* magazine in 1970 called Shakey "the first electronic person" capable of traveling about the moon "for months at a time."[19] In fact, it could "barely negotiate straight corridors," said Daniel Crevier.[20]

Rodney Brooks, the CEO of *Rethink Robotics*, aimed to disagree with McCarthy and Minsky, who wanted to establish a proper foundation

before proceeding with robotics. Brooks thought that such preparation
had gone on long enough, with little success. Maybe it would be better
to put robots out into the real world and hope for the best. Children
learn from their environment, so maybe robots would, too. Brooks told
an interviewer in 1997:

> What we've been able to do is build robots that operate in the world,
> in unstructured environments, and do pretty well, because they use
> whatever structure there is in the world to get the tasks done.[21]

But in one of Minsky's talks, "It's 2001: Where's HAL?" his frustra-
tion was plain. (HAL, for those who never saw the movie, was the ma-
lign computer in 2001 who decided to kill off the crew of the spaceship
heading toward Jupiter.) Here's what Minsky said:

> Tell me something that you've learned from building a physical ro-
> bot, and I'll tell you someone in the 1970s who wrote a paper on
> that. So the student is wasting a whole year or three [years] solder-
> ing connections and working with bad components. Every now and
> then the robot will go down the hall and actually find a door and
> go through it. But you don't know why because next time it won't.
> That's why you'll find that these robotics people treasure their vid-
> eos—because it won't work tomorrow.[22]

Minsky warned researchers going into AI: "If you see a student who
says I'm building another robot, tell him 40 thousand people are doing
that. In 15 years they've discovered 5 things (giving them the benefit of
the doubt)."[23]

In *The Society of Mind*, Minsky's ideas were only tangential to AI. Yet
he was right to insist that if computers are to know how to perceive objects and decide whether to ignore them or pay attention, we must first
understand how humans solve the same problem. Sending robots forth
to blunder about in the world and learn by their mistakes was a counsel
of despair. Nothing came of it.

In comments published in his *Washington Post* obituary, Marvin
Minsky's disappointment was plain. What about IBM's "much hyped"
machine, "Watson"? Wasn't that artificial intelligence?, he was once

asked. "I wouldn't call it anything," he replied. "An ad hoc question-answering machine."[24]

## Mind and Materialism

WHAT DOES David Gelernter think about these matters? A computer science professor at Yale, he was wounded in 1993 when he opened a package mailed by the Unabomber. His father Herbert Gelernter participated in the original Dartmouth conference.

Strong AI was bound to fail, David Gelernter once said. "Alan Turing and his followers were naïve about the mind. At least at the start, they didn't grasp the existence of mental states—of an inner mental world, intentional states, of consciousness."

> Building a mind simulator in software and expecting it to think made no more sense than the idea of building a thunderstorm simulator and expecting it to get everyone wet. No reason has ever been adduced for believing that anyone will ever be able to build a conscious mind out of electronics.[25]

Materialism is the foundation on which the whole notion of thinking machines was built. Gelernter reviewed the topic in "The Closing of the Scientific Mind," published in *Commentary* (January 2014). He invoked Thomas Nagel's *Mind and Cosmos: Why the Materialist Neo-Darwinian Conception of Nature Is Almost Certainly False* (2012). Nagel argued that Darwinism cannot explain the emergence of consciousness—the capacity to feel or experience the world. But as Gelernter pointed out, Nagel was immediately set upon "by all the leading punks, bullies, and hangers-on of the philosophical underworld." Gelernter continued:

> Attacking Darwin is the sin against the Holy Ghost that pious scientists are taught never to forgive. Even worse, Nagel is an atheist, but unwilling to express sufficient hatred of religion to satisfy other atheists. There is nothing religious about Nagel's speculations; he believes that science has not come far enough to explain consciousness and that it must press on. He believes that Darwin is not sufficient.[26]

Gelernter also derided the "Kurzweil cult," the belief that machine intelligence will dominate human intelligence to the extent that "men will no longer understand machines any more than potato chips understand mathematical topology."

In the *Commentary* article, Gelernter said:

Whether he knows it or not, Kurzweil believes in and longs for the death of mankind. Because if things work out as he predicts, there will still be life on Earth, but no human life. To predict that a man who lives forever and is built mainly of semiconductors is still a man is like predicting that a man with stainless steel skin, a small nuclear reactor for a stomach, and an IQ of 10,000 would still be a man. In fact we have no idea what he would be.[27]

The great problem with the Kurzweil cult, Gelernter added, is that there is no reason to believe that progress "in any field will continue, much less accelerate." The truth is that "machines do just what we tell them to." Which is exactly what Ada, the Countess of Lovelace, said in the 1830s. It seems that not much has changed since then.

Actually, one thing has changed: Darwinism has intervened. Ever since Darwin we are disposed to believe that only material explanations deserve to be regarded as scientific.

The mainstream view of mind nowadays "among philosophers and many scientists is *computationalism*," said Gelernter. "This view is inspired by the idea that minds are to brains as software is to computers." He reminded us that Daniel Dennett in *Consciousness Explained* had enjoined us to "think of the brain as a computer." Gelernter commented that in some ways this was apt but in other ways a crazy analogy. "At any rate, it is one of the intellectual milestones of modern times."[28]

Meanwhile, we can confidently expect that computers will remain our obedient servants, whether they are under our desks or strapped to our wrists, and operating with an ever-widening range of applications.

As to their becoming "intelligent" or conscious, that will never happen. Nonetheless, the search for "strong AI" was a worthwhile endeavor, if only because it has helped us appreciate at least some of the marvels of the human mind.[29]

# 20. BIOGEOGRAPHY AND DARWIN'S THEOLOGY

THE *ORIGIN OF SPECIES* INCLUDED TWO CHAPTERS ON THE "GEOgraphical Distribution" of species, comprising ten percent of the book. At one point Darwin contrasted two opposing claims about life: his own theory of "descent with modification," and that of "independent creation." Certain geographical facts, he argued, were "inexplicable on the theory of independent creation."[1]

Here Darwin assumed the role of theologian, telling us what a creator might *not* be expected to do. His purely materialistic theory of speciation seemed more reasonable to him than its supernatural alternative. Raising questions about a creator was perhaps not to be expected in the context of geography, but let's follow Darwin's argument and see where it leads. It turns out that he had a point; but in the end perhaps not a very important one. Then we can turn from biogeography to Darwin's ideas about a creator more generally.

Darwin strayed into theology a number of times in *The Origin*, but conspicuously so in his biogeography chapters. He also had a related purpose: to rebut criticism of his theory made by Louis Agassiz—the first geologist to provide good evidence that the Earth had experienced an Ice Age.

## Darwin and Agassiz

AGASSIZ REVIEWED *The Origin of Species* in 1860, saying that he considered Darwin's transmutation theory "a scientific mistake, untrue in its facts, unscientific in its methods, and mischievous in its tendency."[2] Years later, in his *Autobiography*, Darwin found an opportunity to retaliate, referring to "poor Agassiz," who had been attacked by Thomas Huxley.[3]

Swiss-born, Agassiz was appointed professor of Zoology and Geology at Harvard, where he founded Harvard's Museum of Comparative Zoology. That was in 1859—the year of *The Origin*'s publication. Agassiz, who served as the Harvard museum's first director until his death in 1873, never accepted Darwin's theory of evolution. Today he is sometimes identified as a creationist. His son, Alexander Agassiz, made a fortune in copper mining and made a large gift to Harvard University, supporting what later became the Agassiz Museum of Comparative Zoology. Later, Gould, Lewontin, and Wilson all had offices in the Agassiz Museum.

In 1857, Louis Agassiz had written that the living world shows "premeditation, greatness, prescience, omniscience, providence." All these things "proclaim aloud the One God." Natural history, he wrote, must "become the analysis of the thoughts of the Creator of the Universe, as manifested in the animal and vegetable kingdoms."[4] In short, Louis Agassiz's ideas were about as far from Darwin's as can be imagined.

Their conflict can be summarized in this way: Speciation (by Darwin's theory) was achieved by the chance accumulation of random mutations. Such a time-consuming method rendered implausible the claim that the same species would evolve more than once. To use a modern analogy, believing in the repeat appearance of the same species in different places was like arguing that the same randomly chosen lottery number could be the winning number in successive lotteries.

So a new species could be expected to evolve only once and it would have what Darwin called a "center of origin." Yet we plainly do find the same species in different locations—sometimes widely separated. Darwin's chapters were intended to explain how that happened, and at the same time to cast doubt on the creationist argument.

A question "largely discussed by naturalists," Darwin wrote, is "whether species have been created at one or more points of the earth's surface," or whether they migrated from their center of origin.[5] Darwin's strategy was to substitute the migration or dispersal of species for their independent creation.

## Darwin's Argument

DARWIN ACCEPTED the Harvard professor's views about the Ice Age. But he also thought that the glacial period, to which Agassiz had drawn "vivid attention," afforded "a simple explanation" of some otherwise hard-to-explain facts about the migration of species.[6]

Glaciation and the subsequent retreat of glaciers could account for the migration of species, whether they moved in search of a warmer or a colder climate. It could also explain the isolation of species that had earlier adapted to the cold but now found themselves stranded in what had been inhospitable places—as in the case of the penguins in the Antarctic. The migration argument was flexible enough that it could explain almost any geographical location of a given species.

In contrast, Louis Agassiz didn't need migration because he believed that species had been "created at one or more points of the earth."[7] He noted that fish of the same species live in separate lakes with no waterway connecting them. So he concluded they were independently created at both locations. He also thought that the ready adaptation of creatures to their various environments testified to an intelligent plan. Darwin, in contrast, argued that any and all adaptation of species to whatever location could be explained by natural selection.

Darwin allowed that difficulties sometimes arise in explaining migration in detail; yet, he went on:

> the simplicity of the view that each species was first produced within a single region captivates the mind. He who rejects it, rejects the vera causa of ordinary generation with subsequent migration, and calls in the agency of a miracle.[8]

Agassiz did indeed reject "ordinary generation" plus migration, and did invoke "the agency of a miracle." In ruling out the latter, Darwin was reminding readers of his underlying strategy: to disqualify miracles as a legitimate explanation in science and to replace them with what he called the laws "impressed on matter." Claims about the natural world had to embrace material causes if they were to be regarded as scientific. In fact, materialism undergirded Darwin's whole enterprise.

Darwin's next point was the essence of his reply. Organisms, including plants—through the agency of transportable seeds—migrate:

> If the difficulties be not insuperable in admitting that in the long course of time all the individuals of the same species, and likewise of the several species belonging to the same genus, have proceeded from some one source; then all the grand leading facts of geographical distribution are explicable on the theory of migration.[9]

As to the "centers of origin" that Darwin invoked, they are not known in anyone's theory. In *The Greatest Show on Earth* Richard Dawkins asked:

> Why would an all-powerful creator decide to plant his carefully crafted species on islands and continents in exactly the appropriate pattern to suggest, irresistibly, that they had evolved and dispersed from the site of their evolution?[10]

But no one knows "the site of their evolution." We know very little about the origin of finches on the Galápagos Islands, for example. Did only one species arrive from Ecuador? Or from somewhere else? We don't know. Those found there now seem capable of interbreeding, and vary only in small ways from one island to another.

Nonetheless, those who are critical of Darwinism in other respects have little difficulty in accepting migration as a reality—although questions have been raised about the plausibility of monkeys rafting themselves across the South Atlantic, to account for their presence in South America. In short, Darwin was eager to assure Agassiz, and to reassure his readers, that his theory could account for the appearance of a given species in lots of different places. "It is obvious," Darwin wrote, that the several species of the same genus, though inhabiting the most distant quarters of the world, must originally have proceeded from the same source, as they have descended from the same progenitor. In the case of those species which have undergone but little modification there is not much difficulty in believing that they may have migrated from the same region... [11]

Darwin's critics are for the most part happy to concede the point and to accept migration as a reality. As Jonathan Wells has written, "the migration hypothesis is not equivalent to Darwinism," and "could be espoused by a believer in the divine creation of individual species."[12]

Finally, a pause to note the irony: Louis Agassiz was the Harvard professor, Darwin the self-employed naturalist financed by his own private income. Yet among biologists at least, Darwin is perceived as having won their debate. Such an outcome would be highly improbable today. Professionals are expected to defeat amateurs; and Harvard biology professors no longer appeal to miracles.

## Darwin as Theologian

BARRY G. Gale wrote in his book *Evolution Without Evidence* that "given the relative paucity of evidence then available," Darwin was "forced to rely on the argument that his theory was better than the doctrine of special creation"—and this was "the strongest line of argument" in *The Origin of Species*.[13] But what new evidence surfaced after *The Origin* was written? Fossils, maybe, but they have drawn attention to lack of intermediate forms in the record. Otherwise, new difficulties for Darwinism—especially at the molecular level—have greatly exceeded any new evidence supporting it.

Darwin addressed his religious belief in various places, notably his autobiography, parts of which were censored by his widow. As we saw above, he also raised theological issues in *The Origin*, and in *The Descent of Man*. His voluminous correspondence tells us even more. Some of his letters are particularly valuable because he is less guarded in writing to friends than in his published work.

In 1862, Darwin told the Harvard botanist Asa Gray that there seemed to be "too much misery in the world." He could not accept, for example, "that a beneficent and omnipotent God would have designedly created [digger wasps] with the express intention of their feeding within the living bodies of caterpillars, or that a cat should play with mice."[14]

Asa Gray (1810–1888) admired and praised Darwin, who in turn saw Gray as his "best advocate." In the course of their extensive correspondence (they exchanged over 300 letters) Gray partly accepted Darwin's theory, but also argued that nature was filled with "unmistakable and irresistible indications of design." (One could say that Gray was an early exponent of intelligent design.) He said that "God himself is the very last, irreducible causal factor and, hence, the source of all evolutionary change."[15]

In one of his letters Gray asked Darwin what it would take to convince him of design in nature. Darwin replied: "Your question what would convince me of Design is a poser. If I saw an angel come down to teach us good, and I was convinced from others seeing him that I was not mad, I should believe in design."[16]

Darwin allowed that his theories were "not at all necessarily atheistical," but was unable to share Gray's worldview. He felt "most deeply that the whole subject is too profound for the human intellect. A dog might as well speculate on the mind of Newton."[17]

Replying in 1873 to a different correspondent, this one in Utrecht, Darwin expressed his agnosticism:

> I may say that the impossibility of conceiving that this grand and wondrous universe, with our conscious selves, arose through chance, seems to me the chief argument for the existence of God; but whether this is an argument of real value, I have never been able to decide. I am aware that if we admit a first cause, the mind still craves to know whence it came from and how it arose.[18]

The *Autobiography* included a section explicitly dealing with Darwin's "Religious Belief." On balance, he decided, happiness in the world ultimately prevailed over misery. Natural selection played a key role in shaping that opinion:

> It may be asked how can the generally beneficent arrangement of the world be accounted for? Some writers indeed are so much impressed with the amount of suffering in the world, that they doubt if we look to all sentient beings, whether there is more of misery or of happiness;—whether the world as a whole is a good or a bad one. According to my judgment happiness decidedly prevails, though this would be very difficult to prove. If the truth of this conclusion be granted, it harmonizes well with the effects which we might expect from natural selection.
>
> If all the individuals of any species were habitually to suffer to an extreme degree they would neglect to propagate their kind; but we have no reason to believe that this has ever or at least often occurred. Some other considerations, moreover, lead to the belief that all sentient beings have been formed so as to enjoy, as a general rule, happiness.[19]

Philosopher Stephen Dilley is among those who have studied Darwin's use of theology. He "used an Enlightenment-style theology in order to enhance the credibility of his argument or theory," Dilley said.[20] As to the "pain and suffering" argument, Dilley quoted Darwin saying to a colleague: "What a book a devil's chaplain might write on the clumsy, wasteful, blundering, low, and horribly cruel works of nature!"[21]

In *The Descent of Man* (1871) Darwin included a section on "Belief in God—Religion." He wrote:

> There is no evidence that man was aboriginally endowed with the ennobling belief in the existence of an Omnipotent God. On the contrary there is ample evidence, derived not from hasty travellers, but from men who have long resided with savages, that numerous races have existed, and still exist, who have no idea of one or more gods, and who have no words in their languages to express such an idea.[22]

Darwin preferred the idea of a God who created a few original forms and then let the "laws" of variation and selection govern the outcome.

"It is just as noble a conception of the Deity to believe that He created a few original forms capable of self-development into other and needful forms," he wrote in *The Origin*, "as to believe that he required a fresh act of creation to supply the voids caused by the action of his laws."[23] At one point he said that such laws were "impressed on matter by the Creator."

He took a harder line when it came to miracles, saying that "the clearest evidence would be requisite to make any sane man believe in the miracles by which Christianity is supported." For "the more we know of the fixed laws of nature the more incredible do miracles become." The underlying problem, he thought, was that "men at that time were ignorant and credulous to a degree almost incomprehensible by us."[24]

What were these "fixed laws"? He gave several examples right at the end of *The Origin*. They were:

> Growth with reproduction; Inheritance which is almost implied by reproduction; Variability from the indirect and direct action of the conditions of life, and from use and disuse; a Ratio of Increase so high as to lead to a Struggle for Life, and as a consequence to Natural Selection, entailing Divergence of Character and the Extinction of less improved forms.[25]

But these were not real laws. "Reproduction," for example, is not a law. And is natural selection a law? He clearly said so in his *Autobiography*:

> The old argument of design in nature, as given by [William] Paley, which formerly seemed to me so conclusive, fails, now that the law of natural selection has been discovered. We can no longer argue that, for instance, the beautiful hinge of a bivalve shell must have been made by an intelligent being, like the hinge of a door by man. There seems to be no more design in the variability of organic beings and in the action of natural selection, than in the course which the wind blows. Everything in nature is the result of fixed laws.[26]

It should be redundant to add at this point that natural selection is not remotely law-like. All attempts to state it as a law collapse into the truism that I reviewed in earlier chapters.

Paul Nelson said that Darwin's other laws begged key questions. "Inheritance, for example, requires the prior existence of an organism (or at least two organisms of differing sexes, in a sexually-reproducing species). But Darwin often postulated the existence of the thing he claimed to explain."[27]

In attempting to represent his own theory as a set of "laws," Darwin hoped to show that biology resembled physics. But it may be questioned whether biology really has laws. (One possible law, not mentioned by Darwin: "All organisms die.") In physics, on the other hand, it is reasonable to describe physical laws as existing without reference to a creator of those laws. In expounding his laws of motion, for example, Newton did not rely on and saw no need to appeal to a deity who might have created such laws.

Wounded pride also seems to have played a role for Darwin. He recalled that while on board *H.M.S. Beagle* he was "heartily laughed at by several of the officers for quoting the Bible as an unanswerable authority on some point of morality."[28] So he reconsidered the Old Testament with its "manifestly false history of the world, with the Tower of Babel, the rainbow as a sign, etc., etc." In "attributing to God the feelings of a revengeful tyrant," the Bible was "no more to be trusted than the sacred books of the Hindoos, or the beliefs of any barbarian."[29]

The result was that he "gradually came to disbelieve in Christianity as a divine revelation." The morality of the New Testament was beautiful, he allowed, but its perfection depended on our own interpretation, just as we today have to interpret metaphors and allegories. The result was that Darwin found it more and more difficult "to invent evidence which would suffice to convince me."[30]

Darwin's mounting hostility to Christianity was suppressed by his widow, who removed some inflammatory comments from his *Autobiography*. The following passage was not generally known until it was restored and first published by his granddaughter Nora Barlow in 1958:

> Thus disbelief crept over me at a very slow rate, but was at last complete. The rate was so slow that I felt no distress, and have never since

doubted even for a single second that my conclusion was correct. I can indeed hardly see how anyone ought to wish Christianity to be true; for if so the plain language of the text seems to show that the men who do not believe, and this would include my Father, Brother and almost all my best friends, will be everlastingly punished. And this is a damnable doctrine.[31]

In 1880, he wrote to a correspondent, "I am sorry to have to inform you that I do not believe in the Bible as a divine revelation, & therefore not in Jesus Christ as the Son of God."[32] Rumors of Darwin's deathbed conversion are without any basis. He died in 1882.

# 21. The Rise and Fall of Progress

Nineteenth-century thought accepted that Progress was such a powerful force that it would transform human nature. Darwin was swept along by that faith, perhaps without recognizing its influence on him and on his most famous idea. In his *Autobiography* he said that "man in the distant future will be a far more perfect creature than he now is."[1] He also said at the end of *The Origin of Species* that "all corporeal and mental endowments will tend to progress towards perfection."[2]

Perfection, he said. The climate of opinion of his day was as difficult for him to escape as the air he breathed. (The same applies to us, in our very different time.) For a longer exposition on the nineteenth-century embrace of Progress, read almost anything by Darwin's contemporary, Herbert Spencer (1820–1903). He collected his numerous opinions on the topic in a lengthy book, *Illustrations of Universal Progress* (1864).

Its opening essay, "Progress, Its Law and Cause," written in 1857, is sixty pages long. A mass of abstract nouns, it is difficult to read today. "The current conception of Progress is somewhat shifting and indefinite,"[3] it begins; but a few pages later he commented that "Progress is not an accident, not a thing within human control, but a beneficent necessity."[4] Writing in *Darwin's Metaphor: Nature's Place in Victorian Culture*, the science historian Robert M. Young noted that "Spencer had argued for inevitable progress before he had worked out his evolutionary theory."[5]

Spencer's *Universal Progress* also included a brief chapter, written in 1852, on "The Development Hypothesis," by which he meant the theory of evolution. In another book, *Principles of Psychology*, he wrote that "Life under all its forms has arisen by a progressive, unbroken evolution; and through the immediate instrumentality of what we call natural causes."[6]

Spencer explicitly rejected "special creation" and he supplied Darwin with the phrase "the survival of the fittest" as a summary of natural selection. It's fair to say that he had more influence on Darwin than is generally recognized. Both men were swept along by the then-unquestioned faith in Progress. (Spencer capitalized the word and so shall I, in an attempt to preserve the particular meaning it had in Darwin's day.)

Robert J. Richards, a history of science professor at the University of Chicago, wrote that "Darwin's deeply ingrained sense that his theory explained progress in organisms permeates his text."[7] It might be better to invert that, and say that the deeply engrained belief in Progress explained Darwin's text. It also goes some way toward explaining *The Origin*'s easy acceptance by the educated classes of his day.

As we can now see, the problem was that in the nineteenth century the idea of Progress was so broadly accepted that Darwinian evolution could be swept along in its wake without needing much in the way of evidence. The rising tide of Progress automatically lifted all organismal boats. The *zeitgeist* of universal progress also prevented Darwin and his allies from seeing the central problem of the theory: that of extrapolation from the small changes we do observe from one generation to the next. Such extrapolation embraced what has never been observed: "indefinite departure from the original type."

In fact, Darwinian evolution can be seen as a way of looking at the history of life through the distorting lens of Progress. Given enough time, society in general, including human beings, would be transformed into something superior and perhaps unrecognizably different. As late as 1959, at the Chicago Centennial, the geneticist Hermann J. Muller felt confident "that not only our cultural but also our biological evolution will go on to now undreamed-of heights."[8]

## The Idea in Its Heyday

"THE IDEA of progress," J. B. Bury wrote in his book of that name (1920), was by the 1870s and 1880s becoming a general article of faith. Between 1880 and 1920, there appeared a large literature of social science in which indefinite progress was "generally assumed as an axiom."[9] In sharp contrast, the idea of progress had been unthinkable to the ancients.

Reflecting further on progress in his later book *The Descent of Man* (1871), Darwin wrote:

> Man may be excused for feeling pride at having risen to the summit of the organic scale. And the fact of his having thus risen, instead of his having been aboriginally placed there, may give him hope for a still higher destiny in the distant future.[10]

Earlier in *The Descent of Man*, Darwin had promoted eugenics, which his cousin Sir Francis Galton helped create:

> With savages [Darwin wrote], the weak in body or mind are soon eliminated; and those that survive commonly exhibit a vigorous state of health. We civilised men, on the other hand, do our utmost to check the process of elimination. We build asylums for the imbecile, the maimed and the sick; we institute poor laws, and our medical men exert their utmost skill to save the life of every one to the last moment…

> Thus the weak members of civilised societies propagate their kind. No one who has attended to the breeding of domestic animals will doubt that this must be highly injurious to the race of man. It is surprising how soon a want of care, or care wrongly directed, leads to the degeneration of a domestic race; but excepting in the case of man himself, hardly anyone is so ignorant as to allow his worst animals to breed.[11]

So that's how Progress could be undermined—by substituting human for natural selection. Humans were too nice for their own good! Alfred Marshall found in 1890 that economists were intrigued by the speculations of biologists—Darwin in particular. They were paying ever more attention "to the pliability of human nature." Furthermore, Marshall thought the way wealth was produced and distributed influenced the "character of man"[12]—a preview of socialist thinking.

Perhaps surprisingly, Thomas Henry Huxley edged away from the doctrine of Progress late in life. In 1893, after Darwin's death, he wrote:

> We also know modern speculative optimism, with its perfectibility of the species, reign of peace, and its lion-and-lamb transformation scenes; but one does not hear so much of it as one did forty years ago... The majority of us, I apprehend, profess neither pessimism nor optimism. We hold that the world is neither so good nor so bad as it conceivably might be.[13]

It's worth taking a brief and out-of-sequence look at the views of his two grandsons, Aldous and Julian. Aldous Huxley, the essayist and novelist, assailed "the apocalyptic religion of Inevitable Progress whose creed is that the Kingdom of Heaven is outside you and in the future." Such a doctrine wants to "bully nature into subserving ill-considered temporal ends." Elsewhere, he said that the religion of progress is "in the last analysis the hope and faith... that one can get something for nothing."[14]

In referring to the religion of progress, Aldous might well have had his brother Julian in mind. Julian preached that religion whenever an opportunity arose. In *Evolution in Action* he defined biological progress as "improvement which facilitates or permits further improvement; or, if you prefer... a series of advances which do not stand in the way of further advances."[15]

Does he move around in a self-confirming circle there? You decide. He was certainly more enthusiastic about Progress than his grandfather. Julian also addressed the subject at length in the Darwin Centennial in Chicago. (See my Chapter 3.) And like Darwin, he prescribed for society a dose of eugenics, to limit breeding by the unfit.

## A New Allegiance

HERBERT SPENCER was a libertarian, highly critical of government. But little more than a decade after his death, intellectuals began to shift their allegiance, showing an anti-market preference for the state, and for socialist ideas. Before too long "New Soviet Man" appeared on the horizon. Still, the idea of Progress survived, even as faith in Spencer's libertarianism faded. His reputation declined sharply in the twentieth century, and as his biographer J. D. Peel commented: "Posterity is cruellest to those who sum up for their contemporaries in an all-embracing synthesis the accumulated knowledge of their age. This is what Spencer did for the Victorians."[16]

In the new age to come, loyal Communists believed that the abolition of private property would transform not just society but its inhabitants along with it. Marx had promised as much in the *Communist Manifesto*. Here's an amazing prediction by Leon Trotsky:

> Man will become immeasurably stronger, wiser and subtler. His body will become more harmonized, his movements more rhythmic, his voice more musical. The forms of life will become dynamically dramatic. The average human type will rise to the heights of an Aristotle, a Goethe or a Marx. And above these heights new peaks will rise.[17]

Somehow, that superior human type never showed up. The belief that it would was one of the great delusions of modern times.

As late as 1948 the American historian Richard Hofstadter, who had only recently escaped from his own youthful love affair with Communism, thought our Founding Fathers had erred in accepting "unchanging human nature." Even after World War II, Hofstadter continued to think that human nature was changing for the better.

The socialist faith lasted for almost 100 years and kept many in its thrall. It was not fully relinquished until the fall of the Berlin Wall in 1989. Almost immediately, the conventional wisdom turned 180 degrees and environmentalism appeared on the scene.

At his retirement from the *New York Times* in 2001, the liberal columnist Anthony Lewis was interviewed by an editor of the paper. Perhaps the most interesting thing he said was: "I have lost my faith in the idea of progress."[18] He had in mind the old idea that mankind is getting wiser and better. Then he added:

The most disappointing fact of life in the 20th century was that, contrary to my expectations, after the Holocaust, the century continued to be riddled with the extraordinary ability of human beings to hate others because they look a little different. Or in fact they may not look very different, they just live next door.[19]

In his book *Advance to Barbarism*, Frederick J. P. Veale pointed out that since the Dark Ages the story of civilization had been one of "slow but steady upward progress."[20] Occasional fluctuations aside, it seemed to be "an established law of nature." It became "a kind of religion for most educated men"; faith in Progress survived until the twentieth century. But after the First World War, civilization began "a retrograde movement without a parallel in history." A "profound psychological change" was taking place.[21]

## Progress Rejected

PROGRESS HAS been explicitly rejected by modern philosophers and writers. One of the first to do so was the Christian writer C. S. Lewis. In his essay "The World's Last Night" (1952), he wrote that "no one looking at world history without some preconception in favor of progress could find in it a steady up-gradient."[22] Often we do see Progress within a given field over a limited period, and if this could spread to all departments of life and continue indefinitely, "there would be 'Progress' of the sort our fathers believed in. But it never seems to do so." The idea that the world "slowly ripen[s] to perfection is a myth, not a generalization from experience."[23]

Lewis went further and saw the connection between the old faith in progress and Darwinism itself, suggesting that both might fall together:

> There may be signs that biologists are already contemplating a withdrawal from the whole Darwinian position, but I claim to be no judge of such signs. It can even be argued that what Darwin really accounted for was not the origin, but the elimination of species… For purposes of this article I am assuming that Darwinian biology is correct. What I want to point out is the illegitimate transition from the Darwinian theorem in biology to the modern myth of evolution-

ism or developmentalism or progress in general. The first thing to notice is that the myth [of progress] arose earlier than the [Darwinian] theorem, in advance of all evidence.[24]

Lewis could have added that the myth of Progress may well have given rise to Darwinism itself.

John Gray of the London School of Economics wrote that "One does not want to deny anyone the consolations of a faith, but it is obvious that the idea of progress in history is a myth created by the need for meaning."[25] Spencer, Darwin, and other apostles of Progress were deists at best, so the idea that history somehow tilted in an upward direction may have ameliorated the bleak implications of their godless philosophy.

The doctrine of progressive change was a "compensatory secular simulacrum for Providence," adopted by Victorians "who were sliding into unbelief," John Offer wrote.[26]

Those who could no longer believe in the next life substituted a more glorious future in this. Beatrice Potter, among many others, struggled with, and lost, her Christian faith. For a while, Spencer's *First Principles* replaced Christianity in her mind. Then she married the socialist Sidney Webb. They became Communists and traveled to Moscow to enjoy the promised future while they were still living.

We do indeed benefit from *material* progress, in the form of improved airplanes, computers, and automobiles. But the problem here, John Gray added, is the belief that the sort of advance achieved in science can be reproduced in ethics and politics. "In fact, while scientific knowledge increases cumulatively, nothing of the kind happens in society... The belief that history is a directional process is as faith-based as anything in the Christian catechism."[27]

The Russian dissident and Orthodox Christian Alexander Solzhenitsyn also rejected Progress, inveighing against it in a late work, *The Russian Question* (1995). "It was from that intense optimism of Progress that Marx, for one, concluded that history will lead us to justice without God," he wrote.[28] Like Gray, he saw that technology had progressed; and like the Greens in the Western world, he criticized it on environmental grounds. Solzhenitsyn rejected Progress because it was a secular philosophy, and there he parted ways with the Greens, who were inclined to be both secular and progressive.

In "On the Origin at 150: Is a New Evolutionary Synthesis in Sight?" (2009), Eugene Koonin, a senior investigator with the National Center for Biotechnology Information at the NIH said: "[G]one forever is the notion of evolutionary progress that undoubtedly is central to the traditional evolutionary thinking, even if this is not always made explicit."[29]

A graduate of Moscow State University and a Russian immigrant, Koonin also said that the state of evolutionary theory at the time of *The Origin*'s 150th anniversary (in 2009) was "somewhat shocking":

> In the post-genomic era, all major tenets of the Modern Synthesis are, if not outright overturned, replaced by a new and incomparably more complex vision of the key aspects of evolution.[30]

## Enter Environmentalism, Stage Left

THE U.N.-SPONSORED "Earth Summit," held in Rio de Janeiro in 1992 and attended by numerous journalists, was promoted by the conference Secretary-General Maurice Strong as an "historic moment for humanity."[31]

It's a remarkable fact that planning for this two-week jamboree began in December 1989, just one month after the fall of the Berlin Wall. So the wildly optimistic faith of socialism was replaced almost overnight by the unduly pessimistic cause of environmentalism. It was a momentous change, very much characterizing the world we live in today. "Progress" was dead, hastily buried and replaced by something close to its opposite.

By 2009 *The New Yorker* was attributing the "sixth great die-off," or mass extinction of species, to reckless human activity (reproduction in particular). And things would go downhill from there. Three years later the magazine followed up with "The Case Against Kids: Is Procreation Immoral?" by the same writer (Elizabeth Kolbert).

"We are a plague on the Earth," the BBC's David Attenborough said in 2013, referring to humanity as a whole. "It's not just climate change.

It's sheer space, places to grow food for this enormous horde. Either we limit our population growth or the natural world will do it for us, and the natural world is doing it for us right now."[32]

Attenborough's remarks were attacked by Wesley J. Smith, a Senior Fellow at Discovery Institute's Center on Human Exceptionalism. Smith pointed out that Attenborough was showing that environmentalism is "growing progressively anti-human," which certainly is true.

Today, the intelligentsia has firmly rejected the old belief in Progress. The twentieth century, with its Holocaust and Gulag, its world wars and revolutions, was unhelpful to the cause. Alan Weisman's *The World Without Us* (2007) described what would happen to the natural and human-built environment (such as New York City) if humans suddenly were to disappear. He was not advocating such an outcome, but his vision was seen as an optimistic one and his book became a surprise best-seller.

Less nuanced was Paul Taylor, a professor of philosophy at City College of New York, who said: "Given the total, absolute, and final disappearance of Homo sapiens, not only would the Earth's Community of Life continue to exist but the ending of the human epoch on Earth would be greeted with a hearty 'good riddance.'"[33]

So much for the human race.

Meanwhile, the fertility rates in all developed countries have fallen below replacement levels (which is 2.1 children per woman on average for the developed world). The decline includes the whole of Europe, the United States, Canada, Russia, China, and Japan. This may well be good news for Attenborough, Bill McKibben, and many Green activists. But given the dependence of modern economies on income transfers, paid to an ever-growing number of "seniors," more and more income earners will be needed to keep the economic ball rolling. The present situation looks unstable.

Recently, leaders in the U.S. have taken to placing themselves on "the right side of history" and have criticized their political opponents for moving toward "the wrong side of history." At first glance, this may resemble an attempt to revive the old idea of Progress. But it is something different, surely. It is an attempt to marginalize opponents by hinting that they just don't know what is going on beneath the (political) surface where the current of "history" flows. It is a political strategy rather than an embedded faith.[34]

## Climate of Opinion as It Affects Darwinism

ONE MUST distinguish between the older worldview that accepted and promoted a belief in Progress and the history of biology itself. Progress, as a formerly prevalent doctrine, helps explain why Darwinism was readily accepted. But the old doctrine of Progress was dropped from at least some recent theorizing about biology.

Stephen Jay Gould partially addressed the issue in his book *Full House* (1996). He wrote that the history of life showed no inherent drive toward long-term progress, no tendency for the supposed ladder of life to go straight from bacteria to man. Life formed "a bush, not a ladder," he liked to say. Following in Darwin's footsteps, Gould was also eager to remind us that humans are in no way exceptional. Life can as easily "adapt" towards simplification, he wrote, as happens with parasites. Gould was a reliable Darwinian, but he failed to point out that Darwin himself had been one of the leading apostles of Progress.

The widespread public acceptance of biological evolution in Darwin's day was probably a product of the simultaneous faith in Progress. Darwin's theory was accepted as readily as it was because it shared in the general belief that things were getting better. It's not that the organisms themselves were being swept along, but that European and then American intellectuals believed that everything was improving.

The corollary is worth noting: with Progress rejected, faith in Darwinian evolution is likely to decline along with it. As we have seen in earlier chapters, there is remarkably little evidence for Darwinism. Universal common descent has been disputed; it is mainly a deduction from Darwin's theory, not a physical observation; "indefinite departure from the original type" has never been observed; natural selection merely multiplies existing varieties, and as C. S. Lewis guessed, it more easily accounts for the disappearance of old forms than the appearance of new ones.

It is clear, then, that Darwinism was propped up by the worldview of Progress that dominated the West from the Enlightenment on, particularly in the middle to late nineteenth century. Today, that same worldview is disparaged by the environmentalists, the most extreme of whom think that humans are a plague on the planet.

But one still-widespread philosophy does lend support to Darwinism, and that is materialism, or the belief that mind is reducible to matter and that the universe consists of molecules in motion and nothing else. Starting with the Greek philosopher Democritus and his Roman popularizer Lucretius, materialism is a philosophy that never died out and was strongly revived by Charles Darwin and Karl Marx in the nineteenth century. Marxism has already collapsed. Whether Darwinism will survive the loss of the faith in Progress and the introduction of more careful scientific scrutiny (thanks to the intelligent design movement) is something that should become apparent before too long.

At the moment, I believe, the science of Darwinism amounts to little more than the "wedding" of materialism and Progress. We have seen that if materialism is true, then Darwinism—or something very much like it—must also be true. But materialism is highly implausible and has been widely challenged. At the same time it only takes one partner to break up a marriage, and as we now know, Progress has wandered off the straight and narrow. As a result, the break-up of Darwinism seems likely in the years ahead.

# ENDNOTES

## INTRODUCTION

1. Arthur Koestler, *Janus: A Summing Up* (London: Hutchinson, 1978), 168.

2. Herbert Spencer, *Principles of Biology*, vol. 1 (London: Williams and Northgate, 1864), 444.

3. A. J. Ayer, as quoted by William Cash in "Did Atheist Philosopher See God When He 'Died'?" *National Post*, March 3, 2001..

4. A. J. Ayer, "Postscript to a Postmortem," *London Spectator*, October 15, 1988.

5. Darwin, "To Asa Gray 22 May [1860]," *Darwin Correspondence Project*, Cambridge University, accessed April 20, 2016, https://www.darwinproject.ac.uk/letter/?docId=letters/DCP-LETT-2814.xml;query=22%20May,%201860;brand=default.

6. Karl Popper, in *Darwin Retried* by Norman Macbeth (New York: Dell Publishing, 1973), back cover.

7. *Evolution After Darwin*, Sol Tax ed., vol. 1 (Chicago: University of Chicago Press, 1960), 381–402.

8. Karl Popper, *Unended Quest* (La Salle: Open Court Publishing, 1974), 168.

9. Ibid., 168.

10. "New trends in evolutionary biology: biological, philosophical and social science perspectives," Conference Announcement, https://royalsociety.org/science-events-and-lectures/2016/11/evolutionary-biology/; David Klinghoffer, "Paul Nelson on Intelligent Design and the Royal Society's 'White Bear Problem," Evolution News, November 16, 2016, http://www.evolutionnews.org/2016/11/listen_paul_nel103293.html; David Klinghoffer, "Royal Society Meeting Not Provocative Enough for You?," Evolution News, November 11, 2016, http://www.evolutionnews.org/2016/11/royal_society_m_1103280.html.

## 1. DARWINISM IN OUR TIME

1. C. S. Lewis to Dom Bede Griffiths, July 5, 1949, *The Collected Letters of C. S. Lewis*, vol. 2 (San Francisco: Harper San Francisco, 2004), 953.

2. C. S. Lewis, *The Discarded Image* (Cambridge: Cambridge University Press, 1964), 221.

3. Ibid.

4. Ibid.

5. Charles Darwin, *Charles Darwin —T. H. Huxley, Autobiographies* (London: Oxford University Press, 1964), 221.

6. Charles Darwin, *The Origin of Species* (New York: Penguin Books, 2009), 426.

7. C. S. Lewis, *God in the Dock* (Grand Rapids: William B. Eerdmans, 1987), 22.

8. William Dembski, *The End of Christianity* (Nashville: B&H Publishing Group, 2009), 2.

9. David Gelernter, "The Closing of the Scientific Mind," *Commentary*, January 1, 2014, https://www.commentarymagazine.com/articles/the-closing-of-the-scientific-mind/.

## 2. Darwin's Mistake

1. Charles Darwin, *On the Origin of Species*, 2nd ed. (London: John Murray, 1860), 484.

2. Darwin, *On the Origin of Species*, in *The Harvard Classics*, Vol. 11, Charles W. Eliot ed. (New York: PF Collier & Son, 1909), 529.

3. Darwin, "To J. D. Hooker, 1 February [1871]" *Darwin Correspondence Project*, Cambridge University, https://www.darwinproject.ac.uk/letter/?docId=letters/DCP-LETT-7471.xml;query=warm%20little%20pond;brand=default.

4. Eugene V. Koonin, *The Logic of Chance: The Nature and Origin of Biological Evolution* (Upper Saddle River, NJ: FT Press, 2011), 391.

5. Ibid.

6. Ibid., 390.

7. Darwin, *Origin*, 79.

8. Ibid.

9. Charles Darwin, *The Autobiography of Charles Darwin*, Nora Barlow, ed. (London: Collins, 1958), 128.

10. Alfred R. Wallace, *My Life: a Record of Events and Opinions*, Vol. 1 (London: Chapman and Hall, 1908), 232.

11. Thomas Huxley, *Life and Letters of Thomas Henry Huxley*, Leonard Huxley ed. (New York, London: D. Appleton and Company, 1909), 183.

12. Bertrand Russell, *Religion and Science* (New York: Oxford University Press, 1997), 72.

13. Darwin, *Origin*, 82.

14. Wallace, *The World of Life*, 288–289; see also Michael Flannery, *Alfred Russel Wallace: A Rediscovered Life* (Seattle: Discovery Institute, 2011).

15. Darwin, *Origin*, 21.

16. Ibid., 22.

17. Ibid., 21.

18. For a detailed discussion of Darwin's reaction to Wallace's 1858 essay on natural selection, and the way the question of priority of discovery was settled between Darwin and Wallace, see Adrian Desmond and James Moore, *Darwin* (New York: W. W. Norton, 1991), 466–477, and Michael A. Flannery, *Alfred Russel Wallace: A Rediscovered Life* (Seattle: Discovery, 2011), 45–48.

19. Darwin, *Origin*, 82.

20. Ibid., 97.

21. Ibid., 77.

22. Darwin, *On the Origin of Species*, 1st ed. (London: John Murray, 1859), 84 (Chapter 4).

23. Ibid., 184 (Chapter 6).

24. Darwin, *Origin*, ed. Charles W. Eliot, 120.

25. T. H. Morgan, *Evolution and Genetics* (Princeton: Princeton University Press, 1925), 120.

26. Jerry Fodor and Massimo Piattelli-Palmarini, "Misunderstanding Darwin: An Exchange," *Boston Review*, March 17, 2010, accessed April 27, 2016, http://new.bostonreview.net/BR35.2/darwin_exchange.

27. Darwin, *Origin*, 32.

28. Ibid.

29. Darwin, "1844 Essay," in *The Foundations of The Origin of Species: Two Essays Written in 1842 and 1844*, ed. Francis Darwin (Cambridge: Cambridge University Press, 1909), 109.

30. Darwin, *The Origin of Species*, 2nd ed. (London: John Murray, 1860), 90.

31. Ibid.

32. Ibid., 172.

33. Ibid., 204.

34. Ibid., 243.

35. Ibid., 280.

36. Ibid.

37. Ibid., 281.

38. Ibid., 282.

39. Ibid., 470.

40. Ibid.

41. Ibid., 109.

42. Ibid., 293.

43. For more information on this distinction, see "Lumpers and splitters," *Wikipedia*, May 31, 2016, accessed July 27, 2016, https://en.wikipedia.org/wiki/Lumpers_and_splitters.

44. Ibid., 278.

45. Ibid., 469.

46. Ibid., 481.

# 3. Darwin's Curia at the Centenary

1. *Evolution after Darwin*, ed. Sol Tax, vol. 3 (Chicago: University of Chicago Press, 1960), 143.

2. Ernst Mayr in "Happy 100th Birthday Ernst Mayr!" interview by Michael Shermer and Frank J. Sulloway, *Skeptic Magazine* 8, no. 1 (2000).

3. *Evolution after Darwin*, vol. 3, 63.

4. Darwin, *Origin*, 6th ed., 444.

5. Ibid., 57

6. *Evolution after Darwin*, vol. 3, 57.

7. Ibid., 58.

8. John Horgan, "In the Beginning..." *Scientific American*, February 1991, http://www.scientificamerican.com/article/in-the-beginning-1991-02/.

9. Carl Sagan, quoted in R. Shapiro, *Origins: A Skeptic's Guide to the Creation of Life on Earth* (New York: Summit Books, 1986), 99.

10. *Evolution after Darwin*, vol. 3, 44.

11. Ibid.

12. Ibid., vol. 3, 44.

13. Ibid., 45.

14. Ibid.

15. Ibid.

16. Ibid.

17. Ibid., 46.

18. Ibid.

19. Ibid.

20. Theodosius Dobzhansky, quoted in *Debating Darwin*, ed. John C. Greene (Claremont: Regina Books, 1999), 93.

21. Ibid., 106.

22. *Evolution after Darwin*, vol. 3, 113.

23. Ibid., 52.

24. Ibid., 60.

25. Ibid.

26. Ibid., 47.

27. Ibid., 58.

28. Ibid.

29. Ibid. vol. 1, 239.

30. Frank Thone, "New Discovery Speeds Up Evolution," *Scientific American*, March 1928, http://www.scientificamerican.com/article/new-discovery-speeds-up-evolution/.

31. *Evolution after Darwin*, vol. 3, 51.

32. Ibid., vol. 1, 242.

33. Ibid., vol. 1, 249.

34. Greene, 10.

35. Darwin, *Autobiography*, 92.

# 4. Common Descent: Fact or Theory?

1. See Carl Zimmer's "Editor's Introduction" to *The Descent of Man: The Concise Edition*, ed. Carl Zimmer (New York: Plume, Penguin Group, 2007), 1.

2. Peter B. and Jean S. Medawar, *From Aristotle to Zoos: A Philosophical Dictionary of Biology* (Cambridge: Harvard University Press, 1985), 39.

3. Carl Woese, "On the Evolution of Cells," *PNAS* 99, no. 13 (2002), 8746.

4. Casey Luskin, "A Primer on the Tree of Life (Part 1): The Main Assumption," *Evolution News and Views*, 2009, accessed on April 21, 2016, http://www.evolutionnews.org/2009/05/a_primer_on_the_tree_of_life_p020141.html.

5. Daniel Dennett, *Darwin's Dangerous Idea* (New York: Touchstone, 1995), 61.

6. "About BioLogos," *BioLogos*, accessed on April 21, 2016, http://biologos.org/about-us/.

7. Richard Dawkins, *The Greatest Show on Earth: The Evidence for Evolution* (New York: Free Press, 2009), 8.

8. Ibid., 5.

9. [Samuel Wilberforce] "On the Origin of Species, by means of Natural Selection; or the Preservation of Favoured Races in the Struggle for Life. By Charles Darwin, M.A., FRS. London, 1860," *The London Quarterly Review*, vol. 107, January–April, American Edition (New York: Leonard Scott & Co., 1860): 121.

10. Darwin, *The Origin of Species*, 1st ed., 490.

11. Darwin, "To J.D. Hooker, 1 February [1871]" *Darwin Correspondence Project*, https://www.darwinproject.ac.uk/letter/?docId=letters/DCP-LETT-7471.xml;query=warm%20little%20pond;brand=default.

12. William Dembski, "William Dembski Interview," *TheBestSchools.org*, January 2012 (updated May 2016), accessed July 27, 2016, http://www.thebestschools.org/features/william-dembski-interview/.

13. James A. Barham, private correspondence with author, 2011.

14. Dawkins, *The Greatest Show on Earth*, 408–409.

15. Ibid., 409.

16. Ibid., 409–410.

17. Mayr, in *Debating Darwin*, John C. Greene ed., 144.

18. Mayr, *One Long Argument* (Cambridge: Harvard University Press, 1993), 163.

19. "The Great Debate—What is Life?" panel discussion at *The Science Network*, February 12, 2011, http://thesciencenetwork.org/programs/the-great-debate-what-is-life/what-is-life-panel.

20. "Venter vs. Dawkins on the Tree of Life—and Another Dawkins Whopper," *Evolution News and Views*, March 9, 2011, accessed on April 21, 2016, http://www.evolutionnews.org/2011/03/venter_vs_dawkins_on_the_tree_044681.html.

21. W. Ford Doolittle, "Phylogenetic Classification and the Universal Tree," *Science* 284, no. 5423 (1999): 2124–2128.

22. Dawkins, *The Greatest Show on Earth*, 157.

23. Ibid., 187.

24. Darwin, *Origin*, 2nd ed., 484.

# 5. Natural Selection: A Closer Look

1. Darwin, *Origin of Species*, 2nd ed., 187.

2. David Berlinski, *The Deniable Darwin and Other Essays* (Seattle: Discovery Institute Press, 2009), 367–378.

3. Mivart, letter to Charles Darwin, "Mivart, St. G. J. to Darwin, C.R.," January 10, 1872, *Darwin Correspondence Project*, University of Cambridge, http://learning.darwinproject. ac.uk/entry-8154.

4. Mivart, *On the Genesis of Species* (New York: D. Appleton, 1871), 178.

5. Conrad Hal Waddington in "Discussion: Paper by Dr. Eden," in *Mathematical Challenges to the Neo-Darwinian Interpretation of Evolution: The Wistar Institute Symposium Monograph*, no. 5, eds. Paul S. Moorhead and Martin M. Kaplan (Philadelphia: The Wistar Institute Press, 1966), 13–14.

6. Stephen Meyer, *Signature in the Cell: DNA and the Evidence for Intelligent Design* (New York: HarperCollins, 2011), 205.

7. Stephen J. Gould, "Darwin's Untimely Burial," in *Ever Since Darwin* (New York: W. W. Norton & Co., 1977), 39.

8. Gould, *Ever Since Darwin*, 42.

9. Dawkins, *Blind Watchmaker* (London: W. W. Norton and Company Ltd., 1996), 1.

10. Gould, *The Panda's Thumb* (London: W. W. Norton and Company, Inc., 1980), 24.

11. Gould, "Evolution as Fact and Theory," in *Hen's Teeth and Horse's Toes* (London: W. W. Norton and Company, 1983), 258.

12. Kenneth Miller, *Only A Theory* (New York: Viking, 2008), 42.

13. Gould, *An Urchin in the Storm* (New York: W. W. Norton and Company, Inc., 1987), 213.

14. Ibid., footnote 1.

15. Stephen Gould in Stephen Gould and Niles Eldredge, "Puctuated Equilibria," *Paleobiology* 3, no. 2 (Spring 1977): 145-146.

16. Huxley, *The Uniqueness of Man* (New York: Mentor, 1942), 2.

17. Richard C. Lewontin, *Biology as Ideology: The Doctrine of DNA* (New York: Nyrev, Inc., 1991), 10.

18. Lewontin, "Testing the Theory of Natural Selection," *Nature* 236, no. 5343 (1972): 181–182.

19. Ibid.

20. Jonathan Wells, "Selection and Speciation: Why Darwinism is False," *Evolution News and Views*, May 15, 2009, accessed on April 21, 2016, http://www.evolutionnews. org/2009/05/selection_and_speciation_why_d020411.html.

21. Darwin, *Origin*, 2nd ed., 90.

22. Ibid.

23. Lewontin, "Testing the Theory of Natural Selection," *Nature* 236, no. 5343 (1972): 181–182.

24. James Schwartz, "Oh My Darwin!: Who's the Fittest Evolutionary Thinker of All?" *Lingua Franca* 9, no. 8 (1999).

25. Lewontin, "Billions and Billions of Demons," *New York Review of Books* (1997), http://www.nybooks.com/articles/1997/01/09/billions-and-billions-of-demons/.

26. Karl Marx and Frederick Engels, *Selected Correspondence*, trans. I. Lasker (Moscow: Progress Publishers, 1975), 128.

27. Gertrude Himmelfarb, *Darwin and the Darwinian Revolution* (Chicago: Elephant Paperbacks, 1959), 421.

## 6. What is the Evidence for Natural Selection?

1. Daniel Dennett, *Darwin's Dangerous Idea* (New York: Touchstone, 1994), 21.

2. Dennett, "SPIEGEL Interview with Evolution Philosopher Daniel Dennett: Darwinism Completely Refutes Intelligent Design," *Der Spiegel*, 2005, accessed on April 6, 2016, http://www.spiegel.de/international/spiegel/spiegel-interview-with-evolution-philosopher-daniel-dennett-darwinism-completely-refutes-intelligent-design-a-392319.html.

3. Dawkins, *The God Delusion* (New York: Houghton Mifflin, 2006), 142.

4. Ibid., 117.

5. Dawkins, *The Blind Watchmaker*, 5.

6. *Evolution After Darwin*, vol. 3, 46.

7. Ibid., vol. 3, 113.

8. Jonathan Wells, "Revenge of the Peppered Moths?," *Evolution News and Views*, February 12, 2012, accessed on April 6, 2016, http://www.evolutionnews.org/2012/02/revenge_of_the056291.html.

9. Michael Majerus, "The Peppered Moth: The Proof of Darwinian Evolution," 2007, Department of Genetics at University of Cambridge, http://www.gen.cam.ac.uk/images/researchpages/majerus/peppered-moth-proof-evolution-text/view.

10. Jerry Coyne, "The Peppered Moth Story is Solid," *Why Evolution is True*, February 10, 2012, accessed on April 21, 2016, https://whyevolutionistrue.wordpress.com/2012/02/10/the-peppered-moth-story-is-solid/.

11. Dawkins, *The Greatest Show on Earth*, 132.

12. Lee Spetner, *Not By Chance! Shattering the Modern Theory of Evolution* (Brooklyn: Judaica Press, 2006).

13. "Press Release: HHS, Public Health Partners Unveil New Campaign to Promote Awareness of Proper Antibiotic Use," *Center for Disease Control*, September 17, 2003, accessed on April 21, 2016, http://www.cdc.gov/media/pressrel/r030917.htm.

14. David Lack, *Darwin's Finches* (Cambridge: Cambridge University Press, 1947), preface, v.

15. Jonathan Weiner, *The Beak of the Finch* (New York: Vintage Books, 1994), 9.

16. Jonathan Wells, *Icons of Evolution: Science or Myth? Why Much of What We Teach About Evolution Is Wrong* (Washington, D.C.: Regnery, 2002), 168.

17. H. Lisle Gibbs and Peter Grant, "Oscillating Selection on Darwin's Finches," *Nature* 327 (1987): 512.

18. Wells, *Icons*, 173–174.

19. Jerry Coyne, *Why Evolution is True* (New York: Viking Penguin, 2009), 145.

20. Dawkins, *A Devil's Chaplain: Reflections on Hope, Lies, Science, and Love* (New York: Houghton Mifflin Company, 2003), 211.

21. Ibid., 212.

22. Ibid.

23. T. H. Morgan, *Evolution and Genetics* (Princeton: Princeton University Press, 1925), 127.

# 7. ON EXTINCTION

1. Darwin, *The Origin of Species*, 2nd ed., 109 (Chapter 4).

2. Ibid., 172 (Chapter 6).

3. Ibid., 278 (Chapter 10).

4. Gould, "Introduction," in David M. Raup, *Extinction: Bad Genes or Bad Luck?* (New York: W. W. Norton and Company, 1991), xiv.

5. Norman Macbeth, *Darwin Retried* (New York: Delta, 1973), 118.

6. Ibid., 118.

7. Ernst Mayr, *Populations, Species and Evolution* (Cambridge: Harvard University Press, 1970), 372.

8. George Gaylord Simpson, *The Meaning of Evolution* (New Haven, CT: Yale University Press, 1949), 202.

9. Raup, 17.

10. Ibid., 181–182.

11. Ibid., 182.

12. Ibid., 127.

13. Ibid., 41.

14. Ibid., 39.

15. Ibid., 187.

16. Ibid., 188.

17. Ibid., 41.

18. Ibid., 145.

19. Amy Frearson, "Mass Extinction Memorial Observatory," *DeZeen*, June 21, 2013, https://www.dezeen.com/2013/06/21/mass-extinction-memorial-observatory-by-adjaye-associates/.

20. Suzanne Goldenberg, "Planet Earth is Home to 8.7 Million Species, Scientists Estimate," *The Guardian*, August 23, 2011, https://www.theguardian.com/environment/2011/aug/23/species-earth-estimate-scientists.

21. "Researchers find that Earth May Be Home to 1 Trillion Species," *National Science Foundation*, Press Release 16-052, May 2, 2016, http://www.nsf.gov/news/news_summ.jsp?cntn_id=138446.

22. Denyse O'Leary, personal communication with author, 2014.

23. E. O. Wilson, "Search Until You Find a Passion and Go All Out to Excel in its Expression," interview in the *Harvard Gazette*, April 2014, http://news.harvard.edu/gazette/story/2014/04/search-until-you-find-a-passion-and-go-all-out-to-excel-in-its-expression/.

24. Scott Russell Sanders, "Is Earth's Dominant Species Doomed to Self-Destruct?", *Washington Post*, November 16, 2014.

25. Gus Speth, "The Global 2000 Report to the President," *Boston College Environmental Affairs Law Review* 8, no.4 (1980): 698.

26. Julian L. Simon and Aaron Wildavsky, "Assessing the Empirical Basis of the 'Biodiversity Crisis,'" *Environmental Studies Program*, Competitive Enterprise Institute (May 1993): 7.

27. Wilson, "The Future of Life—Preserving Our Natural Capital," Bradley Lecture Excerpt, American Enterprise Institute, 2001, available online at: https://www.aei.org/publication/the-future-of-life-preserving-our-natural-capital/.

28. Juliette Jowit, "Humans Driving Extinction Faster than Species can Evolve, Say Experts," *Guardian*, March 7, 2010, accessed April 21, 2016, http://www.theguardian.com/environment/2010/mar/07/extinction-species-evolve.

29. "The Extinction Crisis," *Center for Biological Diversity*, accessed September 2, 2016, http://www.biologicaldiversity.org/programs/biodiversity/elements_of_biodiversity/extinction_crisis/.

# 8. Is Variation Indefinite or Limited?

1. Alfred Russel Wallace, "On the Tendency of Varieties to Depart Indefinitely from the Original Type," *The Proceedings of the Linnean Society* 3 (1858).

2. Darwin, "1844 Essay" in *The Foundations of The Origin of Species: Two Essays Written in 1842 and 1844*, ed. Francis Darwin (Cambridge: Cambridge University Press, 1909), 109.

3. Thomas Robert Malthus, *An Essay on the Principle of Population* (St. Paul's Church Yard (London): J. Johnson, 1798), Chapter 9.

4. Loren Eiseley, *Darwin's Century: Evolution and the Men Who Discovered It* (New York: Anchor Books, 1961), 227.

5. Morgan, *Evolution and Genetics*, 127.

6. Norman Macbeth, *Darwin Retried* (New York: Dell Publishing, 1973), 36.

7. Julian Huxley, *Evolution: the Modern Synthesis* (London: Allen and Unwin, 1942), 519.

8. Ibid., 519.

9. Roger Lewin, "Evolutionary Theory Under Fire," *Science* 210 (1980): 883–887.

10. Pierre-P. Grasse, *Evolution of Living Organisms* (New York: Academic Press, 1977), 87.

11. Søren Løvtrup, *Darwinism: The Refutation of a Myth* (New York: Springer, 1987), 351.

12. Dawkins, *The Greatest Show on Earth*, 22.

13. Ibid., 22–23.

14. Dawkins, 23.

15. Coyne, "The Case of the Missing Carpaccio," *Nature* 412, no. 587.

16. Vincent Torley, "Could the Eye Have Evolved by Natural Selection in a Geological Blink?" *Uncommon Descent*, March 18, 2013, accessed on April 21, 2016, http://www.uncommondescent.com/intelligent-design/could-the-eye-have-evolved-by-natural-selection-in-a-geological-blink/.

17. John Stuart Mill, in an editor's note to James Mill, *Analysis of the Phenomena of the Human Mind*, new edition, vol. 2 (London: Longmans Green Reader and Dyer, 1869), 5, footnote 2.

18. Mayr, "What Evolution Is," *Edge*, December 31, 1999, accessed April 21, 2016, https://www.edge.org/conversation/ernst_mayr-what-evolution-is.

19. Ibid.

20. Elliott Sober, "Evolution, Population Thinking and Essentialism," *Conceptual Issues in Evolutionary Biology* (Cambridge: MIT Press, 1994), 165.

21. Ibid., 163.

22. Marjorie Grene, "Evolution, 'Typology' and 'Population Thinking,'" *American Philosophical Quarterly* 27 (July 1990).

# 9. Homology and Its Possible Causes

1. Michael Denton, *Evolution: A Theory in Crisis* (Chevy Chase: Adler & Adler, 1985), 144.

2. "Homology (biology)," *Wikipedia*, April 13, 2016, accessed on April 21, 2016, https://en.wikipedia.org/wiki/Homology_(biology).

3. Darwin, *The Origin of Species*, 2nd ed., 433–434.

4. Ibid., 435.

5. Ibid.

6. This phrase is commonly used, but originated here: Richard Owen, *Lectures on the Comparative Anatomy and Physiology of the Invertebrate Animals, Delivered at the Royal College of Surgeons in 1843* (Longman, Brown, Green, and Longmans, 1843), 379.

7. Mayr, *The Growth in Biological Thought* (Cambridge: Harvard University Press, 1982), 45.

8. Gould, *The Flamingo's Smile* (New York: W. W. Norton and Company, 1985), 366.

9. Mayr, *What Evolution Is*, 26.

10. Dawkins, *The Greatest Show on Earth*, 313.

11. Jonathan Wells and William Dembski, *The Design of Life* (Dallas: Foundation for Thought and Ethics, 2008), 125.

12. Gavin de Beer, *Homology: An Unsolved Problem* (Oxford: Oxford University Press, 1971), 16.

13. De Beer, 15.

14. Lewontin, *The Genetic Basis of Evolutionary Change* (New York: Columbia University Press, 1974), 159.

15. Ibid., 160.

16. Denton, *Evolution: A Theory in Crisis*, 149.

17. Darwin, *The Origin of Species*, 6th ed., 381.

18. Ibid., Chapter 13.

19. Darwin, "To Asa Gray, 10 September [1860]" *Darwin Correspondence Project*, University of Cambridge, April 21, 2016, https://www.darwinproject.ac.uk/letter/?docId=letters/DCP-LETT-2910.xml;query=by%20far%20the%20strongest%20single%20class%20of%20facts;brand=default.

20. Wells, *Icons of Evolution*, 104–105.

21. De Beer, 16.

22. Tim Berra, *Evolution and the Myth of Creationism* (Stanford: Stanford University Press, 1990), 117.

23. Denton, *Evolution: A Theory in Crisis*, 151.

24. Ibid.

# 10. THE CONUNDRUM OF CONVERGENCE

1. Coyne, *Why Evolution is True*, 101.

2. Ibid.

3. Darwin, *The Origin of Species*, Chapter 6.

4. Darwin, *The Origin of Species*, 6th ed., Chapter 4.

5. Mayr, *What Evolution Is*, 222.

6. Ibid., 285.

7. Dawkins, *The Blind Watchmaker* (New York: W. W. Norton and Co., 1986), 94.

8. Dawkins, *Blind Watchmaker*, 94.

9. Denton, *Evolution: Still a Theory in Crisis*, 178.

10. "Evolutionists Hear Whopping Case of Convergent Evolution," *Creation-Evolution Headlines*, November 17, 2012, accessed on April 21, 2016, http://crev.info/2012/11/whopping-case-of-convergent-evolution/.

11. Arthur Koestler, *Janus: Summing Up* (New York: Random House, 1978), 209.

12. Ibid.

13. American Museum of Natural History, "What is a Pterosaur?" *AMNH.org*, accessed August 23, 2016, http://www.amnh.org/exhibitions/pterosaurs-flight-in-the-age-of-dinosaurs/what-is-a-pterosaur/.

14. Gould, *Flamingo's Smile*, 411.

15. Gould, *Eight Little Piggies* (New York: W. W. Norton and Company, 1993), 90.

16. Gould, *Eight Little Piggies*, 81.

17. Simon Conway Morris, "We Were Meant to Be…", *New Scientist*, November 16, 2002, https://www.newscientist.com/article/mg17623695-200-we-were-meant-to-be/.

18. Simon Conway Morris, *Life's Solution: Inevitable Humans in a Lonely Universe* (Cambridge: Cambridge University Press, 2003), 127–128.

19. Gould, *Eight Little Piggies*, 81.

20. Jerry Coyne, *Why Evolution is True* (New York: Viking, 2009), 94.

21. Mayr, *What Evolution Is*, 113.

22. Ibid.

23. Gould, *Eight Little Piggies*, 90–91.

24. Dawkins, *The Greatest Show on Earth*, 409.

25. George Gaylord Simpson, *The Major Features of Evolution* (New York: Columbia University Press, 1953), 171.

26. Lewontin, *The Genetic Basis of Evolutionary Change*, 11–12.

27. Casey Luskin, private communication, May 7, 2009.

# 11. THE FOSSIL RECORD

1. Darwin, *The Origin of Species*, 2nd ed., 280.

2. Ibid., Chapter 9.

3. Huxley, "From T. H. Huxley November 23 1859," *Darwin Correspondence Project*, Cambridge University, accessed April 22, 2016, https://www.darwinproject.ac.uk/letter/DCP-LETT-2544.xml.

4. Denton, Evolution: *A Theory in Crisis*, 160.

5. Phillip Johnson, *Darwin on Trial* (Downers Grove: InterVarsity Press, 1991), 175.

6. Mayr, *What Evolution Is*, 13.

7. Mayr, *What Evolution Is*, 7.

8. Henry Gee, *In Search of Deep Time: Beyond the Fossil Record to a New History of Life* (New York: Free Press, 1999), 2, 113.

9. Casey Luskin, private communication, February 27, 2014.

10. Michael J. Benton, M.A. Wills, R. Hitchin, "Quality of the fossil record through time," *Nature* 403 (February 2000): 534–536.

11. Mike Foote, "Sampling, Taxonomic Description, and Our Evolving Knowledge of Morphological Diversity," *Paleobiology* 23 (1997): 181–206.

12. Stephen Meyer, *Darwin's Doubt* (New York: HarperCollins, 2014), 70.

13. Ibid., 70.

14. Dembski and Wells,, "The Design of Life," 70.

15. James W. Valentine, "How Good Was the Fossil Record? Clues from the California Pleistocene," *Paleobiology* 15, no. 2 (1989): 83–94.

16. Douglas J. Futuyma, *Evolution* (Sunderland: Sinauer Associates, 2005), 528.

17. Futuyma, *Evolutionary Biology*, 1998 ed. (Sunderland: Sinauer Associates, 1998), 146.

18. Dembski and Wells, *Design of Life*, 83.

19. Futuyma, *Science on Trial* (New York: Pantheon Books, 1983), 81.

20. Kenneth Miller, *Only a Theory* (New York: Viking, Penguin Group, 2008), 46.

21. Gould, *Wonderful Life* (New York: W. W. Norton and Company, 1989), 208.

22. James Valentine as quoted by Dembski and Wells, *Design of Life*, 66, citing on 283 n. 8, R.A. Raff and E. C. Raff, eds., *Development as an Evolutionary Process* (New York: A. R. Liss, 1987), 84.

23. Dembski and Wells, "The Design of Life," 62, 66.

24. Gould, *The Panda's Thumb*, 181.

25. Donn Rosen, interview with author, American Museum of Natural History, March, 1982.

26. Steven Stanley, *Macroevolution: Pattern and Process* (New York: Pantheon Books, 1979), 39.

27. Ernst Mayr, "Speciational Evolution or Punctuated Equilibria," in *The Dynamics of Evolution*, eds. Albert Somit and Steven Peterson (New York: Cornell University Press, 1992). Available online at: http://www.stephenjaygould.org/library/mayr_punctuated.html.

28. Futuyma, "Evolutionary Constraint and Ecological Consequences," Department of Ecology and Evollution, Stony Brook University, Stony Brook, New York, 2010. Available online at: http://documentslide.com/documents/evolutionary-constraint-and-ecological-consequences.html.

29. Meyer, 51.

30. Dembski and Wells "The Design of Life," 68.

31. Wells, *Icons of Evolution*, 58.

32. Darwin, *The Origin of Species*, 2nd ed., 308.

33. Meyer, *Darwin's Doubt*, 355.

34. David Raup, "Conflicts Between Darwin and Paleontology," *Field Museum of Natural History Bulletin* 50, Biodiversity Heritage Library (1979), 25.

# 12. EVOLUTION AND SYSTEMATICS AT THE AMERICAN MUSEUM

1. Philip Johnson, *Darwin on Trial* (Washington, DC: Regnery Gateway, 1991), 157.

2. Genesis 2:19.

3. Colin Patterson, "Are the reports of Darwin's death exaggerated?," BBC Radio 4, published in *The Listener* 105, no. 2730 (October 8, 1981): 390–392.

4. Lewontin, *Human Diversity* (San Francisco: W. H. Freeman & Co., 1982), 163.

5. Lewontin, interview with author, Cambridge, MA, 1985.

6. For those interested in the details of his talk, see "Evolution and Creation," Peter Forey, ed., *The Linnean* 18, (2002).

7. Ibid.

8. Patterson, "Evolutionism and Creationism," *The Linnean* 18, no. 2(2002): 18. Available here: http://cas-tls.edcdn.com/Documents/Publications/The-Linnaen/Lin%20Vol%20 18_%20no%202_%20April%202002.pdf.

9. Ibid., 19.

10. Ibid., 15.

11. Ibid., 16.

12. Ibid.

13. Ibid.

14. Ibid., 17.

15. Ibid.

16. Beverly Halstead, BBC Radio, 1984.

17. Aristotle, *On the Parts of Animals*, trans. W. Ogle (London: Kegan Paul, Trench & Co., 1882), 11.

# 13. Intelligent Design and Information Theory

1. Darwin, "To John Frederick William Herschel 23 May [1861]" *The Darwin Project*, University of Cambridge, accessed on April 22, 2016, https://www.darwinproject.ac.uk/letter/?docId=letters/DCP-LETT-3154.xml;query=one%20cannot%20look%20at%20this%20universe;brand=default.

2. Dawkins, *The Blind Watchmaker*, 1.

3. Casey Luskin, "Researcher Almost Admits, then Quickly Retracts, that 'Intelligent Design' Is Needed to Explore Origin of Life," *Evolution News and Views*, July 1, 2015, accessed on April 6, 2016, http://www.evolutionnews.org/2015/07/researcher_almo097301.html.

4. Ibid.

5. Ibid.

6. William Lane Craig, "Q &A with William Lane Craig: Should Christians Accept Intelligent Design?," *Reasonable Faith*, May 3, 2015, accessed on April 22, 2016, http://www.reasonablefaith.org/should-christians-accept-intelligent-design.

7. Philip Johnson, as quoted by Michael Powell, "Doubting Rationalist," *The Washington Post*, May 15, 2005, accessed on April 22, 2016, http://www.washingtonpost.com/wp-dyn/content/article/2005/05/14/AR2005051401222.html.

8. Thomas Woodward, *Darwin Strikes Back: Defending the Science of Intelligent Design* (Grand Rapids: Baker Books, 2006), 15.

9. Miller, "The Flagellum Unspun: The Collapse of 'Irreducible Complexity,'" in *Debating Design: From Darwin to DNA*, eds. William A. Dembski and Michael Ruse (Cambridge: Cambridge University Press, 2006), 84.

10. Ibid.

11. Michael Behe, private communication, September 27, 2013.

12. William Dembski, "The Explanatory Filter," *Access Research Network*, 1996, accessed August 23, 2016, http://www.arn.org/docs/dembski/wd_explfilter.htm.

13. Stephen Meyer, *Signature in the Cell* (New York: HarperOne, 2009), 91.

14. Ian Fleming, *Goldfinger* (New York: Penguin Group, 2002), 166.

15. Bill Gates, Nathan Myhrvold, and Peter Rinearson, *The Road Ahead: Completely Revised and Up-To-Date* (New York: Penguin Books, 1996), 228.

16. Meyer, *Signature in the Cell*, 205–211.

17. Meyer, *Darwin's Doubt*, 176.

18. Ibid., 176–77.

19. Jonathan Wells, private communication, August 25, 2016.

20. James Shapiro, "In the details… what?," *National Review*, September 16, 1996, 64.

21. "Intelligent Design," *Wikipedia*, April 23, 2016, accessed on April 25, 2016, https://en.wikipedia.org/wiki/Intelligent_design.

22. "Kansas board to restore evolution to curriculum, but new fight over 'Intelligent Design' expected," *AANEWS*, January 12, 2001; For more information, see "Intelligent Design (ID): ID Promotional & Political Aspects," *Religious Tolerance.org*, 2001, accessed August 23, 2016, http://www.religioustolerance.org/ev_id3.htm, and "News about Evolution and

Creation Science During 2001," *Religious Tolerance.org*, 2001, accessed August 23, 2016, http://www.religioustolerance.org/ev_news01.htm.

23. As quoted by Peter Slevin, "Battle on Teaching Evolution Sharpens," *The Washington Post*, March 14, 2005, http://www.washingtonpost.com/wp-dyn/articles/A32444-2005Mar13.html.

24. Steve Fuller, "Intelligent Design: Ten Years after *Dover*," *ABC Religion and Ethics*, December 22, 2015, accessed on April 25, 2016, http://www.abc.net.au/religion/articles/2015/12/22/4376838.htm.

25. William H. Jefferys, "Review: The Privileged Planet," *Reports for the National Center for Science Education* 25, no. 1-2 (2005), http://ncse.com/rncse/25/1-2/review-privileged-planet.

26. As quoted by John G. West, "Statement from Astronomer Guillermo Gonzalez about His New Position at Ball State University," *Evolution News and Views*, July 9, 2013, accessed on April 25, 2016, http://www.evolutionnews.org/2013/07/statement_from_074251.html.

# 14. Darwin and the Philosophy of Materialism

1. Gould, *Ever Since Darwin* (New York: W. W. Norton & Company, 1977), 23.

2. Darwin, *Notebook N: Metaphysics and Expression*, transcribed by Kees Rookmaaker, ed. Paul Barrett (1838-1839), 5, available at *Darwin Online*, http://darwin-online.org.uk/content/frameset?pageseq=1&itemID=CUL-DAR126.-&viewtype=text.

3. Gould, *Ever Since Darwin*, 24.

4. Howard E. Gruber, *Darwin on Man: A Psychological Study of Scientific Creativity* (New York: E.P. Dutton, 1974), 203.

5. Ibid.

6. P. H. Barret et al., *Charles Darwin's Notebooks, 1836–1844* (Cambridge: Cambridge University Press, 1987) 291, 564.

7. Stephen Dilley, "The Evolution of Methodological Naturalism in the Origin of Species," *HOPOS: The Journal of the International Society for the History of Philosophy and Science* 3, No. 1 (2013), 20–58, abstract.

8. Alex Rosenberg, "Disenchanted Naturalism," *Kritikos* 12 (2015): 1552–5112, available at, http://intertheory.org/rosenberg.htm.

9. Kai Nielsen, "Naturalistic Explanations of Theistic Belief," in *A Companion to Philosophy of Religion*, eds. Philip L. Quinn and Charles Taliaferro (Oxford: Blackwell Publishers Ltd., 1999), 519.

10. See Stewart Goetz and Charles Taliaferro, *Naturalism* (Grand Rapids: William B. Eerdmans Publishing Company, 2008), 9.

11. Richard Lewontin, "Billions and Billions of Demons," *New York Review Books* (1997), http://www.nybooks.com/articles/1997/01/09/billions-and-billions-of-demons/.

12. Phillip E. Johnson, "Darwin-L Message Log 41: 26-39," *Robert J. O'Hara*, January 1997, accessed August 23, 2016, http://rjohara.net/darwin/logs/1997/9701a.

13. Dennett, *Consciousness Explained* (Boston: Back Bay Books, 1991), 33.

14. Susan Spath, "Science, Religion and Evolution," *National Center for Science Education*, June 18, 2001, accessed August 24, 2016, https://ncse.com/evolution/education/science-religion-evolution.

15. Jerry Coyne, "Ross Douthat Is On Another Erroneous Rampage Against Secularism," *New Republic*, December 26, 2013, accessed on April 25, 2016, https://newrepublic.com/article/116047/ross-douthat-wrong-about-secularism-and-ethics.

16. Francis Crick, *The Astonishing Hypothesis* (New York: Touchstone, 1995), 3.

17. Michael Egnor, "Your Computer Doesn't Know Anything," *Evolution News and Views*, January 23, 2015, accessed on April 25, 2016, http://www.evolutionnews.org/2015/01/your_computer_d_1092981.html.

18. Ibid.

19. Ibid.

20. William Provine, in "Darwinism: Science or Naturalistic Theology?" (debate with Phillip Johnson, April 30, 1994), available in *Origins Research* 16, no. 1 (1995) http://www.arn.org/docs/orpages/or161/161main.htm.

21. Richard Dawkins, "Religion's Misguided Missiles," *The Guardian*, September 15, 2001, accessed on April 25, 2016, http://www.theguardian.com/world/2001/sep/15/september11.politicsphilosophyandsociety1.

22. Meyer, *Darwin's Doubt*, 19.

23. Meyer, *Darwin's Doubt*, 385.

24. Robert Bishop, "Meyer's Inference to Intelligent Design as the Best Explanation (Reviewing 'Darwin's Doubt': Robert Bishop, Part 3,)" *BioLogos*, September 8, 2014, accessed on April 28, 2016, http://biologos.org/blogs/archive/meyers-inference-to-intelligent-design-as-the-best-explanation-reviewing-da.

25. T. H. Huxley, "The Physical Basis of Life," in *Selections from the Essays of T. H. Huxley*, ed. Albury Castell (New York: Appleton Century Croft, 1948), 19.

26. H. Allen Orr, "Awaiting a New Darwin," *The New York Review of Books*, February 7, 2013.

27. Thomas Nagel, *Mind and Cosmos* (Oxford: Oxford University Press, 2012), 27.

28. Lewis, *Miracles* (New York: HarperOne, 1974), 22.

29. Ibid.

30. Lewis, 21–22.

31. Nagel, "The Core of 'Mind and Cosmos,'" *New York Times*, August 18, 2013, accessed on April 25, 2016, http://opinionator.blogs.nytimes.com/2013/08/18/the-core-of-mind-and-cosmos/.

32. Ibid.

33. Darwin, *The Autobiography of Charles Darwin 1809–1882*, ed. Nora Barlow (London: Collins, 1958), 87.

# 15. DNA: God is in the Details

1. Darwin, *The Origin of Species*, 2nd ed. (1860), 189.

2. Michael Behe, "The Edge of Evolution: Why Darwin's Mechanism is Self-Limiting," *Evolution News and Views,* July 18, 2014, accessed on April 11, 2016, http://www.evolution-news.org/2014/07/the_edge_of_evo087971.html.

3. Darwin, *The Origin of Species,* 454.

4. G. H. Lewes, "Mr. Darwin's Hypothesis," *The Fortnightly Review* 4, ed. John Morley (1868), 61, available at http://darwin-online.org.uk/content/frameset?pageseq=41&itemID=A604&viewtype=text.

5. Thomas Huxley, *Lay Sermons: Addresses and Reviews* (New York: D. Appleton and Company, 1872), 129.

6. W. H. Thorpe, "Reductionism in Biology," in *Studies in the Philosophy of Biology,*" eds. Francisco Jose Ayala and Theodosius Dobzhansky (Berkeley: University of California Press, 1974), 117.

7. Richard Lewontin, interview with author, Cambridge, MA, 1985.

8. Steve Jones, "Francis Galton," *BBC News Magazine,* June 16, 2011, accessed on April 11, 2016, http://www.bbc.com/news/magazine-13775520.

9. Francis Crick, *What Mad Pursuit: A Personal View of Scientific Discovery* (New York: Basic Books, 1988), 3.

10. Bill Gates, *The Road Ahead* (New York: Viking Penguin, 1995), 188.

11. Crick, follow-up letter to "Why I am a humanist," *Varsity,* Cambridge University, 1966. Typescript available online at Wellcome Library: http://wellcomelibrary.org/item/b18171552#?c=0&m=0&s=0&cv=3&z=-0.0247%2C0.5324%2C1.1915%2C0.6029.

12. Crick, *Life Itself: Its Origin and Nature* (New York: Simon and Schuster 1982), 51–52.

13. Richard Lewontin and Richard Levins, *Biology Under the Influence: Dialectical Essays on Ecology, Agriculture, and Health* (New York: Monthly Review Press, 2007), 240.

14. Stephen Meyer, *Signature in the Cell,* 134.

15. Crick, *What Mad Pursuit,* 148.

16. Fred Hoyle and Nalin Chandra Wickramasinghe, *Evolution from Space: The Omni Lecture* (New York: Enslow Publishers, 1982), 27–28.

17. Ibid.

18. Hoyle, "Big Bang in Astronomy," *New Scientist* 92, no. 1280 (November 19,1981): 527.

19. Hoyle, *The Intelligent Universe* (New York: Holt, Rinehart, and Winston, 1984), 19.

20. John Maynard Smith, *Problems of Biology* (Oxford: Oxford University Press, 1986), 49.

21. Ibid.

22. David Goodsell, *The Machinery of Life,* 2nd ed. (New York: Springer, 2009), 17.

23. Chandra Wickramasinghe and Brig Klyce, "Creationism versus Darwinism: A Third Alternative," in *Darwinism, Design, and Public Education,* eds. John Angus Campbell and Stephen Meyer (East Lansing: Michigan State University Press, 2003), 543.

24. Crick, *What Mad Pursuit,* 146–147.

25. Crick, *What Mad Pursuit,* 147.

26. Ibid.

27. Ibid.

28. Carol Ezzell, "Beyond the Human Genome," *Scientific American*, 2000, http://www. scientificamerican.com/article/beyond-the-human-genome/.

29. Eric Lander, quoted by Justin Gillis, "Father of DNA Study Honored at Genetic Map's Debut," *The Washington Post*, February 13, 2001, accessed on April 25, 2016, https:// www.washingtonpost.com/archive/politics/2001/02/13/father-of-dna-study-honored-at-genetic-maps-debut/42930d28-bc2a-4429-a82b-85de58a2a0be/.

30. Helen Pearson, "Genetics: What is a Gene?" *Nature* 441 (May 25, 2006): 398–401.

31. James Shapiro, "In the Details… What?" *National Review*, September 16, 1996, 64.

32. Francis Collins, *The Language of God: A Scientist Presents Evidence for Belief* (New York: Free Press, 2006), 129.

33. Jonathan Wells, "Darwin of the Gaps: Review of *The Language of God: A Scientist Presents Evidence for Belief* by Francis S. Collins," *Discovery Institute*, March 26, 2008, accessed on April 25, 2016, http://www.discovery.org/a/4529.

34. Leigh Van Valen, "Deltatheridia, a New Order of Mammals," *Bulletin of the American Museum of Natural History* 132 (1966): 28.

35. Wells, "Darwin of the Gaps."

36. Ann Gauger, "Biology's Blind Spot: Two Views on Human Origins," *Christian Research Journal* 38, no. 04 (2015): 40-45.

37. Evolution News and Views, "To Protect Genetic Information, Cells Go to Extraordinary Lengths," *Evolution News and Views*, March 10, 2016, accessed on April 11, 2016, http:// www.evolutionnews.org/2016/03/to_protect_gene102679.html.

38. Kenneth R. Miller, *Only a Theory: Evolution and the Battle for America's Soul* (New York: Viking, 2008), 57.

39. Kenneth Miller, *Finding Darwin's God* (New York: Harper Perennial, 2007), 193.

40. Jocelyn Kaiser, "The Epigenetics Heretic," *Science* 343, no. 6196 (January 24, 2014): 361–363.

41. Ibid.

42. Alastair Crisp in "Some genes 'foreign' in origin and not from our ancestors," *Phy.Org*, March 12, 2015, accessed on April 25, 2016, http://phys.org/news/2015-03-genes-foreign-ancestors.html.

43. Michael Behe, private communication, unknown date.

44. See Behe, back cover comment for Thomas E. Woodward and James P. Gills, *The Mysterious Epigenome* (Grand Rapids, MI: Kregel Publications, 2012).

# 16. Lenski's Evolving Bacteria

1. Richard Lenski, "Evolution: Past, Present and Future," *Evolution of Evolution—150 Years of Darwin's On the Origin of Species*, National Science Foundation, 2009, accessed on April 25, 2016, https://www.nsf.gov/news/special_reports/darwin/textonly/bio_essay1.jsp.

2. Elizabeth Pennisi, "The Man Who Bottled Evolution," *Science* 342, no. 6160 (November 2013): 790–793, available at http://science.sciencemag.org/content/342/6160/790.

3. Dawkins, *The Greatest Show on Earth*, Chapter Five.

4. Carl Zimmer, "The Birth of the New, The Rewiring of the Old," *Discover Magazine*, 2001, http://blogs.discovermagazine.com/loom/2012/09/19/the-birth-of-the-new-the-rewiring-of-the-old/#.Vx6Ip6ODFHw.

5. Dawkins, *The Greatest Show on Earth*, 117.

6. Michael Behe, "Experimental Evolution, Loss-of-Function Mutations and 'The First Rule of Adaptive Evolution,'" *Quarterly Review of Biology* 85, no. 4 (December 2010): 419–445.

7. Michael Behe, "Rose Colored Glasses: Lenski, Citrate, and BioLogos," *Evolution News and Views*, November 13, 2012, accessed on August 15, 2016, http://www.evolutionnews.org/2012/11/rose-colored_gl066361.html.

8. Michael Behe, *Edge of Evolution* (New York: Free Press, 2007), 141.

9. Lenski, "Evolution: Past, Present, and Future."

10. Michael Behe, private communication, December, 2013.

11. Behe, private communication, December 2, 2013.

12. Michael Behe, "Experimental Evolution, Loss-of-Function Mutations and 'The First Rule of Adaptive Evolution,'" *Quarterly Review of Biology* 85, no. 4 (December 2010), 439.

13. Behe, private communication, December 2, 2013.

14. Michael Behe, interview with author, Lehigh University, September 27, 2013.

15. Pennisi, 793.

16. Ibid.

17. Michael Behe, "Rose Colored Glasses: Lenski, Citrate, and BioLogos."

18. Behe, private communication, December, 2013.

19. From Nell Greenfieldboyce, "Bacterial Competition in Lab Shows Evolution Never Stops," *NPR*, November 14, 2013, http://www.npr.org/sections/health-shots/2013/11/15/245168252/bacterial-competition-in-lab-shows-evolution-never-stops.

20. Conrad Hal Waddington in "Discussion: Paper by Dr. Eden," in *Mathematical Challenges to the Neo-Darwinian Interpretation of Evolution: The Wistar Institute Symposium Monograph*, no. 5, eds. Paul S. Moorhead and Martin M. Kaplan (Philadelphia: The Wistar Institute Press, 1966), 13–14.

21. Behe, "Rose Colored Glasses: Lenski, Citrate, and BioLogos."

# 17. The Sociobiology Wars

1. Edward O. Wilson, *Sociobiology: The New Synthesis*, 25th Anniversary Edition (Harvard: Harvard University Press, 2000), 4.

2. Ibid., vi.

3. Boyce Rensberger, "Updating Darwin on Behavior," *New York Times*, May 28, 1975.

4. Quoted by Wilson, in *Sociobiology*, 550.

5. Wilson, *Naturalist* (Washington, DC: Island Press/Shearwater Books, 1994), 347.

6. Wilson, *Consilience: The Unity of Knowledge* (New York: Alfred A. Knopf, Inc., 1998), 6.

7. Ibid., 7.

8. Darwin, *The Origin of Species*, 2nd ed., 207.

9. E. O. Wilson, interview with author, Cambridge, MA, 1976.

10. E. O. Wilson, *Naturalist* (Washington, DC: Island Press, 2006), 286.

11. Wilson, "Comparative Social Theory," The Tanner Lecture on Human Values (Michigan: University of Michigan, March 30, 1979), 64, available at http://tannerlectures.utah.edu/_documents/a-to-z/w/edwardO.pdf.

12. Wilson, interview with author, Cambridge, MA, 1981.

13. Elizabeth Allen, Barbara Beckwith, John Beckwith, Steven Chorover, David Culver, et al., "Against 'Sociobiology,'" *The New York Review of Books*, November 13, 1975, http://www.nybooks.com/articles/1975/11/13/against-sociobiology/.

14. Wilson, "For Sociobiology," *The New York Review of Books*, December 11, 1975, http://www.nybooks.com/articles/1975/12/11/for-sociobiology/.

15. Wilson, as quoted by Colin Campbell, "Anatomy of a Fierce Academic Feud," *The New York Times*, November 9, 1986, http://www.nytimes.com/1986/11/09/education/anatomy-of-a-fierce-academic-feud.html?pagewanted=all.

16. Dawkins, *The Selfish Gene* (Oxford: Oxford University Press, 1976), 1.

17. Stephen Pinker, "Steven Pinker on Robert Trivers," on "A Full-Force Storm with Gale Winds Blowing," *Edge*, October 16, 2004, accessed June 2, 2016, https://www.edge.org/conversation/robert_trivers-a-full-force-storm-with-gale-winds-blowing.

18. Richard Dawkins, "Forever voyaging: The genius of W. D. Hamilton, 1936–2000," *Times Literary Supplement*, August 4, 2002, http://www.the-tls.co.uk/articles/private/forever-voyaging/.

19. Pinker, *How the Mind Works* (New York: W. W. Norton and Company, 1997), 30.

20. Richard Lewontin, "Conversations with History," Institute of International Studies, UC Berkeley, 2004.

21. Richard Lewontin, Steven Rose, and Leon J. Kamin, *Not in Our Genes* (New York: Pantheon Books, 1984), 244.

22. William Hamilton, "The Genetical Evolution of Social Behavior, I," *Journal of Theoretical Biology* 7 (1964): 1–16.

23. Steven Pinker, "Against Nature," *Discovery Magazine*, October 1997, http://discovermagazine.com/1997/oct/againstnature1241.

24. Robert Wright, *The Moral Animal* (New York: Pantheon Books, 1994), 383.

25. Gould, "Potentiality vs. Determinism," in *Ever Since Darwin* (New York: W. W. Norton and Company, 1977), 256.

26. Jerry Coyne, "Of Vice and Men: A Case Study in Evolutionary Psychology," in *Evolution, Gender, and Rape*, ed. Cheryl Brown Travis (Cambridge: The MIT Press, 2003), 181.

27. Thornhill and Palmer, *A Natural History of Rape: Biological Bases of Sexual Coercion* (Cambridge: The MIT Press, 2000), 12.

28. Martin A. Nowak, Corina E. Tarnita, and Edward O. Wilson, "The Evolution of Eusociality," *Nature* 466 (August 26, 2010): 1057–1062.

29. Richard Dawkins, "The Descent of Edward Wilson," *Prospect*, May 24, 2012, http://www.prospectmagazine.co.uk/science-and-technology/edward-wilson-social-conquest-earth-evolutionary-errors-origin-species.

30. Ibid.

31. Ibid.

32. Wilson, *The Social Conquest of Earth* (New York: W. W. Norton and Company, 2012), 51.

33. Dawkins, "The Descent of Edward Wilson."

34. Coyne, "Big dust-up about kin selection," *Why Evolution is True*, March 24, 2011, accessed on April 25, 2016, https://whyevolutionistrue.wordpress.com/2011/03/24/big-dust-up-about-kin-selection/.

35. BBC2, Newsnight, as quoted by Chris Johnston, "Biological warfare flares up again between E. O. Wilson and Richard Dawkins," *The Guardian*, November 6, 2014, https://www.theguardian.com/science/2014/nov/07/richard-dawkins-labelled-journalist-by-eo-wilson.

36. Wilson, as quoted by Steve Bradt, "The ties that bind," *Harvard Gazette*, August 25, 2010, http://news.harvard.edu/gazette/story/2010/08/the-ties-that-bind/.

37. Jonah Lehrer, "Kin and Kind," *The New Yorker*, March 5, 2012, accessed on August 15, 2016, http://www.newyorker.com/magazine/2012/03/05/kin-kind.

38. Phillip Johnson, interview with author, Berkeley, 2000.

39. Ibid.

40. Wilson, *Half-Earth: Our Planet's Fight for Life* (New York: Liveright Publishing, 2016), 46.

## 18. Human Exceptionalism and Its Enemies

1. Darwin, *Notebook C: Transmutation of Species*, transcriber Kees Rookmaaker (1838), 166, available at *Darwin Online*, http://darwin-online.org.uk/content/frameset?itemID=CUL-DAR122.-&viewtype=text&pageseq=1.

2. Ibid., 196–197.

3. Ibid., 243.

4. Darwin, *The Descent of Man*, 1st ed., vol. 1 (London: John Murray, 1871), 35.

5. Darwin, *The Descent of Man*, 2nd ed. [in one volume] (London: John Murray, 1874), 89.

6. Ibid., 65.

7. Thomas Huxley, as quoted in Ernst Haeckel, *The Evolution of Man: A Popular Exposition*, vol. 1 (New York: D. Appleton and Company, 1879), 363.

8. Huxley, *Evidences as to Man's Place in Nature* (London: Williams & Norgate, 1863), quoted in *British Quarterly Review* 37 (January and April, 1863): 509.

9. Gould, *Ever Since Darwin*, 50.

10. David Barash, "God, Darwin, and My College Biology Class," *New York Times*, September 27, 2014.

11. James Rachels, *Created from Animals* (Oxford: Oxford University Press, 1990), 1.

12. Michael Slezak, "Was the Cosmos Made for Us?" *New Scientist*, May 2015, https://www.newscientist.com/article/mg22630190-400-the-human-universe-was-the-cosmos-made-for-us/.

13. Ibid.

14. Darwin, *The Descent of Man*, 2nd ed. (London: John Murray, 1882), 87.

15. Ibid.

16. Gould, *Ever Since Darwin*, 51.

17. Ibid.

18. Noel Rude, private communication, used with permission, 2015.

19. Gould, *Ever Since Darwin*, 52.

20. Ibid.

21. George Johnson, "Chimp Talk Debate: Is It Really Language?" *The New York Times*, June 6, 1995, http://www.nytimes.com/1995/06/06/science/chimp-talk-debate-is-it-really-language.html?pagewanted=all.

22. Ibid.

23. Ibid.

24. Ibid.

25. Helene Guldberg, "Restating the Case for Human Uniqueness," *Spiked Online*, June 26, 2009, accessed on April 26, 2016, http://www.spiked-online.com/review_of_books/article/7087#.Vx-q6qMrLSw.

26. Darwin, "To J. D. Hooker, 1 February [1871]," *Darwin Correspondence Project*, Cambridge University, https://www.darwinproject.ac.uk/letter/?docId=letters/DCP-LETT-7471.xml;query=warm%20little%20pond;brand=default.

27. Stephen J. Gould, "The Human Difference," *New York Times*, July 2, 1999.

28. Gould, *The Panda's Thumb*, 289.

29. Gould, *The Flamingo's Smile*, 413.

30. Lawrence M. Krauss, *Beyond Star Trek Physics: From Alien Invasions to the End of Time* (New York: Basic Books, 1997), 12.

31. Charles Krauthammer, "Are We Alone in the Universe?" *Washington Post*, December 30, 2011.

32. Steven Weinberg, *The First Three Minutes* (New York: Bantam Books, 1984), 144.

33. Steven Weinberg, "'A Designer Universe?': An Exchange," *The New York Review of Books*, January 20, 2000, http://www.nybooks.com/articles/2000/01/20/a-designer-universe-an-exchange/.

34. Ibid.

35. Steven Weinberg, Address at the Conference on Cosmic Design, American Association for the Advancement of Science, Washington, D.C. (April 1999).

36. Keay Davidson, *Carl Sagan: A Life* (New York: Wiley, 1999), 237.

37. Carl Sagan, "The Quest for Extraterrestrial Intelligence," *Smithsonian Magazine* (May 1978), available here: http://www.bigear.org/vol1no2/sagan.htm.

38. Quoted by Michael Powell in "A Knack for Bashing Orthodoxy," *New York Times*, September 19, 2011.

39. Davidson, 241.

# 19. THE SEARCH FOR ARTIFICIAL INTELLIGENCE

1. John McCarthy, Marvin L. Minsky, Nathaniel Rochester, and Claude E. Shannon, "A Proposal for the Dartmouth Summer Research Project on Artificial Intelligence," *Stanford University*, August 31, 1955, accessed on April 26, 2016, http://www-formal.stanford. edu/jmc/history/dartmouth/dartmouth.html.

2. Alan Turing, "Computing Machinery and Intelligence," *Mind* 59 (1950): 433–460.

3. Max Lungarella, Fumiya Iida, Josh C. Bongard, and Rolf Pfeifer, "AI in the 21st Century— With Historical Reflections," in *50 Years of Artificial Intelligence: Essays Dedicated to the 50th Anniversary of Artificial Intelligence* (Heidelberg: Springer, 2007), 2.

4. Ibid.

5. Ada Lovelace, "Note G," in L.F. Menabrea, *Sketch of the Analytical Engine Invented by Charles Babbage: With notes upon the Memoir by the Translator, Ada Augusta, Countess of Lovelace*, from Bibliothèque Universelle de Genève, No. 82 (October 1842). Available online at https://www.fourmilab.ch/babbage/sketch.html.

6. George Gilder, *The Silicon Eye* (New York: W. W. Norton & Company, 2005), 140.

7. Charles Krauthammer, "Man vs. Computer: Still a Match," *Jewish World Review*, November 21, 2003.

8. Herbert Simon, *The New Science of Management Decision* (New York: Harper & Row, 1960), 38.

9. Arthur Clarke, "The 21st Century: Beyond 2001," *CNN: AsiaWeek*, 1999, http://www. cnn.com/ASIANOW/asiaweek/99/0820/cs2.html.

10. Minsky, *Society of Mind* (New York: Simon and Schuster, 1988), 288.

11. Ray Kurzweil, *The Age of Spiritual Machines* (New York: Penguin Books, 1999), 253.

12. Bill Joy, "Why the Future Doesn't Need Us," *Wired Magazine*, April 1, 2000, accessed on April 26, 2016, http://www.wired.com/2000/04/joy-2/.

13. John McCarthy, interview with author, 2005.

14. Douglas Lenat, in "Firm aims to 'computerize' common sense," *CNN: Sci-Tech*, April 11, 2002, accessed on April 26, 2016, http://www.cnn.com/2002/TECH/industry/04/11/ memome.project.idg/.

15. Ibid.

16. Ramanathan V. Guha and Douglas B. Lenat, "Cyc: A MidTerm Report," *AI Magazine* (Fall 1990): 57, available at www.cyc.com/wp-content/uploads/2015/05/midterm_report_19901.pdf.

17. Marvin Minsky, "Programs, Emotions, and Common Sense," Game Developers Conference, San Jose, CA, March 24, 2001.

18. John McCarthy and Patrick J. Hayes, "Some Philosophical Problems from the Standpoint of Artificial Intelligence" (1969), http://www-formal.stanford.edu/jmc/mcchay69. pdf, 30.

19. Darrach, Brad, "Meet Shakey, the First Electronic Person," *Life Magazine* (20 November 1970), 58–68.

20. Daniel Crevier, *AI: The Tumultuous History of the Search for Artificial Intelligence*, 96.

21. Brooks, as quoted by John Brockman, in "The Deep Question: A Talk with Rodney A. Brooks," *Edge*, November 19, 1997, https://www.edge.org/conversation/rodney_a_brooks-the-deep-question.

22. Minsky, "Programs, Emotions, and Common Sense."

23. Ibid.

24. Joel Achenbach, "The world has lost one of its greatest minds," *Washington Post*, January 31, 2016.

25. David Gelernter, private communication, Villefranche, France, June 2015.

26. Gelernter, "The Closing of the Scientific Mind," *Commentary*, January 1, 2014, https://www.commentarymagazine.com/articles/the-closing-of-the-scientific-mind/.

27. Ibid.

28. Ibid.

29. Gelernter read and made small changes to an earlier version of this chapter.

## 20. Biogeography and Darwin's Theology

1. Darwin, *Origin*, 2nd ed. (1860), 355.

2. Louis Agassiz, "Prof. Agassiz on the Origin of Species," *American Journal of Science and Arts* 2, 1869, 154. Available at The Darwin Project, Cambridge University, http://darwin-online.org.uk/converted/Ancillary/reviews/1860_Agassiz_A45.html.

3. Darwin, *Autobiography, 1876–1882* (Oxford: Oxford University Press, 1974), 63.

4. Louis Agassiz, *Essay on Classification*, 1857 ed. (Harvard: Harvard University Press, 1962), 137. See also Michael Denton, *Evolution: A Theory in Crisis*, 20.

5. Darwin, *Origin*, 352.

6. Ibid., 366.

7. Ibid., 352.

8. Ibid.

9. Darwin, *The Origin of Species*, 6th ed., Chapter 13, Summary.

10. Dawkins, *Greatest Show on Earth*, 270.

11. Darwin, *The Origin of Species*, 2nd ed., 351.

12. Jonathan Wells, telephone interview with author.

13. Barry G. Gale, *Evolution Without Evidence* (Albuquerque: University of New Mexico Press, 1982), 140.

14. Darwin, "To Asa Gray 22 May [1860]," Darwin Correspondence Project, University of Cambridge, https://www.darwinproject.ac.uk/letter/?docId=letters/DCP-LETT-2814.xml;query=too%20much%20misery%20in%20the%20world;brand=default.

15. Asa Gray, as quoted by Randy More in *Evolution in the Courtroom, a Reference Guide* (Santa Barbara, Denver, Oxford: ABC Clio, 2002), 125.

16. Darwin, "To Asa Gray 17 September 1862," *Darwin Correspondence Project*.

17. Darwin, "To Asa Gray 22 May 1860," *Darwin Correspondence Project*.

18. Darwin, "To N. D. Doeds 2 April 1873," *Darwin Correspondence Project*.

19. "Darwin, *The Autobiography of Charles Darwin 1809–1882*, ed. Nora Barlow (London: Collins, 1958), 88.

20. Stephen Dilley, "Charles Darwin's Use of Theology in the Origin of Species," *British Society for the History of Science* 45, no. 1 (March 2012): 29–56.

21. Francis Darwin and A. Seward, *More Letters of Charles Darwin*, vol. 1 (London: John Murray, 1903), 94.

22. Darwin, *The Descent of Man*, Chapter 3.

23. Darwin, *The Origin of Species*, Chapter 15.

24. Darwin, *Life and Letters of Charles Darwin, including an autobiographical chapter*, vol. 1, ed. Francis Darwin (London: John Murray, 1887), 308.

25. Darwin, *The Origin of Species*, 2nd ed., 490.

26. Darwin, *Autobiography*, 50–51.

27. Paul A. Nelson, telephone interview with author, Chicago.

28. Darwin, *Autobiography*, 85.

29. Ibid.

30. Ibid., 87.

31. Ibid.

32. Darwin, "To Frederick McDermott 24 November 1880," *Darwin Correspondence Project*, https://www.darwinproject.ac.uk/letter/?docId=letters/DCP-LETT-12851. xml;query=I%20am%20sorry%20to%20have%20to%20inform%20you%20that%20 I%20do%20not%20believe%20in%20the%20Bible;brand=default.

## 21. The Rise and Fall of Progress

1. Darwin, *Autobiography*, 92.

2. Darwin, *The Origin of Species*, 2nd ed. (1860), 490.

3. Herbert Spencer, "Progress: Its Law and Cause," in *Illustrations of Universal Progress: A Series of Discussions* (New York: D. Appleton and Company, 1864), 1.

4. Ibid., 58.

5. Robert M. Young, *Darwin's Metaphor* (Cambridge: Cambridge University Press, 1985), 16, 251.

6. Spencer, *The Principles of Psychology*, 2nd ed. (London: Williams and Northgate, 1879), 465.

7. Robert Richards, "Darwin & Progress," *New York Review of Books*, December 15, 2005.

8. *Evolution after Darwin*, vol. 1, 239.

9. J. B. Bury, *The Idea of Progress: An Inquiry into its Origin and Growth* (New York: Cosimo Classics, 2008), 230.

10. Darwin, *Descent of Man*, 2nd ed. (London: John Murray, 1874), 133.

11. Ibid., 133–134.

12. Alfred Marshall, *Principles of Economics*, vol. 1, 3rd ed. (London: Macmillan and Co., 1895), 5.

13. Thomas Henry Huxley, "Evolution and Ethics," in *Selections from the Essays of T. H. Huxley* (New York: Henry Holt and Company, 1912), 106.

14. Aldous quoted by Julian Huxley, *Knowledge, Morality & Destiny* (New York: Mentor Books, 1957), 20.

15. Julian Huxley, *Evolution in Action* (New York: Mentor Books, 1953), 100.

16. John David Yeadon Peel, *Herbert Spencer: The Evolution of a Sociologist* (New York: Basic Books, 1971), 1.

17. Leon Trotsky, *Literature and Revolution*, ed. William Keach, trans. Rose Strunsky (Chicago: Haymarket Books, 2005), 207.

18. Anthony Lewis in interview, "After 50 Years of Covering War, Looking for Peace, and Honoring Law," *The New York Times*, December 16, 2001, http://www.nytimes.com/2001/12/16/weekinreview/16WORD.html?pagewanted=all.

19. Ibid.

20. Frederick J.P. Veale, *Advance to Barbarism: The Development of Total Warfare from Sarajevo to Hiroshima* (Ostara Publications, 2013), 7.

21. Veale, 8.

22. C.S. Lewis, "The World's Last Night," in *The World's Last Night and Other Essays* (New York: Harcourt, Brace and Company, 1960), 103–104.

23. Lewis, 104.

24. Lewis, 101.

25. John Gray, "The Atheist Delusion," *The Guardian*, March 14, 2008, http://www.theguardian.com/books/2008/mar/15/society.

26. John Offer, ed., *Herbert Spencer: Political Writings* (Cambridge: Cambridge University Press, 1994), Introduction, xviii.

27. John Gray, "The Atheist Delusion"; see also his book *Straw Dogs: Thoughts on Humans and Other Animals* (New York: Farrar, Straus and Giroux, 2003).

28. Alexander Solzhenitsyn, *The Russian Question at the End of the Twentieth Century* (New York: Farrar, Straus and Giroux, 1995), 117.

29. Eugene Koonin, "On the Origin at 150: Is a New Evolutionary Synthesis in Sight?" *Trends in Genetics* 25, no. 11 (2009): 473–475.

30. Ibid.

31. Maurice Strong, "Closing Statement to the Rio Summit," *MauriceStrong.net*, June 14, 1992, accessed on April 27, 2016, http://www.mauricestrong.net/index.php/closing-statement.

32. David Attenborough in "David Attenborough: Humans are a Plague on the Earth," *RadioTimes*, January 22, 2013, accessed on April 27, 2016, http://www.radiotimes.com/news/2013-01-22/david-attenborough-humans-are-a-plague-on-the-earth.

33. Paul Taylor, *Respect for Nature: A Theory of Environmental Ethics*, 25th anniversary ed. (Princeton: Princeton University Press, 1986), 115.

34. See David A. Graham, "The Wrong Side of 'the Right Side of History,'" *The Atlantic*, December 21, 2015.

# ACKNOWLEDGMENTS

Early on, I read books by two lawyers: Norman Macbeth, whose *Darwin Retried* had a big influence on me; and U. C. Berkeley's Phillip E. Johnson, who played a major role in founding the intelligent design movement. Both Macbeth and Johnson became friends. Without their work, I doubt this book would have been written. I was also fortunate enough to have preliminary discussions with Michael Denton in Washington D.C.

Norman Macbeth introduced me to curators at the American Museum of Natural History in New York. Some of them were surprisingly skeptical about Darwin's theory. Among them: Gary Nelson, at one point the chairman of the department of Ichthyology; and Norman Platnick, one of the world's leading experts on spiders. At the museum I also met Colin Patterson, who was with the Natural History Museum in London but visiting New York at the time. All three were happy to answer questions. I also interviewed Patterson in London.

Turning to full-time biologists, I would like to single out the biochemist Michael J. Behe of Lehigh University. He readily answered my numerous questions. His book *Darwin's Black Box*, with its argument that biological organs are often "irreducibly complex" and therefore non-Darwinian, played a major role in convincing people that proponents of ID were not just creationists in disguise.

I am also grateful to Edward O. Wilson and Richard C. Lewontin, both of Harvard University. I interviewed them several times. I also briefly interviewed the late Stephen J. Gould.

No analysis of Darwinism can avoid philosophical analysis, and so I was lucky to encounter Karl Popper when he was visiting the Hoover Institution at Stanford. He happily sat for an interview.

I would like to thank those who read the manuscript, whether in part of in whole, and made many helpful suggestions. These include James A. Barham, who is working on his own book (on the mysteries of life); and Laszlo Bencze, who is both a philosopher and a professional photographer. He took the photograph of me that appears on the back cover.

I am also grateful for numerous comments by the University of Chicago-trained philosopher and long-time Darwin skeptic Paul A. Nelson. Perhaps most helpful of all has been biologist Jonathan Wells, the author of *Icons of Evolution* and the co-author of *The Design of Life*. Both Wells and Nelson are associated with the Discovery Institute in Seattle.

# INDEX

**P**

Paley, William  39, 244
Palmer, Craig  208
*Panda's Thumb, The* (1980)  62, 135, 221
Panspermia  182
Pasteur, Louis  48
Patterson, Colin  14, 55, 139, 182, 285
Pavlov, Ivan  10
*Pax-6* gene  121
Peel, J. D.  251
Pelger, Susanne  59
Pennisi, Elizabeth  193, 198
Peppered moth experiment  72
Philosophical naturalism  171
*Phylogenetic Systematics* (1966)  141
Piattelli-Palmarini, Massimo  29
Pinker, Steven  206, 219
Placental evolution  117
Platnick, Norman  14, 56, 139, 148, 285
Polanyi Institute  162
Polyphyletic position  49
Popper, Karl  13, 14, 65, 89, 208, 286
Potter, Beatrice  253
*Poverty of Historicism, The* (1960, 1961)  15
*Principle of Population* (1798 and later)  24
*Principles of Geology* (1830–33)  128
*Principles of Psychology* (1855)  248
*Privileged Planet, The* (2004)  162, 216
*Problems of Biology, The* (1986)  183
Progress, idea of  17, 43, 223, 247–257
Provine, William B.  170
Punctuated equilibrium  135

**R**

Rachels, James  216
Raup, David M.  86, 87, 137
Reductionism  10
Religion versus science  12
Rensberger, Boyce  201

Reversion to mean  95
Richards, Jay W.  162, 216
Richards, Robert J.  248
Rosenberg, Alex  166
Rosen, Donn  135, 139, 142
Rude, Noel  218
Ruse, Michael  51, 121, 173
Russell, Bertrand  24, 64
*Russian Question, The* (1995)  253
Ryle, Gilbert  11

**S**

Sachs, Jeffrey  212
Sagan, Carl  38, 222, 223
Sahei, Nita  152
Savage-Rumbaugh, Sue  218
*Science on Trial*  132
Scopes, John  12
Searle, John  167
Seidenberg, Mark  219
*Selfish Gene, The* (1976)  201, 205, 211
Sequence hypothesis  181
Shannon, Claude  158
Shapiro, James  60, 161, 186
Shapley, Harlow  37, 40, 42, 44
*Signature in the Cell* (2009)  61, 158
*Silicon Eye, The* (2005)  227
Simon, Herbert  228
Simon, Julian  92
Simpson, George Gaylord  14, 35, 36, 87, 124
Singer, Peter  219
*Singularity is Near, The* (2005)  229
Skinner, Michael  189
Smith, John Maynard  183
Smith, Wesley J.  255
Sober, Elliot  101
*Society of Mind, The* (1985)  229, 233
Sociobiology  64
*Sociobiology: the New Synthesis* (1975)  64, 201
Solzhenitsyn, Alexander  253
Spencer, Herbert  10, 44, 223, 247, 250, 253